DRY BONES AND INDIAN SERMONS

DRY BONES AND INDIAN SERMONS

*Praying Indians in
Colonial America*

KRISTINA BROSS

CORNELL UNIVERSITY PRESS
Ithaca and London

First published 2004 by Cornell University Press
First printing Cornell Paperbacks, 2004

Printed in the United States of America

Library of Congress Cataloging-in-Publication Data

Bross, Kristina.
  Dry bones and Indian sermons : praying Indians in colonial America /
Kristina Bross.
     p. cm.
Includes bibliographical references (p.   ) and index.
  ISBN 0-8014-4206-0 (cloth : alk. paper)
  ISBN 0-8014-8938-5 (pbk.: alk. paper)
  1. American literature—Colonial period, ca. 1600–1775—History and criticism.
2. Indians in literature.   3. Christianity and literature—New England—History—
17th century.   4. American literature—New England—History and criticism.
5. Christian literature, American—History and criticism.   6. Indians of North
America—New England—Religion.   7. Indians of North America—Missions—
New England.   8. National characteristics, American, in literature.   9. Sermons,
American—History and criticism.   10. New England—Religious life and customs.
11. Conversion in literature.   12. Colonies in literature.   13. Prayer in literature.
I. Title.
  PS173.I6B76 2004
  810.9'352997—dc22

                                                                        2003019729

Cornell University Press strives to use environmentally responsible suppliers and
materials to the fullest extent possible in the publishing of its books. Such materials include vegetable-based, low-VOC inks and acid-free papers that are recycled,
totally chlorine-free, or partly composed of nonwood fibers. For further information, visit our website at www.cornellpress.cornell.edu.

Cloth printing   10 9 8 7 6 5 4 3 2 1
Paperback printing   10 9 8 7 6 5 4 3 2 1

To JoAnn Bross and Billy Bross

Contents

Acknowledgments

This book would not have been possible without the advice, criticism, and generous support of many friends and colleagues. Janice Knight, Janel Mueller, and Clark Gilpin skillfully and patiently guided this project through its earliest manifestation. Shoshannah Cohen, Anne Myles, and Peter Sattler suffered through early revisions with good humor and even better advice. Matthew P. Brown, Joshua Bellin, Joanna Brooks, Susan Curtis, Dane Morrison, and Reiner Smolinski read chapters and provided invaluable comments at a more advanced stage. My sincere thanks go also to David Shields and the anonymous reviewers of Cornell University Press for their encouragement and critique of the book. My editor at Cornell University Press, Sheri Englund, has gone above and beyond in giving of her time and insight. My friends and colleagues at California Polytechnic State University, especially William Fitzhenry and Kathryn Rummell, and at Purdue University, especially Emily Allen, Dino Felluga, Minrose Gwin, Nancy Peterson, Cheryl Oreovicz, G. Richard Thompson, Aparajita Sagar, Siobhan Somerville, and Marta VanLandingham have given of themselves both professionally and personally. I could not have completed this book without their wisdom and encouragement. Most of all, my thanks go to Steven Wereley, my friend and companion on the academic way, whose sacrifices of time too often went unrewarded and whose boundless confidence saw my work through from start to finish.

Research for this book was supported in part by a California State Faculty Support Grant (summer 1998) and by a Purdue Research Foundation Summer Support Grant (2001). Parts of chapters 1 and 5 originally appeared in *Millennial Thought in America: Historical and Intellectual Contexts, 1630–1860*, edited by Bernd Engler, Joerg O. Fichte, and Oliver Scheiding (Trier: WVT Wissenschaftlicher Verlag Trier, 2002). An earlier version of chapter 2 originally appeared in *Messy Beginnings: Postcolonial Early American Studies*, edited by Maline Johar Schueller and Edward Watts (New Brunswick: Rutgers University Press, 2003). Part of chapter 6 was originally published as "That Epithet of Praying," in *Fear Itself*, edited by Nancy Schultz (West Lafayette, Ind.: Purdue University Press, 1999), and reprinted here with permission. An earlier version of chapter 7 appeared in *Early American Literature* 36, no. 3 (2001).

DRY BONES AND INDIAN SERMONS

1 Praying Indians and the Mission upon the Hill

In 1658, William London, bookseller in Newcastle-upon-Tyne, set out to create a list of "the most vendible Books in *England,* Orderly and Alphabetically Digested." It must have been a useful work. During this decade of the English Commonwealth, writers of every political and theological stripe added to the "pamphlet wars" being waged for public opinion. The proliferation of titles flooding the market would have been hard to keep up with, especially because, as London rather immodestly declares on the title page of his catalogue, the "like Work" was "never yet performed by any."[1]

Most of his catalogue is devoted to books of divinity—London lists a collection of eighty sermons by John Donne and a full fifty-two works by the Puritan minister Richard Sibbes as among those texts "of esteem, or of easie purchase" that would be useful to readers "of these Northern parts" (B2r). It is not difficult to imagine William London sitting among a pile of books and making his choices for the catalog. A folio of the "famous Mr *Perkins*[.] Works compleat. In three vol." (Q1r)? Certainly. Richard Baxter's well-regarded *Saints everlasting Rest* (K4r)? By all means. But among the divinity works is a small publication from Massachusetts, that barbarous antipode, penned by a pair of obscure clerics. It is a text written by "Mr *Eliot* and Mr *Mayhew*," which London titles "A relation of the repentance and conversion of the poor *Indians* in *New-England;* shewing the wonderfull work of God in their poor souls" (M3v). He is referring to a 1653 publication, *Tears of Repentance; or, A further Narrative of the Progress of the* Gospel *amongst the Indians in New-England,* which contains accounts of New England evangelism written by Thomas Mayhew, Jr. and John Eliot, both ministers in the Massachusetts Bay Colony. In it, Mayhew gives a brief history of Indians' "feeling" after God, and Eliot presents his translations of the confessions of faith by several of his Indian proselytes, whom he calls "praying Indians."

Why would such a publication be popular and well regarded, even in the far north of England? One answer lies in London's preface to his catalog, which makes clear the attraction of America and of Indians to English writers. London recalls exploration and travel narratives describing Indians as naïve trading partners as he compares the benefits of buying books to the lopsided profits European "adventurers" reputedly enjoyed in America: *"He that gets Books for his money, has in my mind as good a bargain as our Mariners, who trade with the* Indians, *and get Gold for* Knives, Rattles, Glasses, *&c."* (B4r). But a more telling comparison comes earlier, when London laments the neglect by Englishmen of books and learning: *"Had the poor Indians the treasures of knowledg contained in Books, who will not say they would surfet of Knowledg, compar'd with many in this age, that in the midst of means to accomplish* Wisdome *and* Knowledg, *are only like moths in Books?"* (B2v–B3r).

This statement goes beyond common descriptions of Indians as exotic innocents. Here London employs a strategy made possible by the mission literature I analyze throughout this book. Indians are held up as potential examples for the English: learning and civilization are contingent on actions, not on innate characteristics. Such an argument belongs to the missionary rather than the adventurer; if Indians were given the means of salvation (whether books in general or the Bible—*the* book, for Christian missionaries), they would be capable of being "raised," perhaps even above the level of sinning Englishmen. Indians, especially "saved" Indians, signify in such an argument as markers of God's blessings on English colonialism and as one means by which English readers—whether in Boston or London—could gauge their personal saintliness.

Indeed, in the 1640s and 1650s, when William London was taking stock of his vendibles, gauging one's saintliness was a task of considerable importance. The cataclysmic events of the English civil wars, beginning in 1642, the regicide in 1649, and the establishment of Cromwell's Interregnum government a year later persuaded many that the end times were upon God's people, and they cast about for the proper response. Some observers on both sides of the Atlantic suspected now—more than ten years after the Puritan colonization of

New England—that emigration to New England had been a mistake, that New England settlers had fled their home country out of cowardice just when the saints were needed to fight for Christ in Old England. Many colonists repatriated. Others sought ways to understand New England, not as a refuge from a corrupt Anglican church and a doomed English nation, as it had seemed in the 1630s, but as a place of continued significance and vitality.

In this book I examine the effect of the English civil wars and Interregnum government on New England and its literature. What became of colonists' identity after their initial understanding of New England as the "city upon the hill" failed them? The answer, surprisingly, turns on authors and on figures who cannot be understood solely as belonging to New England. For a time, accounts of Indian evangelism were proffered as records of the true role of New England. Praying Indians were at the center of the story, and New England was promoted as a missionary enterprise. These accounts were written by colonists but published with the commentary and under the imprimatur of prominent supporters in Old England. Mission literature, through this joint production, linked events in Old England to those in New England. Evangelical writers argued that just as Cromwell and the New Model Army fought to establish God's kingdom in Old England, colonists who remained in New England to proselytize could be seen as the vanguard of "westerne" reformation. Whereas before, Indians were seen as incidental or inconvenient to English colonization, in writings produced between 1643 and 1671, New England's identity depended on the active presence of Indians. Praying Indians were presented as the colonies' native inhabitants, savage perhaps, but capable of reformation once they were rescued from sin by heroic settlers. They were the "dry bones" of the prophet Ezekiel's vision, brought back to life through the efforts of English missionaries. The Praying Indian was imagined so strongly and described so vividly, that even after interest in Old England waned and colonial wars brought Christian Indians and colonists into violent conflict, the figure continued in colonial literature, shaping Indian representation and self understanding.

A New Errand for New England

The story of Puritan evangelism in America and of the invention of the Praying Indian begins in 1643, with the publication of *New En-*

glands First Fruits. This tract describes the Christian conversion of several Indians and African servants as well as the founding of Harvard College. The belated rise of a sustained and well-supported mission does not mean that Puritans—or English colonists, more generally—were not interested in spreading the gospel. Puritan settlers from the first were intent on imagining a Christian Indian to legitimize their presence in America, but such a construction did not take hold until imagination was matched by active evangelical endeavor. Consider, for instance, the Great Seal of the Massachusetts Bay Colony, struck in 1629 as Puritans were preparing to leave England for America. The seal's central figure is an Indian man holding a bow in one hand and an arrow in the other, naked but for a girdle of leaves. From his mouth issues a ribbon with the words "come over and help us." Evangelism was thus associated with the colony from its very beginnings, although settlers did not heed the fantasized call for help for more than fifteen years.

Part of the delay was due to the colony's attention to physical survival and comfort in the early years of their colony. Part was due as well to the Puritans' ecclesiastical organization. A minister was a minister only if called to a particular pulpit. Until Indians had a church, they could not call a minister; if Indians had no minister, it was unlikely they would found a church. This paradox was resolved only when ministers and teachers in English churches individually took it upon themselves to cheat time and preach to neighboring Algonquians. Indeed, English colonists had done so little to convert native peoples to Christianity that the Northhamptonshire minister William Castell, along with seventy-six other divines, petitioned parliament in 1641 in an effort to spur colonization and evangelism, noting "the great and generall neglect of this Kingdome, in not propagating the glorious Gospel in *America*." Although Castell calls America "a maine part of the world," he dismisses New England as planted "but in the skirts of *America*, where there are but few natives."[2]

So long as Puritan colonists felt they had discerned the right reasons for their migration—had found "warrants" for their removal from England—they paid little heed to such calls for evangelism. In early statements about the planting of their colony, most writers referred to Indians only as impediments to possession of the land. Their deaths through disease and warfare were celebrated as a providential emptying of areas the English wished to occupy. John Winthrop makes note in his *Reasons to Be Considered for . . . the Intended Plantation in New England* of the "great plague" that had thinned Native American

The Seal of the Governor and Company of the Massachusetts Bay in New England, 1629. Courtesy of the Commonwealth of Massachusetts, Office of the Secretary of the Commonwealth, Boston, Mass.

populations.[3] In *God's Promise to his Plantations*, John Cotton lists war, the deeding of land, and finally, sparse Indian populations as the ways God had for "making room" for his chosen people. Cotton does include an injunction to make the "poor natives" "partakers of your precious faith," but that goal is only tentatively suggested: "Who knoweth whether God have reared this whole plantation for such an end."[4] Indeed, until the mid-1640s, the true "end" of the plantation seemed clear enough. In his 1631 sermon "The Danger of Desertion," Thomas Hooker preached that "as sure as God is God, God is going from England." And as for the colonies, "God makes account that New England shall be a refuge for his Noahs and his Lots, a rock and a shelter for his righteous ones to run unto; and those that were vexed to see the ungodly lives of the people in this wicked land [England], shall there be safe."[5]

When, in 1642, the English civil wars broke out, the inscrutability of God's plan was brought home to many who had before been sure of it. Some in New England found themselves wondering whether they could have been so mistaken as to have abandoned England just as God's care for that nation was being made manifest. Archbishop William Laud, whose persecution of Puritan ministers had caused many to emigrate in the 1630s, was arrested in 1640 and executed in 1645. Parliament gained increasing control of the government, and the continual clashes between royalist and parliamentary armies seemed to indicate that events of cosmic significance were taking place in England rather than in the colonies.

The steady stream of goods and immigrants that New England had enjoyed during the early years of its settlement dwindled as supporters found local concerns in England more pressing. As Edmund Morgan argues, just as the initial migration to New England had been sparked by economic concerns, "so now the desirability of returning home seemed to be argued by economic difficulties in New England."[6] Many English colonists repatriated, including the colonies' leaders and the rising generation of educated young men. By the mid-1640s, Massachusetts was experiencing what Andrew Delbanco calls a "reverse migration," arguing that "some [New Englanders] were not so much thinking of the 'counter-emigrants' as deserters but of themselves as stragglers."[7]

As king and parliament fought in Old England, New England colonists found in Indian evangelism a reason for their continual colonization of America. The coincidence of new evangelical endeavors and the civil wars is striking. In 1643, Roger Williams published *A Key into the Language of America,* a work describing his interactions with Indians, couched in "implicite dialogue[s]."[8] Thomas Mayhew, Jr. began his conversion efforts with a man named Hiacoombes, and John Eliot began his study of Algonquian languages. The United Colonies were formed when representatives from four colonies signed the Articles of Confederation. Commissioners from the United Colonies would later be charged with dispersing funds collected in Old England for the support of New England's evangelism of Indians. Also in 1643, the Massachusetts Bay Colony directed its agents in London to publish *New Englands First Fruits.* Thus, at precisely the moment when events in Old England suggested that the saints there faced not God's wrath but God's recognition and were building the "New Jerusalem," New England remembered its charge to evangelize those "poor Indians." The New England mission and the Commonwealth were born at the same political moment. If not quite twins, they are transatlantic siblings.

New Englands First Fruits was but the first salvo against charges that New England did nothing to spread the gospel. Following its publication, Bay Colony Puritans launched a systematic missionary effort, which was met by intense interest in England. Prominent Puritans from both sides of the Atlantic (including some who had signed William Castell's 1641 petition) wrote in support of New England's Indian mission between 1643 and 1660. Several colonists, John Eliot foremost among them, began to proselytize in earnest. Published reports began appearing in London in 1647; by 1660, nine mission tracts were published touting the success of the English mission. The publicity worked. In 1649, the same year that parliament tried and executed King Charles I, it passed *An Act for the Propagating of the Gospel*, which set up mechanisms for soliciting and dispersing money for Indian missions.

Thus, although Praying Indians have been thought of as mediators of the relations of settlers and "wild" Indians across a narrow geographic frontier located on the western edge of the New England colonies, the authors of mission tracts were responding to English national—not New English colonial—events. Their writings link events in Old England to mission efforts in New England.[9] If the New Model Army was truly conquering the king for Christ, then providence dictated that Christ's dominions should be spread in America as well. If American evangelism was successful, it was proof positive that the New Jerusalem was being raised in England. In exchanges largely conducted in the pages of tracts printed in London to promote New England's evangelical activities, the Christian Indian was used to fix English identities on both sides of an Atlantic "frontier." Together, writers in Massachusetts and writers in London constructed a new purpose for the remaining English settlers.

As an early entry in the mid-century "literature of self-definition," *New Englands First Fruits* only tentatively rewrote New England against the backdrop of events in England.[10] Published in London and most likely the work of the Bay Colony's recently repatriated agents, Hugh Peter and Thomas Weld, *New Englands First Fruits* describes individual converts as well as the course of study at fledgling Harvard University.[11] Despite the tracts' claims of success with some Indians, it is painfully clear that *New Englands First Fruits* invents rather than reports a policy of evangelism. As the writers acknowledge, until 1643

Indian-English relations had been characterized (at best) by cautious coexistence: "(mistake us not) we are wont to keep them [the Indians] at such a distance, (knowing they serve the Devill and are led by him) as not to imbolden them too much, or trust them too farre; though we do them what good we can."[12]

This arm's-length approach toward conversion seemed prudent so long as the Bay Colony's primary goals were to establish an English settlement and to protect church purity against English corruptions. When *New Englands First Fruits* was published in 1643, however, colonists needed to answer accusations that they had done nothing to convert Indians despite their charter's charge to do so and to explain their sudden willingness to evangelize so long after migration.[13] This defensive posture clarifies why *New Englands First Fruits* makes only oblique reference to reasons for planting, other than to propagate the gospel among "heathens," either Indian or English. The tract immediately focuses on anecdotal evidence of Indian conversion, noting only in passing that God "hath not frustrated the ends of our Transplanting in sundry other respects."[14] The opening avoids discussion of the original motivations for New England's planting (which at this point seemed to be misguided), turning immediately to Indian conversion. Only after detailing anecdotes of several Indian encounters with Christianity does the tract venture to offer a reading of providence and New England's history:

> See how Gods wisdome produceth glorious effects, from unlikely meanes, and make streight works by crooked instruments: for who would have thought, that the chasing away hence so many godly Ministers, should so farre have promoted the praises of God, and should be a meane to spread the Gospel.[15]

Not surprisingly, *New Englands First Fruits* invokes God's omniscience and omnipotence to explain New England's weaknesses; when colonists had ignored or played down their errand to spread the gospel, they had simply been shortsightedly human. The real reason for migration, they had now discovered, had not been to escape God's wrath or Archbishop Laud's persecution but to carry the knowledge of God's redeeming love to a people held captive by Satan. *New Englands First Fruits* is meant to demonstrate that the colonists had unwittingly been pursuing their true purpose and that they were proselytizing with alacrity now that they understood their divine role.

The transatlantic nature of mission narratives is registered clearly in the accounts of evangelism that followed *New Englands First Fruits*. In 1647, New England agents in London published *The Day-Breaking, if not the Sun-Rising of the Gospell with the* Indians in New-England.[16] The title of this tract, along with the titles of those that followed, sketch out the metaphoric day of the Indians' Christian enlightenment from the "Day-breaking" to the "Clear Sun-shine of the Gospel." These tracts present a consistent, geographically ordered *translatio imperii* (or at least extension) of Christ's empire into America. But the very orderliness is a metropolitan reformulation of colonial materials.[17] Praying Indians provided the ostensible raw evidence of spiritual encounters, while English colonists transcribed and described these encounters. The eyewitness testimony appeared as letters, lists of Indian questions, and hasty, "from the front" narratives. English writers in London gave shape and coherence to the material, appending titles, dedications, prefaces, and epilogues. The result was a series of quick, multigeneric, multivocal publications.[18]

Much of the discussion in the prefaces and dedications is given over to concerns about English competition with Spain in the Americas, to calls for merchant investment in the enterprise, and to millennial speculation on the identity of Praying Indians. The role of the colonial plantation was central to each of these discussions. Thomas Shepard's *Clear Sun-shine of the Gospel* (1648) performs perhaps the most comprehensive rereading of the planters' original motivations. The dedicatory epistle, added by English authors as a preface to Shepard's work, sets a discussion of New England's saints in the context of Old England's struggles. Amid the "present *troubles*" in England, the epistle hearkens back to the "evils" of bishop and king: "Among those who *tasted* of the *first*, I say not the *worst* sort of their cruelty, were these our *Brethren*, who to enjoy the *liberties* of the Gospel, were *content* to sit downe, and pitch their *tents* in the *utmost* parts of the Earth." But, the epistle recalls, God turns men's evil to his own triumphs: "It was the end of the *adversary* to suppresse, but Gods to *propagate* the Gospel."[19] Thus the English supporters of New England's cause reiterate the claim made in *New Englands First Fruits*, distinguishing between security for religious practices and the enterprise of Indian conversion. This passage elevates the colonists' new purpose, arguing that the propagation of the Gospel rivals England's civil wars in the providential design. Whatever events would unfold in England, English colonial writers argued, New England still had a task to complete, a role to fulfill.

Subsequent tracts continue to address the reasons for English migration as they track the success of Indian evangelism. In a 1649 publication, John Dury concluded that "these godly persons who fled into *America* for shelter from *Prelaticall persecution,* doe now appeare to be carried there by a sacred and sweet providence of Christ."[20] By 1651, the rhetoric surrounding mission work was no longer even this tentative: "appearances" have given way to declarations that link the design of Christ's worldwide rule to the conquest of Indian souls in New England. Henry Whitfield, a repatriated Connecticut pastor, proclaims in the conclusion to *The Light appearing more and more towards the perfect Day* (1651), his assurance that the migration had a providential purpose other than "shelter" from Laud: *"The Lord hath now declared one great end he had of sending many of his people to those ends of the earth."* God had dispatched his people to convert the heathens of America, who now *"sing and rejoyce in the wayes of the Lord."*[21]

The letter of dedication to *Clear Sun-shine,* signed by twelve prominent Englishmen, sums up the new disillusionment with the original reasons for colonization. It addresses the temptation to repatriate, employing a lexicon of religious persecution and providential design that critics today more commonly associate with the 1630s:

> Indeed *a long time* it was before God let them see any *farther* end of their comming over, then to *preserve* their consciences, *cherish* their Graces, *provide* for their sustenance: But when *Providences* invited their return, he let them *know* it was for some farther Arrand that hee *brought* them thither.[22]

That "farther Arrand" was to bring Christianity to Indians. With this redefinition of New England's purpose came a new relationship of the English periphery in America to the English center in London, of colony to metropole, as mission writers tried to work out the significance of their evangelical errand to all of the saints—whether in New or Old England—and as they petitioned readers for prayers, goods, and money to further Indian conversions.

In construing the Puritan mission in New England as a belatedly discovered "errand," I am contributing to the recent revisions of the idea of American exceptionalism, of a triumphant errand for New England, present from the very beginning, which became the basis for a U.S. national sense of destiny that continues to this day.[23] Recently, historians have asserted that instead of a progressive and positive sense of self, early New England literature betrays "an embarrassed contradiction of purpose" or even outright primitivism.[24] The history of the missions in New England confirms the conclusions of revisionist scholars about the earliest history of New England. If colonists from the first felt "not only called but chosen, and chosen not only for heaven but as instruments of a sacred historical design," then the delay of fifteen years in vigorous Puritan evangelism is inexplicable.[25] But the sudden appearance of systematic Puritan evangelism in New England years after the initial migration is less surprising if it is understood as evangelical improvisation, a response to events that made the initial colonial self-understanding—whether primitivist or simply confused—inadequate.

Despite my agreement with revisionist accounts of the earliest years of New England, by reading the mission discourse through the lens of literary criticism as well as historical analysis, I see that discourse as more forward-looking than a purely historical analysis may suggest. Theodore Dwight Bozeman argues that the belated adoption of an historic mission had only a limited influence and that, in keeping with other founders' ideas, even John Eliot had little interest in "enacting a New England Errand."[26] Richard Cogley extends Bozeman's reading by following the missionary's shifting eschatology, charting the development of a belief that New England and England would both be inaugural sites for the millennium. Cogley's arguments depend on specific and careful attendance to doctrine and on a detailed reading of Eliot's writings, but he discounts the missionary's more elaborate claims, noting they "should probably be regarded as rhetorical flourishes."[27]

Eliot does express great concern for scriptural purity, and he did not consciously seek to construct a "mission upon a hill" that would surpass England's millennial role. I am certainly not suggesting that we should read these texts more closely to recapture the sense of a glorious American beginning in the writings of the "founders." Nevertheless, the tracts demand a more careful analysis of their ringing assertions of a farther errand. We need to pay attention to the language of the mission tracts—even (or especially) to their rhetorical flourishes—in order to understand how the mission powerfully affected New England's place in transatlantic Puritanism and created a place for Indians in the Bay Colony. These texts do grapple with an errand for New England, with a special role that depended on Indian evangelism and focused on the Praying Indian figure.

This sense of exceptionalism, however, can best be understood in terms of the tracts' transatlantic production. Ironically, the most radical articulations of New England's special providential identity, especially *Clear Sun-shine*'s description of the colonies' new purpose, were penned by English writers for English readers. The publication of Puritan evangelism both took advantage of and was shaped by rising anxieties and expectations during the dramatic events at mid century. Authors on both sides of the Atlantic promised an Indian evangelism that offered a "farther Arrand," one that would contribute significantly to Christ's kingdom, confirm God's blessing on events in Old England, and justify continued English colonization. In this sense, an exceptional American identity is partly an Old World articulation. In evangelist discourse, the Praying Indian is significant to English identity on both sides of a British Atlantic, for New England did indeed become, albeit for a short time, a "mission upon a hill."

Praying Indians in Millennial and Colonial Time

The interest many metropolitan Puritans had in the evangelism of a far-distant people grew out of the radical religious beliefs coming to the fore in the 1640s and 1650s. During this period, many English Christians came to believe that they would live to see (or were already living within) the millennium, the thousand-year rule of saints prophesied to precede or, depending on one's interpretation of difficult scripture, to follow Christ's second coming.

The millennial beliefs of Puritans, whether in Old or New England, are generally traced most immediately to the early seventeenth-century writings of Thomas Brightman, who understood the approach of the millennium to be a gradual affair, but gave 1650 as the specific date of Christ's return.[28] David Katz explains that such prophecies led to an intense interest in readmitting Jews to England and in active proselytizing, for the "calling of the Jews" was understood as immediately preceding the second coming. Thus, "the Jews would be converted to Christianity by 1650," and "Brightman's confident predictions of their conversion before 1650 helped to agitate his English disciples to work as the servants of fate."[29] In other words, some believed that evangelism efforts could help usher in the millennium; for believers of such millennial interpretations, action was needed.[30] Following publication of Brightman's interpretations, general theorizing among Puri-

tans gave way to beliefs that connected millennialism to local situations and immediate action.[31]

In New England, action could take the form of repatriation to do battle against the king in England or of a new diligence in gospelizing Indians. But knowing whether the time was right for Indian evangelism
depended on the right interpretation of people and events. Commentators expressed ongoing uncertainties about the identity of Indians
and the part they would play in these prophesied events. Fixing their
identity was important for determining the start and progress of the
millennium and would indicate whether effective evangelism would
even be possible.

If Indians were Tartars or other gentiles, as mission writer Thomas
Shepard and, seemingly, most New Englanders believed, the millennium might be a good way off, whether they converted to Christianity
or not. Some believed that a seal would be set on Indian hearts until
after the calling of the Jews.[32] If, however, they were descendents of
the lost tribes of Israel, as English authors John Dury and Thomas
Thorowgood argued in the late 1640s and 1650s, it was possible that
the Middle Advent was at hand.[33] If Indians were Jews and their conversion could be documented, then the Praying Indian would serve as
confirmation that the civil wars, regicide, and Commonwealth government were indeed blessed by God, as progress toward the millennium would be indicated by the New World advance in Christ's
dominions. No wonder English observers were so interested in mission reports.

John Eliot himself came to embrace the theory of the Indians' Jewish origins.[34] But whatever his beliefs of their ancestry, he concerned
himself primarily with pragmatic action. He felt Indians were
uniquely ready for a government derived from scripture, because he
believed that Christ would not have to conquer and replace strong human institutions among Native Americans. Indians, even if they were
Jews, were but a remnant of their former selves, holding only vague
memories of their religious inheritance. Compared to other nations,
including England, Eliot argued, they were *"abrasa tabula scraped
board,"* blank slates on which the Christian conversion text could be
written.[35] Like all sinners, Indians needed to be conquered by Christ,
but because they were free from the corruption of a government derived from human wisdom, they did not need to submit to violent conquest, nor need missionaries call for the destruction of an old structure
of government to make way for the new.

Indeed, John Eliot substitutes a "benevolent" conquest—the winning of souls to Christ—for the violence of previous European-Indian encounters and even as a contrast to violence in Old England. From the first, the tracts compare New England's peace to Old England's troubles: geographical isolation afforded the colonies relief from the continual worldly upheavals that had afflicted England and Europe for so long. This colonial peace allowed New England saints to lead the way in conversion. Even *New Englands First Fruits,* published when England's troubles seemed most clearly to call New Englanders back to aid in the struggle against the Antichrist, articulated the strategic promise of New England's isolation. Just five years after the Pequot War (the first major conflict between Puritan colonists and Indians), the tract describes New England as a God-given place of "such peace and freedome from enemies, when almost all the world is on a fire that (excepting that short trouble with the Pequits) we never heard of any sound of Warres to this day."[36]

The tracts suggest that the successful conclusion of the Pequot War in 1638 closed the period of violence in New England permanently, even as England's troubles continued. That peace was central to the new mission. In *Light appearing,* Henry Whitfield describes New England as *"a place of rest, and a little sanctuary . . . in these troubleous times."*[37] In the scope of "troubleous times," the tracts include both the righteous violence of the civil wars and the political and ecclesiastical "brangles"[38] into which England's political and military situation devolved following the execution of the king. So the tracts reassure that violent conquest is a stage to be passed through on the way to the higher good of conversion, even as they also suggest New England would be a good model for Old—an argument some English signatories of the tracts were making elsewhere more directly.[39]

Conversion, as the tracts present it, is both distinct from and better than conquest. When critics of the New England Way or repatriated enemies of the Puritan colonies levied charges of avarice and cruelty on the part of Puritan colonists, Eliot and other missionaries responded with descriptions of Indian poverty and contrasted themselves favorably with Spanish conquistadors. The Spaniards, they charged, only wished to further their self-interest: "Other Nations who have planted in those furthest parts of the Earth, have onely sought their owne advantage to possesse their Land, Transport their gold, and that with so much covetousnesse and cruelty, that they have made the name of Christianitie and of Christ an abomination."[40] By contrast, they argued, English missionaries had nothing to gain. Repeatedly, the tracts stress the Praying Indians' extreme poverty and the missionaries' material sacrifices.[41] New England did not have the mineral wealth of Spanish colonies, but what had seemed a national embarrassment turned out to be a spiritual advantage.

This discourse on Spain served another purpose, one that meshed firmly with English imperial interests and that blurred any distinctions among religious, political, and economic motivations. By the time New England began publicizing Puritan evangelical efforts, accounts of Spanish colonization and Catholic evangelism were well known among English readers. These included fabulous rumors of the discovery of gold, stories of massed conversions of Indians—along with corresponding abuses of Indians—and assurances that England could easily supplant its national rivals in the New World. The stories gained credibility because many of their authors were Catholic priests: José de Acosta, who wrote *Historia natural y moral de las Indias*, published in 1604 as *The natural and moral historie of the East and West Indies*; Bartolomé de Las Casas, who penned *Brevísima relacíon de la destruccíon de las Indias*; and especially Thomas Gage, a lapsed English Dominican friar who published *The English-American: A New Survey of the West Indies* in 1648. Las Casas's work, originally published in 1552, was translated into English as early as 1583. Translations appeared in 1620 and again, significantly, in 1656 during the Interregnum.[42] Gage's work, in particular, influenced English plans to attack Spain. He sent a précis of his account to Cromwell sometime in 1653, summarizing his arguments for Spain's weakness and a sure English victory.[43]

England's imperial competition with Spain had early consequences for New England. As Karen Kupperman points out, in 1640 and 1641, Lord Saye debated John Winthrop as to where God had intended the English to plant, arguing that at most New England would be a temporary "way station" where colonists would await a fit time for settling Spanish holdings.[44] This mid-century English interest in the West Indies as opposed to New England, especially in terms of evangelism, was signaled in Castell's 1641 petition, which specifically names the islands in his title. Winthrop, of course, disagreed, contending that New England was also intended by God as a permanent Christian settlement.

Colonial awareness that metropolitan observers needed convincing that New England had a vital role to play translates in the tracts to an

appropriation of the anti-Spanish Black Legend charges of Spanish
cruelty and avarice and an offering of New England evangelism as a
counter to Spaniards' reputed greed.[45] Catholic conversions were
superficial, mission writers alleged, whereas Puritan conversions ran
deep. In *Glorious Progress,* John Dury concludes that "the Gospel in
its advancement amongst these *Western Indians,* appears to be *not
in word only* (as it was by the *Spaniards* among their Indians) *but
also in power, and in the Holy Ghost, and in much assurance."*[46]
In contrast to the proliferation of papal "hypocrites," the Puritans
characterized their few converts as "leaven," who would gradually
spread Christianity among their brethren, and the Puritan message
itself as a "mustard seed," starting small but branching widely, producing real Christians.[47] The tracts' writers concede that Catholic
priests had nominally converted thousands, but, as Thomas Shepard
predicts, the Spanish tenure in America was destined to be short-
lived:

> The beginnings and foundations of the *Spaniard* in the Southerne parts
> of this vast continent, being laid in the blood of nineteene Millions of
> poor innocent Natives (as Acosta the Jesuite a bird of their own nest re-
> lates the story) shall certainly therefore bee utterly rooted up by some
> revenging hand; and when he is once dispossest of his Golden Mansions
> and Silver Mines, it may be then the oppressed remnant in those coasts
> also may come in.[48]

Thus violent Spanish conquest not only produced false converts but
also tempted the "revenging hand" of God, a punishment that the Puritan dedication to evangelism would divert from the English. Spanish missionaries belonged to the pope—the Antichrist, according to
Puritans—and the realms of the Antichrist would surely be destroyed
when Christ ruled. It was then that the saints would witness the wisdom of the English colonists' slow but steady efforts. By invoking the
Black Legend and then contrasting themselves with Spanish competi-
tors, English mission writers claimed a benevolent colonial role, one
being fulfilled by the English presence in New England.

   All this might seem high-flown rhetoric, but the possibility of
Protestant Indians and the vilification of Spanish conquest had a con-
crete effect on English national policies. As Bumas points out, Spanish cruelties toward Indians were used as excuses to justify revenge on
all Catholics.[49] But the Black Legend and Indian conversions had an

importance for Cromwell's plans for America as well as the closer colonies of Ireland and Scotland. In 1651, Cromwell wrote to John Cotton in Boston, asking "what is the Lord a doing? What prophesies are now fulfilling?" Cotton at this time was a notable exegete; William London would list Cotton's *Powring out of the 7 vials, being an Exposition of the 16ᵗʰ Chap. of the* Revelation *of St John* among his best-sellers.[50]

Cotton's reply to Cromwell, as reported by Samuel Sewall in his diary, confirmed the Lord Protector's interest in attacking Spain in America. The New England divine "advis'd him that to take from the Spaniards in America would be to dry up Euphrates."[51] Cotton's interpretation was linked to the end-time prophecy of Revelation 16:12: "And the sixth angel poured out his vial upon the great river Euphrates; and the water thereof was dried up, that the way of the kings of the east might be prepared." Sewall reports that Cotton's advice had an effect on Cromwell; Cotton's interpretation of scripture "was one thing [that] put Him upon his Expedition to Hispaniola."[52]

Thus, during the 1650s, Cromwell set himself on a course of action meant to fulfill prophecy. Cotton's reading of scripture underscored Cromwell's sense that other signs pointed to the right time for an attack. The recent end of the Anglo-Dutch War left him with a large and well-equipped navy at his command, and Cromwell saw its deployment in the West Indies as providentially determined.[53] Then, too, some reported that settlers in New England were ready to relocate to lands south when England should take possession of them.[54] The fleet sailed in December 1654 to fulfill its "Western Design." Some New England Puritans did indeed see the expedition as worth support. Sewall writes that had the expedition succeeded, "Mr Higginson and 3 more wer to have gon to Hispaniola."[55] And Edward Winslow, former governor of Connecticut and New England's agent in London, proved his willingness to relocate in response to ongoing events when he joined the expedition as a commissioner.[56]

The first attack, on Hispaniola, failed miserably; English forces succeeded only in taking a much less fortified Jamaica. Despite this limited success, most observers, including Cromwell himself, saw the expedition as a profound failure.[57] Nevertheless, plans continued to settle and take advantage of the Jamaican colony. In September 1655, Cromwell selected Daniel Gookin as his agent to recruit New Englanders for immigration to Jamaica.[58] And here the connections between New England evangelism and Cromwell's Western Design are most striking. Gookin's career attests to the connections between England's imperial interests in the West Indies, New England's colonial purposes, and the common religious motivations of both. Gookin's errand to resettle New Englanders failed, but he quickly redirected his energies to local concerns, becoming the superintendent of Praying Indian towns the year after his appointment as Cromwell's agent, a position he kept with only a brief interruption until his death in 1687.[59]

So the players in the Western Design and the New England mission overlap, and the motivations for both are entangled. The Western Design—a plan that promised to redefine New England's identity as ancillary to other, future English colonies and that would concretely connect colonies to the spiritual and material fate of England—had an effect on New England mission literature. As we have seen, mission writers employed anti-Spanish sentiment almost from the first to prove that Puritan apostles were really about God's business. So it is not surprising that Eliot, in *A Late and Further Manifestation of the Progress of the Gospel*, a mission tract published in 1655, argues that converting Indians is more valuable than gold: "Let the gaining of any of their souls to Christ, and their turning to God from Idols to serve the living and true God, be more pretious in our eyes then the greatest gaine or return of Gold and Silver."[60]

Reports published a year or two earlier are more anxious to capitalize specifically on Cromwell's newly awakened interest in the Americas and to assert New England's importance. It may only be coincidence, but it is a striking one, that just as Cotton was corresponding with Cromwell about the millennial interpretation of scripture, the New England divine begins making appearances in the mission tracts. As he does for Cromwell, Cotton interprets providence and prophecies for John Eliot. In *Light Appearing* (1651), Eliot reports that he has "advised with Mr. *Cotton* and others" about the form of "civil gov't" that Praying Indians should adopt.[61] He reportedly confers with Cotton on several matters in this and the next tract and sends his proselytes to hear Cotton preach. Once, when Eliot feared that England's failure to supply the Praying Indians with necessary tools was a rebuke of his overly heavy reliance on man's strength rather than God's, Cotton counseled him to hold a day of fasting and prayer.[62] If Cotton is Cromwell's theological advisor in America, he is John Eliot's as well.

But in *Tears of Repentance* the close connections between Cromwell's deliberations on the Western Design and the mission literature resonate the most. Indeed, Bumas argues that the title of the tract is a Protestant reworking of *Tears of the Indians,* the well-known translation for Las Casas's title. Kupperman notes the usefulness of the Las Casas translation for whipping up anti-Spanish sentiments and drumming up support for English attacks on Spain.[63] But *Tears of Repentance* was published three years *before* John Phillips's translation of *Tears of the Indians.* It is possible that reports coming out of New England could have shaped Phillips's presentation of other American stories, and it is certain that the trope of tears and England's belief in its precedence over Spain by virtue of its relationship with Indians was circulating widely at this time.[64] In any event, Eliot's dedicatory letter for *Tears of Repentance,* addressed to Cromwell, engages in just the kind of language calculated to attract the attention of those who were pondering providence and deciding the fate of England in America.

Here, Eliot extends his arguments about England and Spain in America to focus on a more daring strategy: a comparison of colonial and metropolitan endeavors. New England saints, mission literature argues, had moved beyond mere violence and destruction to begin the constructive work of Indian conversion while England remained mired in schism and uncertainty. By 1653, at the height of millennial fervor in England, Eliot characterized providential history as twofold. In his letter to Cromwell, Eliot declares, "*The design of Christ in these daies is double, namely, First, To overthrow Antichrist by the Wars of the Lamb; and Secondly, To raise up His own Kingdom in the room of all Earthly Powers which He doth cast down.*"[65] On Parliament and Cromwell had fallen the obvious burden of violence. They had struck the first blows against Antichrist, defeating the king, and now Eliot urges the Cromwell to the second task:

> And as the Lord hath raised and improved You, to accomplish (so far as the Work hath proceeded) the first part of His Design, so I trust that the Lord will yet further improve You, to set upon the accomplishment of the second part of the design of Christ . . . so the Word of Christ might rule all. (212)

In the vertical imagery of "raising" and "casting down," Cromwell had so far only reached ground zero—old evils had been torn down; the building of new, godly structures awaited.

Although Eliot deferentially predicts that Cromwell will accomplish the second task, he elsewhere makes the point that while England was preparing the ground, he himself had already begun to raise Christ's kingdom. In an address "To the Reader," Eliot cites the prophecy "that the Gospel shall spread over all the Earth, even to all the ends of the Earth . . . all Nations shal become the Nations, and Kingdoms of the Lord and of his Christ" (214). In his own work of converting Indians, he asserts, *"Such Prophesies are in part begun to be accomplished"* (215). Cogley argues that when Eliot wrote this preface, he believed the "millennium was imminent at Natick because it was imminent in England.⁶⁶ The preface as a whole, however, urges Cromwell to greater action, pressing on him the significance of New England, whether as a sign of England's imminent transformation or a claim for the colonies' preeminence.

In *Tears of Repentance,* Eliot repeatedly refers to "Christ's design" in America (as opposed to Cromwell's "Western Design"?). His language suggests that he may have been privy to Cromwell's questions to Cotton about divine providence. Eliot and Cotton were close colleagues, and Samuel Sewell's discussion of the Cotton-Cromwell exchange so many years later indicates that news of the correspondence circulated. Eliot's dedication to Cromwell reads like an implicit answer to the Lord Protector's question for Cotton, "What is the Lord a doing? What prophesies are now fulfilling?" In this tract, dedicated by Eliot to Cromwell, the missionary assures his readers that whatever God may have been doing in parts south, He is clearly present in the mission work of New England:

> *I doubt not, but it will be some Comfort to Your heart to see the Kingdom of Christ rising up in these Western Parts of the His Blessed Kingdom, which shall (in his season) fill all the Earth: and some incouragement to your heart to prosecute that part of the Design of Christ, namely, That Christ might Reign.*⁶⁷

And, *"In these times the Prophecies of* Antichrist *his downfall are accomplishing"* (214). To those who had heard Cotton preach on the pouring out of the seven vials—or who, like Cromwell, received personal assurances from him about scripture meaning—Eliot presents the confessions of his converts as external confirmation: *"For this Cause I know every beleeving heart, awakened by such Scriptures, longeth to hear of the Conversion of our poor Indians, whereby such Prophesies are in part begun to be accomplished"* (214). New England's mission is important, Eliot maintains. To the careful observer, colonial evangelism and the Praying Indians it produced are part and parcel of a divine plan that included both England and America.

The Figure of the Praying Indian

Thus, for a time mission writers made evangelism and the Christian Indians it produced the focus of New England's identity. For a time English colonial discourse came to depend on the presence rather than the absence of Indians in New England. But if English desire (both colonial and metropolitan) for Christian Indians first made the invention of the Praying Indian possible and desirable, actual Indians who were Christians gave shape to the figure of the Praying Indian. Careful attention to mission literature as colonial narratives that reflect encounter rather than as historical archives to be mined for facts allows us to uncover—tentatively or suggestively—Massachusett, Narragansett, Nipmuck, and Wampanoag experiences at a moment of heightened English interest in evangelism.

Such glimpses of Indian agency are difficult to achieve and are subject to the limitations of the literary sources, written almost exclusively by English authors. Nevertheless, close reading of the mission tracts reveals both individuals who found in Christianity the means to understand better their colonized position as well as those who never ceased to resist the demands English evangelists placed on them. We can see moments in which the English preachers are taken aback by the persistence of Indian interlocutors, and we can see examples of Indians who learned to use Christianity and scripture to negotiate their place in the English colonial order.

Most of the tracts' descriptions of Praying Indians come from the letters John Eliot wrote to friends and supporters in England. Eliot was among the first generation of Puritan emigrants, coming at the age of twenty-six to New England. He soon became the teaching elder at Roxbury, Massachusetts, where he lived and worked until his death in 1690. Sometime in 1646 he preached his first sermon to Indians in their own language. Immediately thereafter he began writing accounts of his mission endeavors.[68] Eliot was a masterful self-publicist; he soon became *the* name in Puritan evangelism, and the ten mission tracts published in English between 1646 and 1671 are associated almost solely with him.

Tears of Repentance is a good example of Eliot's savvy publishing tactics. The missionary had his finger on the pulse of events even far across the Atlantic. He dedicates his part of the tract to Oliver Cromwell ("His Excellency, the Lord General *Cromwel*") in an address that at most was written a few months before Cromwell took the position of Lord Protector, a time when many in New England were uneasy about the radical changes taking place in their homeland.[69] Despite this lofty address, Eliot appealed to supporters in London primarily to describe the confession narratives of several Praying Indians. These had been delivered before English church elders in the hopes of founding an Indian church. However optimistic about New England's role in God's plan the prefatory materials are, Eliot must report that the trial did not go well. The confessors ran out of time, the elders were unconvinced that even the most well-respected among them were ready for church membership, not to mention leadership, and the Praying Indians failed to meet with approval. Nonetheless, as Eliot explains in a later tract, he thinks their narrative confessions are worth printing, both in order to see "what acceptance the Lord gave unto them, in the hearts of his people" in England, and also to influence New England authorities in the converts' favor: "My desire was, that by such Books as might be sent hither, the knowledge of their Confessions might be spread here, unto the better and fuller satisfaction of many, then the transacting thereof in the presence of some could doe."[70]

Eliot's approach here is a reminder of the interconnectedness of transatlantic English communities. The missionary-Indian encounter interested English readers and eventually influenced parliamentary debate and the print industry in London. The opinion of colonial affairs that resulted in turn influenced the tenor of Indian-settler relations in New England. The writings of John Eliot and other missionaries who celebrated a successful Indian mission stimulated the flow of good opinion and hard cash from metropolitan writers and investors. Moreover, because a successful mission depended upon them, the literature mandated a role for Indians. And so as the writings constructed a new evangelical errand in service to English colonialism, they also afforded Indians an identity with which they could negotiate a place—if painfully circumscribed—within the English colonies.[71]

Dubbed "praying Indians" by Eliot, a term that was generally accepted by other mission writers, Indian converts to Christianity in New England probably numbered around eleven hundred.[72] They were drawn from the Pawtucket, Massachusett, Wampanoag, Narragansett, Pequot, Mohegan, and Nipmuck peoples of southeastern New England.[73] Beginning in 1650, they settled in "praying towns," which were created out of lands set aside by New England authorities. As many critics have pointed out, these settlements were tantamount to reservations—and they became especially restrictive after King Philip's War, when Indian movement within English colonial borders was closely regulated. Physical restriction was met by other forms of control. Mission writings repeatedly explained the need to make Indians "men" before they could become Christians.[74] Thus missionaries ignored Indian cultures as nonexistent or discounted traditional Algonquian forms of dress, religious practices, labor, and gender roles as bestial and sinful. Missionaries began a program to reform these outward traits as they attempted to bring the inward soul to saving grace. As one missionary put it, "I thinke no great good will bee done till they bee more civilized."[75]

Missionaries and their supporters judged Indians to be most "civilized" when they spoke English, produced and wore English-style clothing, and gave over their traditional forms of medicine, government, and religion. This demand by the English for a cultural transformation to match the Indians' spiritual conversion constituted, in James Axtell's evocative phrase, a terrible "invasion within."[76]

Although mission writers recognized that outward signs were no sure indication of an Indian's salvation, the physical manifestation of grace in converts was taken as seriously in Indian conversions as it was in New England's tradition of public confession for church membership or in the debates over sanctification during the Antinomian Controversy. Richard Mather's prefatory epistle to the Indian confessions in *Tears of Repentance* notes that "sober and godly" critics demand evidence that Praying Indians conform themselves to English ways: "If there be any work of Grace amongst them, it would surely bring forth, and be accompanied with the Reformation of their disordered lives, as in other things, so in their neglect of Labor, and their living in idleness and pleasure."[77] Mather agreed; he and others demanded visible signs of internal grace; the efficacy of Indian conversion was gauged by the convert's appearance and demeanor. When Nataôus, or William of Sudbury, tells Edmund Browne that "[he] will pray to God as long as live [*sic*]," Browne demands an external confirmation: "He said, I doubt of it, and bid me cut off my hair."[78] Monequassun's deliberation on the same dilemma shows that Praying Indians themselves understood the connections between profession and behavior that they were to internalize. He confesses the difficulty he had in deciding to cut his hair, finally doing so by taking a scripture passage semiliterally: *"If thy right foot offend thee cut it off."*[79]

Praying Indians in the tracts manifest their internal change in other ways. Their transformation of traditional forms of dress in particular was taken to be constructively blurring the boundaries between Indian and English. In 1648, Eliot argued that converts grew in material wealth as they grew in the wisdom of God, and chief among their newly acquired goods were English textiles and clothing. Compared to the "wicked *Indians*," those who pray "have some more cloths then they."[80] At the first meeting of Puritan missionaries with Indians held in the home of a man named Waban, the Indian's son, who had been given to the English to be educated, appears "standing by his father among the rest of his *Indian* brethren in English clothes."[81] At another lecture, Thomas Shepard notes that many of the people attending were dressed in English-style clothing: "You would scarce know them from *English* people."[82] *Strength out of Weaknesse* published John Wilson's report of an Indian preacher "clad all in *English* apparrell (as most if not all others of them are)."[83]

No less impressive to the missionaries and to their readers was the use of English architecture and construction technologies. One of the primary prerequisites for gathering Praying Indians into church fellowship was their ability to erect "well sawen" structures.[84] Indians interested in Christianity began to impose English styles on their traditional dwellings several years before the organization of Praying Indians into the "orderly" space of the praying town of Natick, in which streets would be laid out with geometrical precision and each house would have its private garden plot. John Eliot reports proudly:

> The *Wigwams* of the meanest of them equallize any *Sachims* [Indian rulers, more often, "sachems"] in other places, being built not with mats but barks of Trees in good bignesse, the rather that they may have their partitions in them for husbands and wives togeather, and their children and servants in their places also.[85]

The new construction style reinforced Puritan hierarchies of husband-wife, parent-child, master-servant, discouraging a "looseness" of association of which Puritans disapproved, even as it undermined traditional Indian hierarchies by "equallizing" politically undistinguished converts with their sachems.[86]

Indians had, since first contact, appropriated useful English ways and technologies—as the English themselves had adapted Indian modes of warfare, farming, and local knowledge to their own use.[87] Often they did so without English sanction, and early accounts detail the efforts of colonists to control or restrict Indians' access to English goods, especially weapons.[88] Earlier English commentators assumed that Indians adopted the English language, dress, trade, and customs out of poverty, admiration, or fear, but Puritan missionaries welcomed and insisted on such changes. They believed Indians were "raised" both materially and spiritually when they cut their hair, sang psalms in their own language to English meters, or learned to spin yarn.

As mission writers praised Indian transculturalism, they constructed a new, recognizable Indian figure. Careful attention to the contours of this figure can tell us something about the lives of Christian Indians. After all, the interest some Indians had in acquiring the goods that so elevated them in English eyes indicates their motivation for participating in Puritan evangelism. But if we simply note such an interest, we do little to move beyond the most cynical assessments of early modern English commentators, who were sure that Indians converted to gain material wealth rather than out of spiritual belief. Without careful analysis, we risk slighting seriously and sincerely held religious beliefs or missing other motivations for conversion in this complex contact zone.[89]

A more important consideration is the ways Indians experienced Christianity—*were* Christians. But although Indian experiences are only partly suggested by descriptions of externals, any attempt to go further smacks up against the tracts' authorship. Although we draw our assumptions about missionaries' motivation, converts' agency, colonial identities, and, say, Nipmuck resistance from texts designed for specific rhetorical functions, their forms largely go unremarked. They were written by English authors in service to pedagogic, propagandistic, or economic aims, but the tracts are often treated as transparent windows to the missionary-convert encounter or as numbingly conventional. Ironically, such assessments—that mission literature is easy to interpret or simplistic in form and content—assume that colonial writers were unable to see their own productions in anything but the most naïve terms, and so wrote straightforward, formulaic descriptions, and that reading them against the grain reveals only our latter-day sense of evangelical exploitation. Such a reading is limited and risks erasing Indians from the accounts altogether. While we must remain alert to such exploitation, it is equally important to attend to what Thomas Scanlan calls the "interpretive status of native people" within English literature of the colonial period.[90]

A careful reading of mission literature reveals the unpredictable figurations of the Praying Indian and the varying, sometimes even conflicting representation of Indians and their significance to the colonial enterprise. As I maintain throughout this book, the conventions of evangelical writing should interest us very much, not least because we cannot understand these reports of encounter without accounting for the genres and figures with which the authors worked.

Understanding the difficulties of listening to Praying Indians in texts mediated by white authors must lead to creative interpretive approaches. Where the English missionaries recorded overt resistance, we can be sure it is for a purpose counter to the speaker's own. It may be that we hear Indians' voices most clearly in these tracts when they are speaking most conventionally, not because the English author lets his or her guard down and an "authentic" voice slips through but rather because all such moments inscribe Indian-English evangelical encounters.[91]

The presence of Indians, not just the idea of Indians as related to the frontier, savagism, natural nobility, or removal, shaped colonial evangelical literature. However much the English may have approved of their converts' use of English goods, it is clear that they were not in complete control of such exchanges. Indian converts fully understood that they could make demands once they had entered into a relationship with missionaries. For example, on first hearing John Eliot preach, Indians began making requests for land and eventually followed those demands with suits in English courts.[92] Out of a desire to find resistance and out of the equation of resistance with authenticity, it may be, as Hilary Wyss argues, that "we have ignored those who wrote and thought from a Native perspective that included a sense of their colonial position."[93] This perspective is (perhaps) easier to identify in the later works of literate Indian converts than in seventeenth-century English-authored descriptions of them. Nonetheless, by reading mission texts for the ways Christian Indians speak within the mission discourse, we can hear individuals commenting on their experiences with English colonialism through the forms we associate most often with Reformed Protestantism—the catechistical question, the conversion narrative, and the deathbed confession.

To the English identities constructed or affirmed by mission texts,

then, we must add a colonial Indian identity, that of the Praying Indian and see the lines of mission influence as triangular rather than
binary, as encompassing Indians, settler-colonists, and metropolitan
subjects alike. In keeping with such complexities in the mission discourse, *Dry Bones and Indian Sermons* does not follow a strict chronology, although the first half of the book focuses on Interregnum-era
representations and the second half on post-Restoration figurations.
Rather, I proceed generically and thematically, examining forms of Indian religious expression recorded by missionaries and other English
colonial writers and as often as possible considering the experience of
the Christian Indians that the tracts reflect.

As a close examination of the mission discourse makes clear, the
figure of the Praying Indian helped shape the belief, at a time of spiritual, economic, and political crisis in the colonies, that New England
had a place and purpose in God's plan that was special to itself but in-
timately connected with events in Old England. The chapters to follow explain that the Praying Indian was a figure in transatlantic
meditations on scriptural prophecy and colonial clashes over town
boundaries; in colonial translation practices and the early Christian
Indian church; in reports of the Antinomian controversy and in transatlantic debates over the New England Way; in experiments in early
American fiction and English-Indian diplomacy; in war histories and
in captivity narratives.

Finally, when the figure was abandoned by the white writers who
had originally published it, Christian Indians used the Praying Indian
figure as an expression of their community's viability and persistence.
The Praying Indian and seventeenth-century mission literature were
involved in a wide constellation of events and issues that have shaped
the scholarly and popular understanding of colonial America. This
was true even after the figure's particular cultural and historical moment had passed and colonial identities turned to policies of extermination rather than evangelical assimilation.

2 Seeing with Ezekiel's Eyes

Indian Resurrection in Transatlantic Colonial Writings

During the turbulent years of the English civil wars and the Interregnum, New England settlers found themselves faced with a dilemma. Should they return to England to take part in the new political, military, and religious battles taking shape there, or should they remain in New England? And if they were to remain, what purpose could the colonies possibly serve as divinely significant as that of Cromwell and his New Model Army? For many in New England, the answer was "none." Samuel Morison notes that out of twenty-four Harvard students who were graduated between 1642 and 1646, fourteen returned to England or Ireland. Of some twenty who were graduated in 1647, 1649, and 1650, only eight remained in New England.[1] The "city upon a hill" had been constructed, just as John Winthrop had promised in his migration sermon of 1630, but its residents found, contrary to his assertion then, that the eyes of *no* people were upon them, whether they had dealt falsely with God or not.[2] As I discuss in chapter 1, among other responses to these changes, colonists turned to the long-neglected project of proselytizing the Indians to identify for the United Colonies a "farther errand" that promised a new and unique role for New England on a transatlantic stage.

In England at this time, writers had taken up the difficult task of divining God's plan in the exciting but tumultuous events that engulfed them and in particular of discerning England's national identity within that plan. What polity was most appropriate to the rule of saints? How should recalcitrant subjects be brought into line, whether they were individual Christian dissidents or whole colonies? Civil order, toleration, Cromwell's military actions in Ireland: these were endlessly debated in Parliament and in print. Indians became important to metropolitan England, as they were understood to support or confirm various attempts at religious and national self-fashioning. For some in England, the most exciting and exotic speculation concerned the possibility that Native Americans were Jews, members of the lost tribes of Israel. English and European writers presented their theories of Native American origins in works such as the writings of John Dury, an enthusiastic millennialist who returned from continental exile to England after the execution of Charles I, and of Menasseh Ben Israel, a rabbi living in Amsterdam. Both men's speculations were included in Thomas Thorowgood's *Jewes in America* and referenced in William Greenhill's commentaries on Ezekiel.[3]

The discussion in the 1640s and 1650s depended on the belief that conversion of Jews would precede universal Christianity. Thus if Indians were gentiles, their conversion to Christianity could not signal the initiation of end-time events but was rather a taste of the massed conversions to come. If, however, Indians were members of the lost tribes of Israel, their conversion to Christianity could indicate Christ's imminent return.

Such theories of Indian origin and the accompanying millennial speculation were folded into English mission writings, to be met with anxiety by some and enthusiasm by others. In exchanges about Indian identity, conducted largely in the pages of tracts printed to publicize New England evangelical activity, a seemingly exceptional American figure was constructed—the Praying Indian. Whatever this figure's usefulness to Christian Indians, English writers contested the figure in order to fix not Native American but English national and English colonial identities. During this period, as Michael Warner explains, colonists were more interested in connecting to England than separating from their homeland: "Some of the North American colonies . . . were far from renouncing the English imperial project. They were still in the process of inventing it."[4] In the mission literature of the 1640s and 1650s, they invented it by "remembering" what earlier colonial writers had pointedly ignored; they invented it by insisting that Indians, not settler-colonists, were the sole and true focus of their errand into the Wilderness. In this way, English colonists could remain decisively, discursively English.

But of course by doing so, they marked themselves as emphatically non-English.[5] In the figure of the Praying Indian, the colonial strategy of stereotyping—exhibited as biblical typing in mission texts—is employed differently by English writers on either side of the Atlantic. Although the English mission effort is usually seen as work that united all English Protestants, a close examination of mid-century English speculation about Indians allows us to perceive colonial discourse as complex and contradictory.

Metropolitan writers' eager embrace of the Praying Indian figure, which confirmed their hopes for an imminent millennium, was met by an ambivalent colonial response. Wampanoags, Massachusetts, and Narragansetts, as well as New English Bostonians, Lancastrians, and Dedhamites, were enmeshed in colonial identities that corresponded to different axes of colonial-metropolitan influence.[6] Reminders of these various configurations of colonization may help to sort out the contradictory impulses present in the mission texts and in continuing critical assessments. We should keep in mind that different colonial power relations were simultaneously enacted in New England. English colonists' anxious relationship with their metropolitan mother country and the settlers' domineering relations with indigenous peoples profoundly shaped mission theology and practice. The literature of the mission discourse held these seemingly contradictory colonial formulations in tension. More broadly, a careful examination of mission literature reveals the extent to which the New England "city upon a hill," no less than the Indian mission itself, was a fragmented rather than unified outpost of empire.

Reading Millennial Signs

English colonists began to contribute significantly to the discussion of Indian conversion in 1643, with the publication of two competing representations of evangelism, *New Englands First Fruits* and Roger Williams's *A Key Into the Language of America*, which were followed closely by the first of the New England mission tracts, *Day-breaking . . . of the Gospell*, in 1647. The tracts initiated a flurry of publications directed toward English readers. In these works, Praying Indians were variously represented as redeemed captives of Satan, as warnings to English saints against apostasy and, significantly, as members of Israel's lost tribes. As I discussed in chapter 1, their progress in the faith would help observers determine the start and progress of the millennium. If Indians were truly "coming in," one then had only to discern their identity—Jewish, gentile, or pagan—to predict whether Christ's second coming was at hand.

For Puritan writers, discerning legitimate millennial identities for Indian converts depended on uncovering biblical types. Mission discourse found in the Hebrew prophet Ezekiel's vision of dry bones coming back to life an especially rich application to Christian Indians—people who, English writers asserted, had been "dead" in their sin before hearing the Word. Converts became important to the Puritan millennial imagination, and for a time the figure of the Praying Indian shaped a colonial discourse and fired the imagination of English writers on both sides of the Atlantic.

Mid-century conjectures about Indian origins and the millennial significance of conversion were not met with universal welcome. Understandably, writers who eagerly anticipated Christ's Second Coming and expected England to be the site of the New Jerusalem seized on signs that indicated Christ's rule among Native converts. If Christ's approach could be seen in New England, surely his rule in Old England was near at hand. Others, who understood the Second Coming as a time of disruption and fear, who simply did not believe in a literal rule of saints, or, as is likely, who disliked making their purpose dependent on continuing English-Indian coexistence, approached the theory conservatively. In the mission tracts at least, these differences seemed to fall along transatlantic lines. New Englanders were perhaps less interested in the identification of Indians as Jews than more radical millennialist thinkers in Old England. As Theodore Dwight Bozeman points out, "Millennial hope was a far more modest factor in early American Puritan theology than usually assumed and . . . Puritan millennialism in its formative phases generated hope for the future primarily by refocusing *retro*spective priorities."[7] In other words, New England Puritans hoped for a return to apostolic practices rather than a cataclysmic apocalypse. In the 1640s and 1650s, millennial hopes increased in New England but never approached the enthusiasm in Old England.

Even colonists who supported Indian evangelism and recognized the importance of the work to New England were cautious about identifying converts as end-time Jews. Thomas Shepard, minister at Cambridge, Massachusetts, acknowledged the momentous events shaping transatlantic Puritanism but held a tentative view of the Praying Indians' identity and prophetic promise. In *The Clear Sun-shine of the*

Gospel Breaking Forth upon the Indians in New-England, he admits that "the Lord Jesus seemes at this day to bee turning upside down the whole frame of things in the world, Kings, Parliaments, Armies, Kingdomes, Authorities, Churches, Ministers." The tract makes clear, however, that he remains skeptical about an imminent millennium:

> If Mr. *Brightmans* interpretation of *Daniels* prophesie be true, that *Anno* 1650. Europe will hear some of the best tidings that ever came into the world . . . I shall hope then that these Westerne *Indians* will soon come in, and that these beginnings are but preparatives for a brighter day then we yet see among them, wherein East & West shall sing the song of the Lambe: but I have no skill in prophesies, nor do I beleeve every mans interpretation of such Scripture.[8]

Such lukewarm sentiments confirm Janice Knight's argument that Shepard's views of the millennium were pessimistic. He "not only rejects radical typologizing, but also repudiates the orthodox practice of [John] Cotton that was dependent on a progressive reading of history." He was much less interested in projecting future joy than in identifying present failures.[9]

The preface to Shepard's tract, added in London by missionary supporters, does not contradict Shepard's cautious reading of unfolding providence, but the tone is surely at odds with his. While Shepard holds himself to a careful subjunctive tense ("If . . . then . . . I shall hope . . . if these be such times"), the epistle dedicatory by contrast seems giddy with hopeful expectation. Like Shepard, the writers do not offer an assured interpretation of Indian conversion, but they seem much more enthusiastic about present signs. They invoke and expand on Shepard's millennial discussion, without the New Englander's tentative tone:

> If the *dawn* of the *morning* be so delightfull, what will the *clear* day be? If the *first fruits* be so precious, what wil the *whole harvest* be? if some *beginnings* be so ful of joy, what will it be when God shall *perform* his *whole* work, when *the whole earth shall be full of the knowledge of the Lord, as the waters cover the Sea,* and East and West shal sing together the song of the Lamb?[10]

Whereas Shepard immediately follows his biblically allusive discussion with a corrective, "But I have no skill in prophecy," the dedication erases that rhetorical loss of energy and maintains a rising crescendo of speculative joy; the ending directly echoes Shepard's words but recasts his meaning. The next paragraph of the dedication begins not with Shepard's retreat but with a call to further the mission work: "What doth God *require* of us, but that we should *strengthen* the hands, *incourage* the hearts of those who are at *work* for him."

A problem in understanding these subtle differences is that they must be traced within a seemingly unified discourse. The figure of the Praying Indian was produced in reports and letters from New England but prefaced and published in London by Independent, Congregational, and Presbyterian authors who, as we see in the passages above, echo one another. Despite any discomfort, New Englanders had very pragmatic reasons for encouraging such radical millennial readings of their efforts. Colonists who were otherwise cautious about ascribing such significance to Native Americans, but who also had a voice in transatlantic discourse, understood the need for New England to acquiesce to those more enthusiastic Puritans in Old England.[11] After all, mission supporters in London told others on the basis of an imminent end time that donations to the missions would "add to the *comfort* of your owne *accounts* in the day of the Lord."[12] At a moment when all eyes were on Old England, when New England's economy, dependent on the regular infusion of people and wealth, had collapsed, enthusiastic supporters of Indian evangelism, eager to channel support from the imperial center, commanded "Masters of money" to "Come forth" and "part with your Gold to promote the Gospel."[13] In an even more telling admonishment, the financial support of New England missions was likened to financial speculation in a religious marketplace:

> This gaine of soules is a *Merchandize* worth the glorying in upon all the *Exchanges,* or rather in all the *Churches* throughout the world. . . . And of this the ensuing Discourse presents you with a Bill of many particulars, from your spirituall *Factory in New England,* as the improvement of your former adventures thether, for the promoting of that heavenly Trade.[14]

Nor were these admonishments mere rhetorical flourishes. Largely because of such publicity, colonial authorities did collect money and goods from individuals. In 1649, parliament passed an act establishing a corporation to finance and administer the mission, and ministers throughout England used their pulpits to appeal for funds.[15] This circulation of news, goods, and millennial beliefs directly affected colonial Indian policy. Colonial authorities established praying Indian towns and, as I discuss below, protected converts from local English encroachments on their lands and livelihoods.

Thus, by a powerful coincidence of theological, political, and economic needs and desires, otherwise disparate perspectives were stitched together in a series of tracts that described a linear progress of Protestant English missions, from *The Day-Breaking, if not the Sun-Rising of the Gospell with the* Indians in New-England (1647), to *The Light appearing more and more towards the perfect Day* (1651). And the most prominent "tailor" of this consensus was John Eliot. As Philip Round argues, Eliot was a prolific missionary author, "able to knit together areas of the English cultural field that would otherwise have been torn asunder by religious dissent, mercantile greed, and geographical distance."[16]

Dry Bones

John Eliot's role in shaping the transatlantic mission discourse can hardly be overstated.[17] In terms of the Atlantic divide I have been describing, Eliot straddles the gulf. A staunch supporter of the New England Way (he helped translate the *Bay Psalm Book*, he was a respected minister at Roxbury, Massachusetts, and was one of Anne Hutchinson's interrogators), Eliot's millennialist views were nonetheless extreme for New England, more in line with the signatories of *Clear Sun-shine*'s dedication than with Shepard. However, his skills as a fundraiser earned his support in New England even as his testimonies about converted life and Praying Indian beliefs appealed to readers in Old England.

Eliot began preaching regularly to Indians in 1646. Early in his mission work, he delivered a sermon for which he took a passage from Ezekiel as his text: "The children being catechised, and that place of *Ezekiel* touching the dry bones being opened, and applyed to their condition; the *Indians* offered all their children to us to bee educated amongst us."[18] Eliot based his sermon on Ezekiel 37, in which the prophet is carried to a valley full of "very dry" bones. God commands him to prophesy to the bones:

There was a noise, and behold a shaking, and the bones came together, bone to his bone. And when I beheld, lo the sinews and the flesh came up upon them, and the skin covered them above: but there was no breath in them. Then said he unto me, Prophesy unto the wind, prophesy son of man and say to the wind, Thus saith the Lord God; Come from the four winds, O breath, and breathe upon these slain, that they may live. So I prophesied as he commanded me, and the breath came into them, and they lived, and stood up upon their feet, an exceeding great army.[19]

The application of this verse to Christian Indians depended on the English perception that the Massachusett and other Native people were the "*saddest* spectacles of *degeneracy* upon earth."[20] Combining this sense of degeneracy with the trope of spiritual rebirth, Indian conversion to Christianity seemed an almost literal resurrection to Puritans, who had taken for granted that Indians were marked for death so that God's chosen—the English—could inhabit their lands. Allusions to spiritual rebirth abound, of course, in mission discourse as they do in Puritan literature more generally. However, Eliot's use of Ezekiel's vision as a type of his converts' resurrection received special elaboration and notice from his readers as millennial speculation about them grew.[21]

In the mission publications, Thomas Shepard was the first observer to respond to Eliot's use of Ezekiel to identify Christian Indians as the dry bones whose resurrection would establish the New Jerusalem. Shepard's *Clear Sun-shine* appeared the year after Eliot made his first published report. In his tract, Shepard commented on the seeming coincidence of providential signs surrounding Indian conversion:

It is somewhat observable (though the observation bee more cheerfull than deep) that the first Text out of which Mr. *Eliot* preached to the *Indians* was about the dry bones, *Ezek.* 37. where it's said, *Vers.* 9, 10. *that by prophesying to the wind, the wind came and the dry bones lived;* now the *Indian* word for Wind is *Waubon,* and the most active *Indian* for stirring up other *Indians* to seek after the knowledg of God in these parts, his name is *Waubon,* which signifies Wind . . . some of the *Indians* themselves that were stir'd up by him took notice of this his name and that Scripture together.[22]

Despite reporting on possible correspondences between scripture and converts in this passage, Shepard has faint interest here in seeking after such connections. He confirms that Waban has been an effective evangelist but downplays the coincidence of name and providential role. However instrumental Waban had been, Shepard writes, "we thinke there be now many others whom he first breathed encouragement into that do farre exceed him in the light and life of the things of God."[23] We might further see in his description a reproof of laymen who presume to interpret providential signs for themselves, since he finds the meaning Indians read into Waban's name only "somewhat observable." Shepard by implication equates an Indian custom of naming with an overzealous Christian reading of millennial signs.

Compare Shepard's rather tepid descriptions to the eager correction offered by John Dury, an enthusiastic millennialist in England. He was asked to contribute to a follow-up mission tract, published the following year, in which he critiques Shepard's "modesty":

> The observation is not to be sleighted (though the observer modestly said it was *more cheerfull then deep*) that the first Text out of which Mr. *Eliot* preached, was about the dry bones. . . . It may be there is not much weight in the observation, that the word which the Indians use for wind, is *Waubon:* and that an *Indian* of that name is, and hath been very sedulous for their conversion: Yet to me there is ground for a very weighty thought; that, that portion of Scripture should be first of all openned to them, which clearly foretold the conversion of *Israel.* . . . Why may we not at least *conjecture,* that God by a special finger pointed out that text to be first openned, which immediately concerned the persons to whom it was preached.[24]

Note Dury's suggestion that Ezekiel 37 had "immediate" significance for Native Americans. He assumes both a millennial interpretation of Ezekiel (the verse "clearly foretold the conversion of Israel") and the Indians' identity with Israel.

The differences in Shepard's and Dury's accounts can be attributed to personal beliefs as well as the divergent theological cultures developing in New England and in Old during and after the English civil wars, and they demonstrate the fragmented nature of colonial culture. The differences may also arise from the more pragmatic realities of settler colonialism, which resonated with Ezekiel's prophecy. Either way, these differences upend the notion of American exceptionalism. Millennial readings of Indian identity were understood as signs of the chosen status of England, not America. The lukewarm reception New

Englanders gave to Eliot's theorizing about Indian identity, in contrast to the metropolitan enthusiasm for the idea, can be attributed to the radical meaning Ezekiel's vision gave to Indian deaths and spiritual rebirth. While Londoners heard in these reports evidence of a fast-approaching millennium that they had helped to initiate, colonists may have perceived Indian "resurrection" as a military threat—Ezekiel's "dry bones," after all, are the remains of "an exceeding great army." The vision of dead Indians rising may have seemed uncomfortably like a nightmare reversal of the earliest reports of New England colonization or a judgment on recent military conflicts.

The challenge a "resurrected" people posed to New England's self-understanding is clear if we consider earlier descriptions of mass deaths. As so many of their writings show, Puritans believed that the land they settled had been "emptied" for them, granting them right to the land by *vacuum domicilium*. John Winthrop reported that God had "consumed the natives with a great plague," thereby providing a "warrant" for Puritan plantation in New England.[25] William Bradford called the plague a "late great mortality," which was so devastating in Indian communities that "thousands of them died. They not being able to bury one another, their skulls and bones were found in many places lying still above the ground."[26] Thomas Morton called the heaps of dead "a new found Golgotha."[27] When English colonists clashed violently with the Native residents they were displacing, military victories were likewise ascribed a providential meaning. John Mason, describing the vicious English attack on the Mystic Fort massacre in 1637, exulted, "Thus did the Lord judge among the Heathen, filling the Place with dead Bodies."[28]

Repeatedly, in the earliest writings about the Puritan migration, settlers (actual and potential) wrote that dead Indian bodies would give way to the living body of Christ. Winthrop's foundational sermon, "A Modell of Christian Charity," provides perhaps the best-known example of the bodily metaphor applied to English colonies. He describes the ideal organization for the new community that would be "planted" in New England: "All true Christians are of one body in Christ," and the body is "knit together" by love.[29] Winthrop uses imagery drawn from Ezekiel to explain how Christ's love, which connects men one to another, effects spiritual transformation:

> Now when this quallity [of Christian love] is thus formed in the soules
> of men, it workes like the Spirit upon the drie bones Ezek. 37. bone came

to bone, it gathers together the scattered bones of perfect old man Adam
and knits them into one body againe in Christ whereby a man is become
againe a living soule. (229)

Once reassembled, the body of Christ in the wilderness would be visible to all the world.

As we have seen, when England's civil wars began in the 1640s, both
New England's identity as the body of Christ in the wilderness and the
providential understanding of Indian deaths proved problematic. In
Eliot's work and in mission writings, the representational focus
shifted from the dead to those Indians who had survived, and the resulting vision directly competes with Winthrop's use of Ezekiel's
prophecy to describe an anglicized body of Christ in America. Even before John Eliot fully embraced the theory of Jewish Indian origins, mission descriptions altered the providential significance of the early
plagues:

> They being but a remnant, the Lord using to shew mercy to the rem-
> nant; for there be but few that are left alive from the Plague and Pox,
> which God sent into those parts, and if one or two can understand [the
> Christian message] they usually talke of it as wee doe of newes, it flies
> suddenly farre and neare, and truth scattered will rise in time, for ought
> we know.[30]

This identification of the survivors as a "remnant" is significant, as
the word was associated biblically with a small number of the house
of Israel who would renew the covenant with God. The providential
nature of the plagues thus is no longer directed toward Puritan settlers,
but rather has meaning for the Indian survivors converting to Christianity. Again, for the idea of a scattered "remnant" people waiting for
the word of God to cause them "to rise," Eliot finds his biblical type
in Ezekiel. Whereas Thomas Morton had seen a Golgotha in the heaps
of dead, Eliot saw the resurrection of Ezekiel's dry bones in the living
converts.

Eliot's typology challenged the hegemonic understanding of the
colonists themselves as the focus of God's particular favor, and his
publication of Christian Indian piety was not always seconded by New
England colonists. Eliot was obviously well aware of his fellow
colonists' unease with his work and with his application of Ezekiel to
the converts. In a 1649 letter, he openly addresses criticism by developing the notion of his converts as a religious spectacle, viewed cor-

rectly only by the righteous. He complains that critics have had no actual experience of the converts:

> Some, (as I am informed) who came from us to *England*, are no better friends to this work then they should, and may speak slightly of it: I do intreat that such may be asked but this question; Did they so much regard to look after it here, as to go three or four miles to some of our meetings, and to observe what was said and done there? if not, how can they tell how things be?[31]

Spectatorship is important here. If English critics cannot be eyewitnesses to the Praying Indians' performance, they had better attend to Eliot's testimony. Only his reports, Eliot implies, allow the world to see Praying Indians truly and judge them fairly.

By reading his reports, English supporters—however far removed from actual events—stand in Ezekiel's place and witness the miracle of resurrection. In this and in subsequent letters, Eliot repeatedly includes lists of the converts' spiritual questions so that English readers "might perceive how these dry bones begin to gather flesh and sinnews."[32] He implies that his readers, although an ocean away from the Bay Colony itself, have a more accurate, eyewitness view via written reports than those unscrupulous sorts recently come from New England, who, Eliot suggests, had been given eyes to see but saw not. Thus Eliot redirects the rhetoric of spectacle and covenant that appeared in Winthrop's sermon to colonists on board the Arbella. Then, Winthrop employed what Michael Warner calls "a creepy erotics of visibility," in which the New England saints were always to consider that the "eyes of all people are upon us."[33] In mission literature, visibility is no less creepy; Christian Indians are constantly subject to surveillance, even unto their bones, flesh, and sinews. Moreover, the gaze is no longer directed *at* colonists but *by* them. Eliot becomes Ezekiel, prophesying to England, enabling his readers to see and understand as he redirects the same metaphors of Christian embodiment Winthrop used twenty years earlier.

Performing Resurrection

Most significant to an analysis of this trope of resurrection in a transatlantic context is Eliot's description of his converts' civil organization. In his report the missionary touches on both the global and local consequences of evangelism. Eliot saw his experiences with Praying Indians as experiments (in the sense of experiential knowledge) in the ideal civil and ecclesiastical organization of Christian communities. This experience led directly to the invention of so-called praying towns—reserves set aside for converts; in turn, the praying towns became examples for the kind of godly rule he sets out in his *Christian Commonwealth*.[34] According to his very pragmatic millennialism, this rule would be the means by which he and his converts and all who submitted themselves to scriptural rule would usher in the worldwide kingdom of Christ.[35] Eliot modeled praying-town rule on Exodus 18, in which Moses organizes his people by hierarchies of tens, fifties, and hundreds. When the town of Natick was organized along these lines, male residents dramatically enacted the biblical scheme. Following a sermon, Eliot reports, the residents of the first praying town chose their immediate governors: "Every man chose who should be his Ruler of ten, the Rulers standing in order, and every man going to the man he chose."[36]

As he continues his report of the town's formation, Eliot's brief description of Natick's rulers suspends time for a brief moment. He describes himself as an Ezekiel rather than a Moses as he watches the men of Natick arrange themselves behind their rulers: "It seemed unto me as if I had seen scattered bones goe, bone unto his bone, and so lived a civil politicall life" (172). Here he is gazing, like Ezekiel, at the vision of dry bones reassembling themselves into human form. At this moment, he does not see contemporary Massachusett men but the remains of Israel. Ezekiel's vision of resurrection is realized by this performance—as the men choose their rulers, the body of Christ is assembled.

Eliot's reading of this dramatic spectacle of Natick's "tithing men" (171) articulates a new providential identity for English colonists. Whereas in earlier publications, settlers themselves were to form the body of Christ, now Praying Indians embodied Christ's rule. In Eliot's descriptions of the praying town's formation, he offers a direct challenge to the settlers' self-understanding—Praying Indians not only figuratively construct the body by entering into covenant, but they also dramatically perform their spiritual resurrection with their own, real bodies, arranging themselves "bone to his bone."

On the one hand, this presentation in all its performativity is problematic, given the Puritans' suspicion of role-playing and especially of possible Praying Indian hypocrisy. But in the mission discourse, par-

ticularly on the part of New England, Puritan antipathy to the "artifi-
cial" gives way, time and time again, to the demand that Indian converts take on the proper appearance of visible saints, in other words,
that their dress, hair, speech, gesture, and visages conform to English
expectations. New England writers reported their observations of Indian worshippers' clothing and demeanor in meetings, even when they
could not report on the substance of the prayers and sermons because
they did not speak the language. Moreover, the inherently theatrical
spectacle of public confession is perhaps nowhere so well documented, certainly nowhere as well publicized as in the spectacle of
Praying Indians.[37]

In *Theater Enough*, Jeffrey Richards argues that performativity and
theatrical metaphors infuse Puritan identity and action generally. In
particular, he points to Winthrop's "Modell of Christian Charity" as
providing "a governing metaphor for religious mission":

> The city on a hill becomes in essence a substitute theatrum mundi,
> more limited in space and action than the broadly interpreted figure
> from English drama; yet, because biblically derived, it gives legitimacy
> to an image of actor, platform, and spectator that commands behavior
> rather than simply expresses it.[38]

Eliot's biblically derived "governing metaphor"—the dry bones—
likewise lends legitimacy to the Praying Indians. Clearly, Eliot has
been awed by the performance before him. Moreover, his presentation
of the theatricalized town formation solves the problem of hypocrisy
that is always lurking for Puritans. The performers' reaction is unre-
coverable (even for the English at the time, no less than for us today).
At most, we are left with questions: How is the moment experienced
by the men of Natick? Are these new Christians performing this physical arrangement of their bodies to placate or please Eliot? Does this
ritual resonate for them as it does for him? Perhaps, as Jean O'Brien
suggests, Ezekiel's vision "reverberated" among native Christians.
But we cannot hear those echoes through Eliot's noisy mediation, nor
does the record suggest that he himself tried to sense such reverbera-
tions.[39] In fact, Eliot does not say that he communicates to the men
of the town the perceived parallel between the valley of the dry bones
and Natick. Ezekiel is not explicitly described as a part of direct, cross-
cultural dialogue, and one has the impression that the new Christians
and their preacher do not share this vision: "It seemed unto me as if I

had seen scattered bones goe, bone unto his bone." The "seeming" is private; it belongs to Eliot-Ezekiel, not to the "resurrected" men. Although Eliot tells us he had opened and applied this verse to them, the sermon is not mentioned here. He reminds us only of his preaching on Exodus 18, the model for the praying town's organization.

From the English perspective, then, Praying Indians can perfectly match "being" and "seeming" in a way that English colonists could not. In the tracts, Praying Indians "authentically" inhabit their divine roles because they do so "naturally." They are not described as seeing themselves in Ezekiel's vision, and Eliot's personal vision of Indian resurrection keeps the self-consciousness that can lead to artful self-presentation at bay. Only he—and by extension his English readers—have the perspective of Ezekiel.

Nevertheless, Eliot does construct an "Indian" subjectivity, attaching it to an alternate biblical allusion. His role as spectator allows him to witness a vision of resurrection, but the actual display of the men's bodies is meant to represent Exodus 18:19–22, which, Eliot assures his readers, his converts have heard "expounded" several times."[40] In these verses, Jethro, Moses' father-in-law, counsels Moses to spare himself direct oversight of the people of Israel by providing a hierarchical civil organization, with "rulers of thousands, and rulers of hundreds, rulers of fifties, and rulers of tens." Thus, Eliot cannily creates a double meaning for this moment of town formation. Praying Indians act their exilic parts self-consciously, performing civil organization for Eliot-Moses who, as their spiritual leader, must be a participant. But they are innocent of artifice when it comes to their millennial identities, which only Eliot-Ezekiel recognizes. This doubled significance of Praying Indians is politically conservative, however radical it might have been theologically. As Eliot explains, his converts "look onely into the Scriptures" for their government, but they submit that local, scriptural government to the larger English power: "In this Government among themselves they doe reserve themselves in that poynt to owne [the English] as their superiors" (171).

Natick and Dedham

Regardless of Eliot's attempt to place Natick within the Bay Colony's control, and regardless of Eliot's lifelong support of New England hegemony, the performance of resurrection at Natick—despite, perhaps,

Eliot's intentions—was deeply subversive of the Bay Colony's polity and identity, a challenge that came to the fore in settler-Indian litigation. Almost immediately after Natick's founding, the occupants of Dedham, an adjacent English town, were concerned about losing land to the Praying Indian settlement. Their concern soon changed to open contention with the Indian converts and their leaders and to litigation in the Massachusetts courts.[41]

In this fight over land use, millennial representation meets the material entanglement of Native peoples and settler-colonists. In 1651, the Massachusetts court ordered the town of Dedham to yield two thousand acres to Natick. In 1652, just after the Praying Indians delivered confessions before English church elders in hopes of forming an Indian church, the court appointed a committee to lay out "meete bounds" for the Indian plantation. Dedham objected to the Indians' land claims, and the boundary survey was protracted for several years. Eliot and the Praying Indians came forward to press Natick's rights in this disagreement; court records show a rancorous debate between the evangelist and Dedham officials. Although the records comprise only transcriptions of white colonists' petitions and testimonies, it is evident that prominent Natick residents actively challenged Dedham's land claims. In May 1653, the records note that "there beinge a difference betweene the inhabitants of Dedham & severall of the Indians about land which the Indians doe challenge within the bounds of there [sic] town," a committee was appointed to "consider & determine what they shall judge necessary in relation to" the request of Dedham residents.[42]

The Dedhamites were particularly incensed by "some affronts offred them by the Indians, as also some difference in relation to land betweene them" (243), suggesting that there were some ongoing personal as well as legal encounters. In 1661, the constable of Dedham was directed to "Attach the Goods, and for want thereof the body of John Speene the Indian at Natick & Thomas Speene an Indian at Natick" for "Illegall possessing, and improveing, and Detaineing a parcel of Land Due" several Dedham residents. Attachments were also served on Waban, Nawanitt, "Peeter Indian & Divers others." Although Eliot is always named in these actions, he was not present at the jury trials of the cases, as his later petitions to the court mention.[43] Praying Indians were fully involved on their own behalf in these disputes, and the trials seem to have been quite contentious.

In two cases, the jury found for the Dedham plaintiffs, but the mag-

istrates refused the verdict. The colonial hierarchy was split on the issue of how to treat Praying Indians. Eventually, the Massachusetts
court ruled in the Indians' favor, granting Natick four thousand acres.
In "Red Puritans," Neal Salisbury notes that antagonism to Praying
Indian populations "came principally from those settlers in immediate contact with them. . . . The other English generally offered less resistance. This was due largely to the missionaries' success in
presenting conversion as a positive solution to the problem of Indian
'savagery.' "[44] The Dedham-Natick land dispute follows this pattern,
which parallels the disparate reception of millennial typology by colonial and metropolitan readers. Dedhamites resisted the praying town's
claim to land, but Bay Colony magistrates, who were not immediate
neighbors to the Indians, granted acreage to Natick on John Eliot's rec-
ommendation.

Eliot extends his evangelistic ideals to his understanding of this English-Indian land dispute, making repeated recourse to idealized notions of mission and town founding. Although he wished to adhere to
the law (indeed, his arguments were based on his interpretation of the
law and the Indians' legal rights), the effect that an adverse decision
might have on the Praying Indians was equally important: "If these
lands now sued for be taken from us Natick is overthrown from being a Towne."[45] Moreover, he reminds the court in 1662, less friendly
Indians are watching and learning from their dealings with converted
Indians:

> These actings of the English, doe make the prophane Indians laugh at
> the praying Indians, and at praying to God, as I heard with my owne ears
> at Conecticot, with respect unto Ogquonikongquamesit [Okom-
> makamesit, a praying town], which is in effect overthrown, some gone
> as I am informed to one place, some to another, some to the non pray-
> ing Indians among their kindred, others know not what to doe. To
> Natike they dare not come because of Dedhams actings. Now if Natik
> also be overthrowne, let wise men look upon the consequences, in re-
> spect of God and man. (259)

Eliot is reminding the court of the colony's responsibility and interest
in an Indian policy that extends beyond this local dispute to both temporal and spiritual concerns.

In contrast to Eliot's learned and careful, but idealistic arguments,
Dedham brought forward learned and careful, but legal arguments.
They adduced multiple testimonies, cited grants and deeds, and dis-

cussed the principle of *vacuum domicilium*, which Eliot accepted but claimed was not in effect for Natick.[46] Dedhamites were uninterested in the importance of a settled and secure Praying Indian town, whether to satisfy New England's local desire for a pacified Indian population or to prove transatlantically that New Englanders were accomplishing their new errand. In response to Eliot's 1662 petition, they assert that not only have the Indians settled on and improved land that belongs to Dedham, but by doing so, they also forfeit claim to the two thousand acres the court granted to them in 1651. They are "legally Cutt off of having any Lands in Dedham bounds" (252). In light of such a claim, Eliot's belief that the Dehamites wished to drive the converts out of English colonial bounds does not seem extravagant.

Throughout the dispute, the court sought to placate Dedham by its decisions and recommendations. Nevertheless, its rulings ultimately supported Natick Indians because, during this period, the court saw its role as protector of special Indian claims. In 1660, the "Christian friends and Neighbors" who adjudicated the case had suggested that Eliot confess his actions to be "very irregular, and such as he will not justify in himselfe or Any other." Further, the ruling requires that Natick Indians acknowledge that they possess their land by virtue of "the Love and Christian condesendency of the English of Dedham and not from the right of Any Indian Title out bidding theirs" (249). Thus the court reinforces the notion of New England's special care for Indian converts. But even as it continues the colonial investment in Indians as millennial figures, the court makes clear that it does not intend to set any other precedent. Such grants of land to Indians reflect special circumstances.

Although the final ruling favors the Natick Indians, it also foreshadows later treatment. Natick had retained its lands by virtue of its inhabitants' favored status as symbols of New England's sacred purpose. When the Praying Indians ceased to embody millennial promise, New England authorities withdrew their "encouragement," and the converts were left vulnerable to the avarice and antagonism of their English neighbors.

Indian Sermons

As the example of Dedham's rivalry indicates, detaching material effects from the spiritual was difficult in New England, where Native and English residents regularly competed for resources and for military dominance. The image of "resurrected" Christian Indians put added pressure on English colonists, who were contending in the courts and in the fields with the original residents over land use and possession. Before 1646, when the few Christian converts were perceived as simple objects of charity, they could be removed and resettled at will. But one doesn't evict the body of Christ out of His settlements. And one certainly doesn't raze a New England mission "factory" that is a significant force in the colonial economy.

Throughout the 1640s and 1650s, then, colonial authorities gave their support to Eliot's mission, recognizing the political and economic need to do so. The mission created capital for the colonies, and Eliot was too well connected to ignore. If, however, colonists were only reluctant supporters, readers in Old England were eager to embrace Eliot's optimistic reports. In London, unlike in Dedham or in the Massachusetts General Court, English Puritans had no pesky real-world issues to contend with as they seized on signs indicating the millennial identity of Christian Indians. English contributors to mission publications display enthusiasm for the notion of Indian resurrection, and it is clear that these writers do not consider the animation of Indian "dry bones" an immediate threat. Rather, they assume England is the focus of divine interest and see in the reports of Indian conversions good material for chastening their backsliding English brethren. These writers employ Ezekiel's lexicon of "resurrection" and "rising" to characterize the relative spiritual states of the English and the Indians. So the preface to *Clear Sun-shine of the Gospel*, signed by twelve prominent Congregationalists and Presbyterians, laments that while Indians are being resurrected spiritually, the English are apostate: *"Oh that* England *would be* quickened *by their risings, and* weep *over her own declinings!"*[47] Part of the power of these admonishments is that the lesson comes from so unexpected and exotic a source: "O that Infidelity should do that which those who professe themselves beleevers cannot do!" (34).

On its face, such rhetoric continues the tactics of sermons and tracts from the years of the Great Migration, when Puritans articulated the reasons for emigration and warned that God's wrath would descend on England.[48] As in those earlier texts, New England is held up as a lesson and model for the world. The letter to the reader in *Clear Sunshine* speculates, *"Who knows but God gave life to* New England, *to* quicken Old, *and hath* warmed *them, that they might* heat *us,* raised *them from the dead, that they might* recover *us from that consumption, and those sad* decayes *which are come upon us?"* It goes on to offer the mission report as a foreboding "Indian Sermon" in the hopes that *"though you will not hear us* [the 12 signers of the letter], *possibly when some* [converts] *rise from the dead you will hear them."*[49] The tracts do more than imagine the transformation of the wilderness into a favored nation or Indians into Englishmen. Rather, they describe a complete reversal: Indians quicken; English die.

The Light appearing more and more towards the perfect Day, a tract penned by a former New Englander, Henry Whitfield, provides a point-by-point comparison of Indian piety and English apostasy. He envisions England's judgment if warnings are not heeded: *"These Indians will rise up in judgment against us and our children at the last day. Brethren, the Lord hath no need of us, but if it please him, can carry his Gospel to the other side of the world, and make it there to shine forth in its glory, brightnesse, power and purity, and leave us in Indian darknesse."*[50] Although Whitfield is a representative of New England, his prose here indicates that he sees himself as an Englishman inhabiting a space far removed from a New England on "the other side of the world." The Indian threat, for him and for his fellows in London, is a distant one. And in his vision, Praying Indians—the new recipients of the Gospel—are witnesses, accusers, and perhaps executioners of sinning Englishmen.

Such a reversal of national and providential identities might seem to favor New England's colonists over metropolitan observers, because through their mission work they would become the means by which Christ would establish his new Kingdom. They were Ezekiels, prophesying to Waban-wind, and Eliot certainly embraced this role. But New Englanders were not accustomed to such casting. In settler literature, *Indians* were God's instruments for blessing or punishing the English colonists as a chosen people, not the other way around.[51] Again, the small differences between Shepard and the English writers are instructive. Shepard also looks to English sinfulness to illuminate the mission discourse, but the English prefacers to *Clear Sun-shine* saw a great contrast between Indian and English faithfulness, one that would cast shame on the English. Shepard says, "I dare not speake too much, nor what I thinke about their [i.e., Indians'] conversion, I have seen so much falsenesse in that point among many English, that I am slow to beleeve herein too hastily concerning these poore naked men."[52] English sin leads him to doubt the fullness of Indian conversion, since the latter, as "poore naked men," have far fewer helps to faith.

The differences are a function of colonial proximity. London writ-

ers viewed resurrected Indians from a comfortable distance—one almost detects a *frisson* of excitement at the exotic danger of being
plunged into "Indian darknesse." In contrast, the notion of Indians
"rising up in judgment" against Englishmen was being read by
colonists who had lived through the cycles of conflict in the early settlement period. The positive vision of Indian resurrection was terribly
fragile, as the vilification of Praying Indians during King Philip's War
in the 1670s demonstrates. The decision many converts made to fight
against the English confirmed settlers' suspicions that Indians who
"rose" were doing the work of Satan, not of God. Wartime literature
widened the gap in colonial and metropolitan representations, and as
I discuss in chapter 6, the war caused mission representations to re-
vert to racist stereotype.

Walls of Prejudice

Eliot, by contrast, seems to have kept his interest in Ezekiel's
prophecy all his life. Samuel Sewall reports hearing of a "small Paraphrase of Mr. Eliot's upon Ezek. 37. written about half a year before
his death."[53] But other colonists illustrate New England's underlying
distrust of Eliot's mission formations. In his 1694 biography, *The Life
and Death of the Reverend Mr. John Eliot*, published four years after
the missionary's death, Cotton Mather dismisses the methods of
Eliot's evangelism and creates a Christian Indian figure who is little
more than a brute animal. Most revealing is the way Mather deals
with Eliot's millennial beliefs. Mather reviews how Eliot, led by
Thomas Thorowgood and his publication of Menasseh ben Israel's
ideas, endorsed the theory that his converts were members of the lost
tribes of Israel: "I confess there was one, I cannot call it so much guess
as wish, wherein he was willing a little to indulge himself; and that
was *that our* Indians *are the posterity of the dispersed and rejected* Israelites."[54] Clearly, Mather considers this a crackpot idea and Eliot's
endorsement somewhat of a weakness. Then again, according to
Mather, the missionary must have been a little crazy in the first place
to have devoted so much of his life to Native American evangelism:
"To think on raising a Number of these hideous Creatures unto the
Elevations of our holy Religion, must argue more than common or little Sentiments in the Undertaker" (88). As Mather painfully argues,
Eliot's mission was a lost if noble cause. He calls Native Americans

"the veriest *Ruines of Mankind*" (82), whose capacity for Christian salvation was little better than beavers, those other native inhabitants of New England.[55]

Mather's dismissal of Eliot's theory is a distressingly familiar-sounding articulation of America's continuing settler racism. He describes Eliot as a Pauline fool for Christ, at least in terms of his mission work. Indian evangelism is a worthwhile effort, he suggests, but it does not do to get too worked up about it.[56] Reading through Mather's account of Eliot's life, one suspects that Mather rather wished he could pay homage to a respected founder without having to account for Eliot's nutty ideas of Indian origins. But Mather could not ignore Eliot's belief. However quickly he passes over it, a half century earlier the theory had been taken earnestly and had been a source of significant metropolitan support for the colonies. Eliot's views on Indian origins were sought out and respected. His reputation for pious endeavors continued until long past the high point of his mission activity and well into his old age. But after the Restoration, especially in the wake of King Philip's War, the theory simply did not have the power to merit continued New England attention. Despite the seeming differences between Mather and earlier New England writers, Mather's patronizing account of Eliot's beliefs and motivations is an extension of colonists' longstanding reservations about enthusiastic millennial theorizing. It participates in colonial anxieties about the threatening presence of Massachusetts, Pequots, Narragansetts, Nipmucks, and all living Indians—Christian or not—in the Bay Colony.

Not until the threat of actual Indian "rising" was perceived to be past did white writers in New England safely employ the trope of resurrection Eliot and his English supporters popularized—and then only in such a way as to affirm the notion's bloodless impotency and to engage in what Renato Rosaldo has called "imperialist nostalgia."[57] Rather than real renewal, a physical embodiment of Christ's kingdom, Indian resurrections in later writings are ghostly, and the real bodies that rise up to inhabit the land are those of white settlers.[58]

William Cullen Bryant's poem "The Prairies" provides a nineteenth-century American example of this discourse, which draws on the trope of resurrection to lay claim to the land for white settlers. The poem describes a "race" of "mound builders" who occupied the prairies in ancient times and who were conquered by "the red man." "All is gone," Bryant laments, "all—save the piles of earth that hold their bones."[59] This loss is perceived as inevitable. Rising from the dead is described as a cyclical phenomenon, once again with a providential meaning:

> Thus change the forms of being. Thus arise
> Races of living things, glorious in strength,
> And perish, as the quickening breath of God
> Fills them, or is withdrawn."
>
> (ll. 86–89)

Bryant concludes his poem with a dream of white settlers who seemingly rise out of the mound builders' burial grounds to displace the "red man":

> I hear
> The sound of that advancing multitude
> Which soon shall fill these deserts. From the ground
> Comes up the laugh of children, the soft voice
> Of maidens, and the sweet and solemn hymn
> Of Sabbath worshippers
>
> (ll. 115–20)

As Bryant's poem suggests, nationalist writers used the trope of resurrection to articulate U.S. manifest destiny. This appropriation only works, however, once the power of the seventeenth-century vision is defused. "All is gone," Bryant asserts, and in the words of another nationalist poet, only "timorous fancy" conjures the images of Indians.[60]

Throughout this chapter, we have seen how English writers used the trope of Indian resurrection and the Praying Indian figure in their so-called Indian sermons. Although mission tracts give some indication of the reception by converts of Christian millennial theorizing on their origins and of the application of Ezekiel's vision to their lives, it is difficult to penetrate the layers of mediation. But the archive does provide later writings in which Indian authors respond to and employ the tropes early colonial writers constructed. Counter to Bryant's nineteenth-century example—and to the nineteenth-century assumption of the "vanishing" Indian—is the powerful writing of William Apess, a Pequot Methodist orator and author, who skillfully draws on the missionary discourse to argue for Native rights in the 1830s. In "Eulogy on King Philip," he uses Increase Mather's castigation of

Philip as an Indian "of cursed memory." Apess goes on to critique Mather's unchristian sentiment, employing the tactics of reversal colonial writers used some two hundred years before:

> He ought to have known that God did not make his red children for him to curse. . . . Now, we wonder if the sons of the Pilgrims would like to have us, poor Indians, come out and curse the Doctor, and all their sons, as we have been by many of them. And suppose that, in some future day, our children should repay all these wrongs, would it not be doing as we, poor Indians, have been done to? But we sincerely hope there is more humanity in us than that.[61]

In his writings, the militant threat of Indian "rising" in retribution is barely contained by the Christian promise of future divine judgment. Take heed, he warns, the English settler-colonists built "walls of prejudice" with "untempered mortar, contrary to God's command; and be assured, it will fall upon their children" (288). Thus, in a reversal that could not have been imagined by seventeenth-century writers, Apess preaches *his* "Indian sermon," a work that confirms the challenging power of the trope in colonial American literature.

3 Wielding the Sword of God's Word

Translating and Reading the "Indian Bible"

If Indian conversions seemed threatening to English colonists, the "resurrection" of Ezekiel's dry bones a fearsome vision, the settlers saw themselves as sufficiently armed, at least spiritually, to meet the Indian challenge. The "sword of God[']s word" is the phrase Thomas Shepard used to describe the divine power behind the Puritans' feeble efforts to convert Indians. Borrowing language from the letters of the apostle Paul and from the Book of Revelation, Shepard asserts that whatever the failings of Puritan evangelists, as Ephesians 6:17 puts it, the "sword of the Spirit, which is the word of God" would overcome them. His allusive metaphor is a reminder that Puritans saw the evangelism of native peoples as a conquest no less militant for being (as they insisted) spiritual rather than physical.

John Eliot more than once compared his efforts to those of the apostle Paul, whose letter to the Ephesians explained that the sword of God's word was directed "not against flesh and blood, but against principalities, against powers, against the rulers of the darkness of this world, against spiritual wickedness in high places" (Eph. 6:12). The consequences for those who would resist are described in Hebrews 4:12, a verse in which the line between the spiritual and material is blurred: "For the word of God is quick, and powerful, and sharper than any two-edged sword, piercing even to the dividing asunder of soul and spirit, and of the joints and marrow, and is a discerner of the thoughts and intents of the heart."

In this conquest, Puritan missionaries employed the Bible as a potent weapon, which they considered the singularly reliable record of

God's Word. The translation of scripture was yet one more means of conquering, one more weapon for accomplishing the "invasion within."[1] One confessor, Monequassun, learned to identify his failure to "reade right" and even his failure to "rightly *desire* to read Gods word" as sinful, the "right" presumably being defined by Eliot and other English evangelists.[2] And yet, as Kathleen Bragdon argues, "Vernacular literacy in Massachusett had effects not intended by its sponsors."[3] Puritan evangelists saw the translation of the Bible as tangible evidence of their success. But they could neither predict nor control how it would be used by Native American readers, nor how it would be received by their brethren in England who paid for the press, the paper, the ink, and the type that produced it. The translation, publication, and interpretation of the "Indian Bible" were complex acts that constructed a New English identity within a mid-century context of colonial anxiety and metropolitan millennial enthusiasm and that at the same time interpellated Indians as both colonial and resistant subjects.

By the end of the seventeenth century, more than three thousand copies of the Indian Bible had been printed, distributed to converts and English friends.[4] Although Europeans who could read the translation were unusual, quite a few Indian people had become literate in their language—perhaps thirty percent—and more gained access to scriptural translations by hearing kinfolk and friends read aloud.[5] Nonetheless, despite the central importance of literacy and the Bible to Puritans and to the Praying Indian community throughout the seventeenth century, little is known about the dissemination or the reception of the Bible translated into the language variously known as Natick, Massachusett, or, recently, Wôpanâak.[6] Rather, the so-called Indian Bible, published in full in 1663 and reprinted in 1685, has become a fixed object, understood as the printed artifact of a successful conquest, a failed mission, or both—and in a "dead" language to boot. As early as 1710, New England officials were counseling the Society for the Propagation of the Gospel in London *not* to reprint Eliot's translation: "There are many words of Mr. Elliott's forming which [Indian converts] never understood. . . . Such a knowledge in their Bibles, as our English ordinarily have in ours, they seldom any of them have."[7] By the mid-nineteenth century, discussions of the Bible appear as sentimental nostalgia. *Putnam's Monthly Magazine* published "Eliot's Indian Bible," a poem in quatrains by S. H. Brown, which uses one of Eliot's Massachusett neologisms, "Up Biblum God," as an exotic refrain, asserting that the "Holy old relic" is written in a language "evermore unspoken."[8]

That language *is* being spoken, however, revitalized through the efforts of the Wampanoag Nation.[9] The revitalization is a reminder that eulogies pronounced over indigenous languages are dangerous, often relegating peoples as well as words to "extinction," to historical and political invisibility.[10] Similarly, if we categorize the Indian Bible as simply a rare artifact, as always and only the "first Bible published in North America," we overwrite the dynamic and complex negotiations that produced it, erasing the participation of Praying Indians in its production. Rather than *Mamusse wunneetupanatamwe up-biblum God*, a title that at least acknowledges the text's bicultural production with its mixture of Wôpanâak and English words, the text is most often known as "John Eliot's Indian Bible," a description that implies an individual, English-settler ownership of the translation. The story is, of course, much more complicated.

Any colonial publication, most especially of translated scriptures, is enmeshed in complicated and even contradictory motivations. If Christian Indians were meant to be the *primary* consumers of the translation, they were by no means the only ones. Puritans in New England were always aware (sometimes painfully so) of the metropolitan gaze on their works and words, and the publishers of this Bible intended it to mean something to the Christian reader in London, even though he or she was not literate in Wôpanâak. The Indian Bible, then, is a transatlantic document, with a readership both in New and Old England, and it is significant both to England's religious and political debates as well as to settler-Indian relations in the colonies.

Moreover, if Christian Indians were meant to be primarily *consumers*, from the first they were active translators and inspired users of translated scripture as well. As Joshua Bellin reminds, "Indians and Christians shared and contested not only the material but the immaterial territory they traversed."[11] The realities of what Bellin calls the "intercultural" nature of the New England mission include a long history of religious exchanges, dialogues, and misunderstandings among Indians and European colonists. More immediately, they include the assistance—willing, coerced, or otherwise enlisted—of Eliot's teachers and translators, including a man captured during the 1636–37 war between the English and the Pequots, and John Sassamon, a bilingual convert whose death precipitated the war of 1675–76.[12]

Later, Indian translators mediated the confessions of Praying Indians to Puritan elders and worked with Eliot to print a translated Bible, which was then used by Christian Indians to negotiate their relations with colonial authorities. The results of this negotiation extended from the ecclesiastical—the founding of an independent Natick church, for example—to the secular—written materials, such as deeds and petitions. In *Writing Indians,* Hilary Wyss argues for a reconsideration of the Native American literacy reflected in such documents, challenging the neglect of early writings, particularly those produced in the Protestant Christian tradition, as mere overlays of English Puritanism. She sees in these works "a Native perspective that included a sense of their colonial position." She further claims that "native converts attempted not only to acquire literacy but also to create an identity through literacy that marked them as different from missionaries as well as from other Native Americans."[13]

Bellin and Wyss demonstrate the importance of adding literary analysis to ethnographic and historical approaches, but their work primarily focuses on a later period, in which at least some writings by Indians in New England exist. What has been missing from accounts of English spiritual colonization and Indian responses to it is a thorough analysis of the earlier literature of mission encounter. Here, I reach back to the mid-seventeenth century, considering the first generation of literate Praying Indians for whom reading, especially reading scripture, was as important a marker of colonial identity as writing was for their children and grandchildren.

In the discussion that follows, I rely on descriptions of scriptural translation and circulation published in the mid-century mission tracts. This approach has obvious problems, relying as it does on the biased accounts written by white missionaries (in English, of course) as evidence not only of their own translation and evangelical practices but also of the Praying Indians' reception and use of the Indian Bible. These materials can yield only partial evidence of the use of the vernacular Bible by either English missionaries or Praying Indians. Nevertheless, the mission narratives offer some real riches, and unless we push the limits of textual analysis, we will forego a fuller understanding of colonial contact and identity formation. In their detail and in their eagerness to assert Christian knowledge on the part of the converts, these tracts give us a view—obscured, to be sure—on the exegetical habits of Christian Indians and the transatlantic, intercultural production of colonial mission writings.

To take into account the mediated nature of these texts, I do not at-

tempt a seamless, teleological history. Rather, I consider three interlocking scenarios that suggest the fluid transatlantic and intercultural
nature of the Bible's production and use. In scenes of translating,
preaching, and reading, missionaries and Praying Indians create a literature of complex religious encounter in which the Bible is constructed as a New World text, is exported to England, and then
becomes available for interpretation by Praying Indian readers.

Translating the Word

Although John Eliot is the Puritan evangelist with both transatlantic
and transhistoric name recognition, Thomas Shepard provided some
of the pithiest descriptions of Puritan evangelism. His writings have
the knack of identifying and spinning important elements of the mission discourse for his metropolitan readership. In *Clear Sun-shine of
the Gospel*, Shepard reports that "my brother *Eliot* who is Preacher"
to neighboring Indians "can as yet but stammer out some peeces of
the Word of God unto them in their own tongue."[14] Shepard then uses
the "sword of God's word" metaphor to explain how this seeming
weakness is actually a spiritual strength. Because Eliot admits to an
imperfect command of Wôpanâak, observers can readily assume that
a divine rather than human power was the source of missionary success: "God is wont to be *maximus in minimis*, and is most seene in
doing great things by small meanes. The Sword of Gods Word shall and
will pierce deep, even when it is half broken" (64). Shepard asserts here
a perfect Protestant explanation for any problems; Eliot's inadequacies, especially his linguistic inadequacies, become, in Puritan fashion, divine efficacy.

   Shepard's description of the role of a stammering bilingual preacher
exemplifies both the overweening confidence and the intense anxiety
of New England Puritans. On the one hand, missionaries were "Soul-
diers of Christ," joining his lists as he rode out "Conquering and to
Conquer."[15] On the other hand, they were negotiating the tricky political terrain of a settler colony with a shaky charter. "God's word,"
most especially the vernacular Bible produced by John Eliot and Indian translators, was touted by colonial authorities as a weapon for
subduing and making tractable the native population, but it was also
used as an apology to metropolitan critics and a return on the invest-
ments of sponsors of their work.

As I discuss in chapter 1, it is no accident that New England missionaries began systematic work just as the civil wars broke out in England. The tracts describe Indian evangelism as continuous with efforts in England to complete church reform and establish godly rule, both civil and ecclesiastical. And while colonial presentations of the "New England Way" raised some hackles in Old England, discussions of evangelism were a safer alternative to debates over polity. As Francis Bremer argues, both Congregationalists and Presbyterians could "unquestioningly" assent to Indian evangelism, "a noncontroversial cause on which all could agree."[16] Such flexibility allowed both ardent metropolitan millennialists and more cautious colonial authorities to endorse it; we find Presbyterians and Congregationalists alike signing accounts of evangelism penned by Thomas Shepard, John Eliot, and Thomas Mayhew, Jr.

Thus, despite their differences, the various voices within the mission discourse seem to sound in unison. Since so many authors agree as to the desirability of the mission, each statement, letter, or section seems a variation on a single theme. The resulting illusion of a unified, orderly mission is so successful in these tracts that the seams where the pieces have been sewn together often go unremarked. Even the term "Eliot tracts," used to describe the mission publications that appeared between 1647 and 1671, reflects a scholarly continuation of the tracts' assertion of consensus, since the tracts were written and edited by several divines, even if Eliot was the best known among them.[17] Indeed, the first mission tract, published anonymously in 1647, rather than under Eliot's name, describes the encounter of Waban and his followers with not one but four Puritan missionaries.

The title and subtitle of that first tract illustrates the fissures within the mission discourse: *The Day-Breaking, if not the Sun-Rising of the Gospell with the* Indians in New–England; *and A True Relation of Our Beginnings with the Indians.* Significantly, the main title suggests metropolitan distance—this will be an account of evangelism over there, "in New England"—while the secondary title represents the colonial perspective of the tract—"our beginnings." The subtitle contrasts with and is perhaps even at odds with the main title.[18] As an account of the Puritan mission, *A True Relation* makes promises different from *The Day-breaking . . . in New England;* the latter inscribes the Indian mission within a Christian timeframe and makes conversion a matter of translating the Gospel from England to America. The "true relation," by contrast, was a useful genre for the "busy man in Europe who want[ed] a factual report on the progress of his American enterprise in the shortest possible form."[19] By placing their work within that genre, colonial mission writers inscribed the spiritual dialogues of Indians and colonists—and of colonists and metropolitan supporters—within the discourse of merchandising and financial exchange. As Philip Round argues, "The act of reporting facts to a metropolitan reader (and thereby producing one's own truth-telling character) recapitulated in discourse the transatlantic mercantile network in which the colonists themselves, their furs and timber, and their much-needed English provisions every day participated."[20]

Nevertheless, the bare-bones profit report became something else as authors of "factual" reports gained (and authored) experience in America.[21] Nowhere is this more apparent than in the tract's efforts to redefine the "beginnings" it describes. As is clear in a close reading of the account, and indeed, by reading virtually any other New England account prior to this, English colonists and Native peoples had been in dialogue about religious faith and practices for years before this meeting or this publication.[22] But the subtitle overwrites those earlier accounts of evangelism, such as the Bay Colony's own account of Christian conversions in *New Englands First Fruits* (1643) and recasts the rather impersonal spiritual encounters detailed there into idealized colonial contact. In *Day-Breaking*, four Puritan ministers approach a gathering of Indians "with desire to make known the things of their peace to them."[23] They are met by "five or six of the chief of them," who greet the Puritans in English. Here we find an echo of Samoset's greeting of Plymouth colony settlers in 1620: "a certain Indian came boldly amongst them and spoke to them in broken English, which they could well understand but marveled at it."[24] This 1646 salutation is not met, as in Samoset's case, with astonishment, but rather with complacent approval. If this is a first encounter, it is one that conforms to a divine script already available to its Puritan actors. What follows is an account of the Englishmen's proselytizing, which continually turns on questions of language and translation.

On the one hand, the missionaries at this meeting are careful to avoid difficult theological topics or to discuss notions that might seem ridiculous to non-Christians. They repeatedly are assured—and reassure the reader—that the Indians understood everything they said perfectly.[25] On the other hand, Indians and English in the account do not have a common language of worship, and so the description of the Puritans' opening prayer seems especially bizarre for these fervent Protestants: "We began with prayer, which now was in English, being not so farre acquainted with the *Indian* language as to expresse our hearts herein before God or them . . . but thus wee began in an unknowne tongue to them, partly to let them know that this dutie in hand was serious and sacred."[26] The Latin mass overtones of this performance—worship in a language the congregants do not understand—are mitigated only by the promise of future prayer in the Indians' own language.[27]

From the mystification of the language of prayer to repeated professions that the proselytes "understood all that which was already spoken," these "beginnings" echo European descriptions of first encounters, from Columbus on. The tract seems to encompass both of the possibilities that Tzvetan Todorov describes as characteristic of the colonists' understanding of the Other—complete linguistic transparency or complete linguistic opacity; radical similarity or radical difference.[28] But this binary cannot entirely describe the encounter detailed in *Day-Breaking*. After all, the initial greeting shows that some Indians there present would have understood the prayer, and there is the clear expectation that Indians would learn Christian prayer themselves. The account more closely resembles what Eric Cheyfitz calls the "primal scene of eloquence," which he explains as "the act whereby savages are converted through the power of eloquence to civility"[29] or to Christianity—which for the missionaries, of course, was the same thing.

This mission tract—any mission tract—is a text that describes an encounter with an "exotic," indigenous people to a "local" audience of English readers, employing eloquence both in the missionaries' speech to potential converts and in the appeal to potential investors. For Cheyfitz, simultaneous "intercultural communication" and "intracultural communication" is a defining element of the primal scene of conversion (109). And, indeed, by casting this meeting into a "beginning," by invoking the "true relation" genre, the missionary writers are positioning themselves in relation to events in Old England. Above all, this report erases the history of secular colonial contact with Indians (insofar as it is possible to make such a distinction) and presents this "initial" dialogue as a fresh start. Colonial writers thereby contrast their efforts with those of the Saints in England, describing the simplicity and efficacy of colonial conversion efforts. The scene implies that whereas Old England is embroiled in civil wars, internecine theological disputes, and faces destruction, New England has embarked on a successful mission that promises to swiftly and easily raise up Christ's kingdom in America.

For all these transatlantic and representational complexities, this scene lays bare the mechanism of translation in a colonial context. In "the field," at some unnamed Indian settlement, the English missionaries work through partial truths and misdirection. They withhold information, judging the Indians (rather than their own persuasive skills) too weak for some basic Christian doctrine. The Indians, who assert their presence by speaking English at the outset of the encounter, are quickly relegated to a more passive role in the written scene (whatever the tenor of encounter at the meeting). Once the tract moves to the incomprehensible prayer in English, the "beginnings" can be enacted. The narrative rolls back the history of encounter to a time of (almost) mutual unintelligibility and then stages the primal scene of the eloquent missionary who instantly brings savage listeners to full understanding. This moment becomes metonymic of European theological disputes.[30] It is the reformation in miniature, turning on vernacular scripture. If at one time mystic language in worship awed savages—whether Indian or Briton—full conversion required knowledge. The next step was therefore to translate the word of God for these almost-Christians.

Preaching the Word

Besides "primal scenes" of evangelical eloquence, we find in the tracts descriptions of continuing religious encounters characterized by double meanings and by translation as obfuscation. However successful the mission encounter as represented in the first tract, subsequent publications acknowledged missteps and misunderstandings. In the apology for Eliot's linguistic skills that Thomas Shepard offers in *Strength out of Weaknesse,* he goes on to posit explanations for translation problems other than Eliot's poor Wôpanâak. Indians who had difficulty understanding Eliot's preaching, he argues, did so simply because they spoke different dialects. More importantly, however, they were not "accustomed unto sacred language about the holy things of God."[31] Shepard asserts here a difference between the common languages of diplomacy or trade and the "spiritual" language of conversion. In other contexts, these languages overlapped. Roger Williams's *Key Into the Language of America,* for instance, shows just such a

mix, and colonial authorities found it convenient to fulfill their pledge
to convert Indians by linking talk of Christianity with trade negotiations; later, they would ask Thomas Stanton, chief translator in secular matters for the colonies, to assist Eliot. In this tract, however,
Shepard maintains that while some (such as Stanton, perhaps) may
have been more fluent in the Indians' language,

> Mr. *Eliot* excells any other of the *English*, that in the *Indian* language
> about common matters excell him: I say therefore although they did
> with much difficulty understand him, yet they did understand him, al-
> though by many circumlocutions and variations of speech and the helpe
> of one or two Interpreters which were then present.[32]

Shepard's description suggests that Eliot may have constructed a
special language for discoursing with Indians about the Bible and
Christianity. Moreover, Shepard implies that "circumlocutions and
variations" were only natural under the circumstances. And indeed,
the tracts elsewhere report that in the early days (at least) he avoided
translating and preaching on the more difficult passages of scripture.[33]

The phrase "circumlocutions and variations" is frustratingly vague,
and we have few indications of just what Shepard and Eliot considered
appropriate variations in spiritual language. One key to their methods
is a description Eliot gives of an early encounter with potential Indian
converts, in which the interconnection of translation and colonization
is especially clear. In *The Glorious Progress of the Gospel, amongst the
Indians in New England* (1648), Eliot describes a sermon on Malachi
1:11, which he delivered to a gathering of potential converts. His account suggests the "variations" he presumably employed, and to an
even greater degree than the description of "beginnings" in *Day-Breaking*, this account suggests a "primal" scene of an eloquent apostle.

The passage is deceptively simple, a seemingly transparent account
of a sermon preached to interested Indians, but the insertion of the
scene into mission propaganda complicates matters. We are dealing
here with translations of translations; Eliot preached in his broken
Wôpanâak, yet he describes the scene in English. In his account we
hear how he presented Malachi 1:11 to Indians, a verse his English
readers would have seen as it appeared on the title page of the tract.
The account thus registers a double audience: those Indians immediately at the gathering place who heard the sermon and English readers of the tract far distant from the site of encounter. By keeping these

two audiences in mind, we can see how Eliot's desire to meet the expectations of a readership in London and to speak meaningfully to the Indian congregation in New England resulted in a sermon that articulated a peculiar, American theology.

Malachi 1:11 seems to have had special significance for the New England missionary effort. As I noted above, it is not simply a text for Eliot's particular sermon but also appears on the title page of this 1651 mission tract: "From the rising of the Sun, even unto the going down of the same, my Name shall be great among the Gentiles, and in every place incence [*sic*] shall be offered unto my name, and a pure Offering; for my Name shall be great among the Heathen, saith the Lord of Hosts." The verse concludes Roger Williams's preface to *Key Into the Language of America* (1643), and appears again on the title page of Eliot's *Indian Grammar* (1666) as well as his *Indian Dialogues* (1671). In this tract, Eliot reports that he used the verse as the text of a sermon delivered at Pawtucket, a place on the Merrimack River where Indians annually gathered to fish—an event Eliot describes as "like Faires in *England*."[34] Malachi 1:11 may have seemed especially appropriate at that time and place, since he was preaching to a group drawn from many places. Such an audience lends special emphasis to the idea of a new diaspora of God's chosen who would be spread "from the rising of the sun, even to the going down of the same."

Whatever inspiration led Eliot to choose the text for his sermon, for the English reader, both the choice and its delivery would have resonated with the whole history of New England's colonization. In this encounter with Pawtucket listeners, even as he invokes Malachi's prophecy in the Hebrew scriptures, he inhabits a type drawn from the New Testament, the apostle Paul, who immediately converts those who hear him.[35] The typological connection is clear if we consider the Great Seal of Massachusetts, with its representation of an Indian man pleading "Come over and help us." The seal alludes to Paul's dream in Acts 16.9, in which "there stood a man of Macedonia, and prayed him, saying, Come over into Macedonia, and help us." Paul's response is to go to Philippi, "which is the chief city of that part of Macedonia, and a colony" and to preach "out of the city by a river side." Eliot's mission as he describes it in *Glorious Progress of the Gospel* is a parallel one: responding to the dream of colonial welcome, he claims that he successfully preaches by the Merrimack River: "thus you see by this short intimation, that the sound of the Word is spread a great way."[36]

What did "the Word" sound like, exactly? Despite, or perhaps because of his impeccably orthodox credentials as a minister and translator, it seems that Eliot may have taken some liberties with the ideals of plainness and absolute fidelity to the original text that mark other Puritan translations of scripture, as he reports that he made some modification to the verse:

> I preached out of Malachi 1.11. which I thus render to them; *From the rising of the Sun, to the going down of the same, thy name shall be great among the Indians, and in every place prayers shall be made to thy name, pure prayers, for thy name shall be great among the Indians.*[37]

Eliot makes telling adjustments to the verse in his translation, as compared to that appearing on the title page of the tract. "My name" becomes "thy name"; rather than offering "incence . . . a pure Offering," converts will offer "prayers . . . pure prayers"; and, most significantly, "Gentiles" and "Heathen" become "Indians." Lest we assume these changes are accidental, a simple concession to language differences, or the result of intervention by Indian translators, Eliot draws attention to the special translation, "which I thus render to them." Eliot means for his readers to notice the differences. After all, he could easily have reported his translation as conformable to the English translations of the Geneva or the King James Bible. It appears that "render" in this context is used to refer to a deliberate choice in translation, one that performs discursive work on several levels and speaks both to his immediate hearers and to readers in London.[38]

First, the substitution of "prayers" for "incense" and "offerings" seems relatively straightforward: a concession to the Indians' inexperience with the trappings of Judeo-Christian ritual. Moreover, the change is authorized by commentaries such as the Geneva Bible's marginalia: "Here the Prophet that was under the Law framed his wordes to the capacitie of the people, and by the altar, and sacrifice he meaneth the spiritual service of God, which shulde be under the Gospel, when an end shulde be made to all these legal ceremonies by Christs onely sacrifice."[39] Thus "prayer" as "the spiritual service of God" is an effective translation from an *anno Domini* and Protestant perspective.

However, the use of "prayer" here is of a piece with Eliot's deliberate shaping of Puritan Indian religious expression. In later tracts, Eliot easily explains the Indians' ubiquitous use of the word "praying" to describe their Christian religious practices as a native idiomatic expression; hence the name given to Eliot's converts—"praying Indians." However, the seemingly stolid derivation and application of the name mask its fluid signification in transatlantic Puritan discourses. In tracts written in English, the term is not simply descriptive but also, even primarily, metaphoric. As a trope, it connects to seventeenth-century linguistic theory and in turn to fervent English millennialism.

As I discuss in chapter 2, millenarians in Old England were eager to find in colonial experiences confirmation of their hopes for an imminent Second Coming. As I have argued, some began speculating that Indians were Jews, members of the lost tribes and that their conversion signaled the end time, as the conversion of the Jews to Christianity was a prophesied harbinger of the Christ's return. English observers who hoped to find Jews in America were especially interested in physical and cultural traits that seemed to prove the lost-tribes theory of Indian origins, while colonists found a new, viable identity in such theorizing.

Among other kinds of evidence, English writers pointed to certain modes of Indian speech that seemed to indicate the Indians' millennial identity as Jews. Early on, the tracts report that Indians "usually expressed what eminent things they meane" with "metaphoricall language," and Eliot reports that he modeled his explanations of Puritan doctrine after what he imagines as an Indian mode, remarking to his readers, "For you know they use and delight in demonstrations."[40] These descriptions build on even older ones, such as William Wood's report in *New England's Prospect* that Indians were "merrily conceited in discourse."[41] Beginning in 1649, however, missionary observers reevaluated such tropes. The English millenarian John Dury notes in *Glorious Progress* that "the *better and more sober sort of them, delight much to expresse themselves in parables.* A thing peculiar to the Jewes, as those who read their writings, or consider Christs manner of expressing himself, will easily see."[42]

The term "Praying Indian" is one example of "metaphorical language" that the English connected to theological speculation, but it is such a common term, both in historical and current critical discussions, that its tropic significance is all but invisible. Eliot introduces the description of Christian Indians as "praying" Indians in a letter dated September 1647. He claims that detractors initially coined the phrase, reporting that powwows discouraged other Indians from "praying unto God, for that they account as a principall signe of a good man, and call all religion by that name, praying to God; and beside they mock and scoffe at those *Indians* which pray, and blaspheme God when they pray."[43] Later, Eliot's etymology for the phrase changes, and he describes the word "praying" as the converts' own "general name of Religion."[44]

It seems clear from studies of other Algonkian-European interaction that "Praying Indian" is a literal translation of an Algonquian term.[45] Robert James Naeher claims that "prayer was a central element of Eliot's message to the Indians, but it was they who made it the central motif of their Christianity, for it met, in a meaningful and emotionally satisfying way, deep human needs that the Indians shared with the New England Puritans."[46] Indians were unlikely to have accepted prayer unless it did meet such needs, but whatever the Indians' usage, the designation continues in the mission literature because of choices Eliot made in translation.[47] Eliot here may be interested in validating his converts by recording a persecution akin to that which the English Puritans themselves had faced, as well as likening the origins of his converts' name with the naming of Puritans; both groups reportedly took what was meant to be a slur and adopted it for their own.[48] He retains the description in *Tears of Repentance*. In that tract, he anticipates the objections of uninitiated English readers to the Indians' use of the word "praying" to refer to the whole range of Puritan religious practices. The word, he asserts, *"comprehendeth the same meaning, with them, as the word [Religion] doth with us."*[49] He implies that "praying" is merely an Indianism, an approximation of what they truly mean, although of course he could have translated the phrase into a more "accurate" English term. Eliot's choice has gone unremarked, despite evidence of alternatives. Thomas Mayhew, for example, working on Martha's Vineyard, initially termed his converts "meeting Indians."[50] "Praying Indian," especially as compared with Mayhew's alternative, implies a less institutional, more direct access to God.

Both Mayhew's term and Eliot's equate Christianity with a particular practice rather than an ontological identity (leaving open the possibility that the identity might one day be revoked). Unlike Mayhew's term, however, Eliot's "Praying Indian" has specific millennial implications. David Katz, discussing the Puritans' search for a universal language, argues that by "the mid-seventeenth century, after much discussion, most Englishmen agreed that God spoke Hebrew." Hebrew was the ideal universal language, Puritan linguists believed, because in it, as in the language used in the Garden of Eden before the fall, "words and things were perfectly congruent."[51] The phrase "praying Indian" gains importance in light of this theory. Unlike "Christian Indian" or "Puritan Indian," it equates the act of praying with the convert and becomes a linguistic sign implying that the Indians' name for themselves follows a Hebraic pattern, suggesting their Jewish identity and therefore their place within millennial prophecy.

This discussion of the origin and use of the name "Praying Indian" illustrates the overlooked nuances of these mission writings. Despite their cobbled-together appearance, the tracts contributed to the most complex political and theological debates of the day. The bent toward millennial meaning in Eliot's rendition of Malachi continues with what is perhaps the most striking difference from the English version—the substitution of "Indians" for "gentiles" and "heathens," which occurs twice and is linked to the substitution of "prayer" for "incense" in his translation. These choices insert his converts explicitly into millennial prophecy and were read by an English audience within the context of unfolding events in Europe and England. Once again, the Geneva Bible illuminates Eliot's translation. The commentary elucidates a standard Puritan interpretation of the verse in which the prophet predicts that the Israelites' "ingratitude and neglect of [God's] true service shall be the cause of the calling of the Gentiles." This "calling" is read as an anticipation of the Christian diaspora in the New Testament, the result of Christ's first coming.

By changing "gentiles" to "Indians," Eliot inserts his converts directly into a new prophecy of Christ's return. His sermon text specifically predicts the conversion of *Indians*, already marked as Jews in the mission discourse, and while New England missionaries are God's apostles, Christians in Old England are in the place of the ingrate Israelites of Malachi.

So the account of Eliot's Pawtucket sermon stages shifts and reversals in identities, underscored by an urgent millennial drumbeat. Those who once were heathen gentiles have become Christian apostles ministering to those who once were Jews. Insider and outsider status are impossibly confused. Moreover, as the translation attempts to place English and Indian identities within prophetic time, it alters the verse's point of view. By changing "my name" to "thy name," Eliot erases the accusatory thunder of Malachi, adding yet another level of complexity. Instead of a prophet speaking the word of God (already a translation, which the King James version recognizes by calling the recorded words the "burden of the word of the Lord") to remind a sinning people that they can at any time be supplanted by the "heathen," a preacher describes inevitable Indian conversion to those he would convert. Stripped of its original prophetic context (or replaced by another), the translation suggests that Indians will join the English as Christians—latecomers at that—rather than be substituted for them as the new chosen people, as the Geneva and King James versions threaten. The verse is now an address to God rather than from God, promise rather than prophecy. The proper audience for this passage thus becomes the Indians who are being instructed on their right attitude toward God.

Nevertheless, the attempt to fix identities narrowly is framed by the composition of the tract as a whole. In yet another variation on the insider/outsider design, Eliot's editors in London restore the vocabulary and first-divinity point of view to the scriptural text and emblazon it on the title page. By presenting such an epigraph, the editors identify their English readers with the stiff-necked, sinning Israelites addressed by the prophet. If Eliot with his "rendering" of scripture articulates a mission project that retains the English people as God's chosen, English enthusiasts make sure readers have a ready reminder that Malachi prophesied to the chosen nation, and the gentiles were a foil for the Israelites' faithlessness. Eliot desires the conversion of his immediate hearers; his editors desire those conversions to be useful examples to a sinning English nation.

It could be argued that neither Eliot's practice nor his editors' here is especially radical. As the Geneva Bible's commentary demonstrates, Eliot is, in one sense, following good Reformation practice by fitting his preaching style to his listeners' needs, and the significance of his changes within colonial discourse is incidental to purely pragmatic translation choices. However, other Puritan translations claimed to avoid any special consideration of audience. In the preface to the Bay Psalm Book, the translators, including Eliot, discuss Ainsworth's practice of paraphrasing psalms:

> Yet it is not unknowne to the godly learned that they have rather presented a paraphrase then the words of David translated according to the rule 2 chron. 29. 30. . . . Wee have therefore done our indeavour to make a plaine and familiar translation of the psalms and words of David into English metre, and have not soe much as presumed to paraphrase to give the sense of his meaning in other words.[52]

Rather than avoiding any human "polishing" of the text, then, Eliot's "rendering" of Malachi 1 is a moment of scriptural translation responding both to the exigencies of contact and to transatlantic concerns.

Reading the Word

When the New England mission began printing Eliot's translations of scripture, in addition to describing oral performances such as his sermon on Malachi, the significance of his work to the colonial discourse was heightened. The necessity of the printed word for a Protestant mission effort cannot be understated. Linda Gregerson argues, "This was what the Reformation had been *about*. Christ is represented in a book, as the Word that at once fulfils and supersedes an earlier testament, the mere letter." But, she asks, "what can this mean to . . . those for whom the letter itself is an innovation?"[53] With the publication of *Mamusse wunneetupanatamwe up-biblum God,* that question was assumed to be answered, as the vernacular Bible made Indian readers possible.

The printing of the "Indian Bible" also had material effects in New England. As Matthew Brown points out, the presses set up to create the "Indian library," the translations and other works designed to inculcate Indian piety and literacy, made a "second-generation white archive" possible when they were co-opted by white colonial authors. The significance of this appropriation on contemporary scholarship has been profound. Brown suggests that English literatures printed on the Indian presses became archival materials for the "exceptionalist" thesis of American studies, inaugurated by Perry Miller and debated ever since. Early American literary and intellectual history as we know it today "is itself a product of publication technologies that were predicated on the use-value of indigenous peoples."[54] The publication history of the "Indian Bible" reveals that even those works published by the first generation of colonists and explicitly designed for Indian converts were turned to English use; they were used to create a vital colonial identity that confirmed the power of the imperial center. Thus, just as Eliot's sermon on Malachi appealed to a double audience years earlier, the "Indian Bible" had two readers: the Indian convert and (colonists hoped) the king.

Eliot's translation of Malachi 1 is a subtle expression of the millennial fervor experienced by the missionary and many of his supporters. In other writings, Eliot articulates his beliefs much more avidly, arguing that the praying-town governments he is establishing for his converts are ideal, predicting that "unto that frame [i.e., Natick's government] the Lord will bring all the world ere he hath done."[55] And in *The Christian Commonwealth*, a work written at about the same time (although published years later), Eliot rejoiced that the execution of Charles I had cleared the way for scriptural rule in England. After the Restoration in 1660 of Charles II to the throne, these sentiments were dangerous, and colonial authorities, fearful of royal reprisals, sought to realign mission work and downplay the strain of anti-monarchism among them. When the New Testament was published a year later, the Commissioners of the United Colonies supplied a dedication for Eliot's translation of the New Testament that not only avoids his millennial sentiments but also takes the opportunity to "congratulate Your majesties happy Restitution, after Your long suffering."[56] They also attribute the further success of the mission effort to the king, assuring Charles that the translation "will be a perpetual monument, that by your majesties Favour the Gospel of our Lord and Saviour *Jesus Christ* was first made known to the *Indians*" (225).

When the entire Indian Bible was published in 1663, it was prefaced by the earlier New Testament dedication, to which the commissioners added a new one for the whole, claiming Eliot's work on behalf of the colonies. The commissioners promise the king that the propagation of the Gospel in New England is "a Nobler Fruit (and indeed, in the Counsels of All-disposing Providence, was an higher intended End) of *Columbus* his Adventure" (227). Indian converts here are the express reward of imperialist expansion, the victory of England over the aspirations of other countries, which is intended by God but is obtained by the New England colonies:

> And though there be in this Western World many Colonies of other European nations, yet we humbly conceive, no Prince hath had a Return of such a Work as this; which may be some Token of the Success of Your Majesties Plantation of *New-England.* (227)

When the Bible was printed, copies were bound separately, depending on the recipient. Twenty copies of the Indian Bible, with the commissioners' special dedication to the king, were in the first shipment sent hot off the press to notables throughout Old England. In these pre-

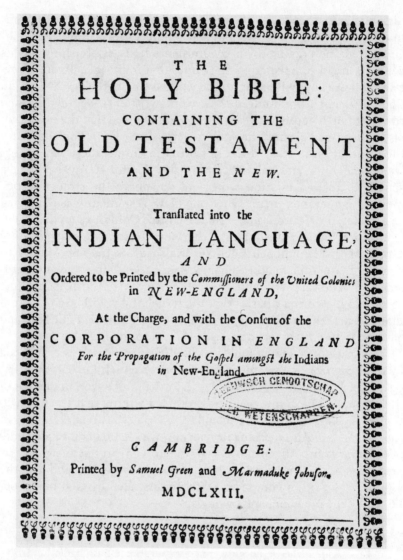

THE
HOLY BIBLE:
CONTAINING THE
OLD TESTAMENT
AND THE *NEW.*

Translated into the

INDIAN LANGUAGE,
AND

Ordered to be Printed by the *Commiſſioners of the United Colonies*
in *NEW-ENGLAND,*

At the Charge, and with the Conſent of the

CORPORATION IN *ENGLAND*
For the Propagation of the Goſpel amongſt the Indians
in New-England.

CAMBRIDGE:

Printed by *Samuel Green* and *Marmaduke Johnſon.*
MDCLXIII.

English title page bound with the 1663 edition of the Massachusett Bible, published in Cambridge, Massachusetts. Courtesy of the Newberry Library, Chicago, Ill.

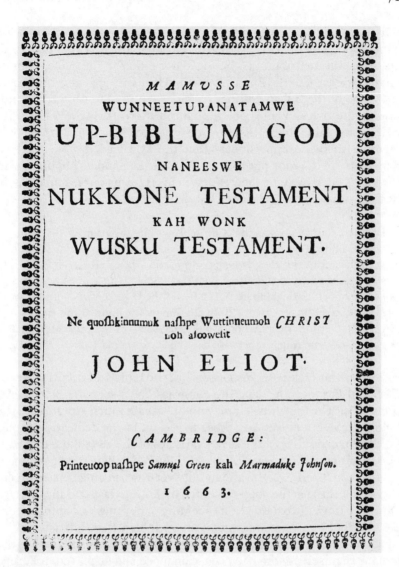

MAMUSSE

WUNNEETUPANATAMWE

UP-BIBLUM GOD

NANEESWE

NUKKONE TESTAMENT

KAH WONK

WUSKU TESTAMENT.

Ne quoſhkinnumuk naſhpe Wuttinneumoh *CHRIST*
noh aſoowelit

JOHN ELIOT·

CAMBRIDGE:

Printeuꝏp naſhpe *Samuel Green* kah *Marmaduke Johnſon.*

1 6 6 3.

Title page bound with copies of the 1663 Massachusett Bible distributed to Praying Indians. Courtesy of the Newberry Library, Chicago, Ill.

sentation copies, Eliot's radical tendencies are erased; although his name appears on the title page of those copies designed for Indian readers, he is not mentioned as the translator either in the dedications or on the title page to the English version. His name appears only on the title page of the Indian edition.[57] More such presentation copies followed, and one imagines colonial authorities waiting anxiously for news of the Bible's reception. In an April 21, 1664 letter, Robert Boyle reported to the commissioners that the king had received and remarked upon his copy of the Bible. To New Englanders hoping to win the king's favor by tying their efforts to his rule, his interest in the publication must have been somewhat disappointing:

> I waited this Day upon the King with your translation of the Bible, which, I hope I need not tell you, he receved according to his custome very gratiously. But though he lookd a pretty while upon it, and shewd some things in it to those that had the honour to be about him in his bed-chamber, into which he carryd it, yet the Unexpected comming in of an Extraordinary Envoyé from the Emperour hindred me from receveing that fuller expression of his grace towards the translators and Dedicators that might otherwise have been expected.[58]

Despite this lackluster response, with the Bible's distribution to English and European readers, the commissioners scored a public-relations coup. The king himself may not have paid much attention to the Indian Bible, but apparently those in receipt of the dedication copies kept them carefully. Of the seven varieties of the 1663 Bible that contain the English title page, Pilling's *Bibliography* lists nineteen, many in "fine condition." Of the Indian-only versions, Pilling lists eighteen, and one of these is the copy presented by Eliot to Jasper Danckaerts, a Dutch visitor to Roxbury.[59] The seeming parity masks disproportionate distribution; there were many more Indian than English copies. Apparently, the Indian Bible was treated by the English (as were the Indians themselves who had been kidnapped and displayed in Europe by early explorers) as a curious exhibit—a tradition of rare-book collection that continues today. The "Eliot Bible" regularly appears in exhibits on colonial printing, religious history, or Native American cultures. Individual leaves of the Bible are marketed as collector's items on the internet, and libraries consider the Bibles among their rare books treasures.[60]

A complicating factor in the discussion of the Bible as a colonial text is that, once forged, the "sword" could be wielded by the people who were supposed to be pierced by it. And the archive of Christian Indian testimony and writing, fragmentary though it is, shows the dynamic uses to which Native readers put translated scripture in contrast to the fixed place of the Indian Bible in the king's bedchamber. In an early eighteenth-century letter, residents of Gayhead, Massachusetts, petitioned against the appointment of the Englishman Elisha Amos as their judge. Along with charges that Amos engaged in corrupt land deals, the petitioners mobilize scripture in support of their argument. They use the transliteration Eliot had employed over half a century earlier:

> kunnanabassummunnumun woh yo kuttomman wutche nonnauwa[n] kuttummake Gayhead Indiansog uskont woh yeu usseit anuhkasueonk woh moocheke kooche nukkuttumakeyeumun wutche yo Elisha amos ne annoowat wuttinnoowaonk God ut Job 34–30.

> We beseech you that you would take away this (person) from us poor Gayhead Indians, lest if he should do this work we would be much more miserable . . . Just as the word of God says in Job 34:30.[61]

The supplicatory tone of the letter, written by "poor Gayhead Indians," is belied by the content of the verse cited, which editors Goddard and Bradgon translate as "Let not the hypocrite rule." The petitioners thus combine tactics within the single petition, assuming an appropriate humility even as they use scripture to support a more commanding position.[62]

As the Gayhead example demonstrates, Native readers made creative use of the Bible and perhaps not always as English missionaries imagined they would. Goddard and Bragdon note that "surviving copies of religious and instructional works in Massachusett . . . are well worn, summoning the vision of generations of native readers, persevering in spite of lack of materials."[63] One such "persevering" reader is Samuel Ponampam, who asserted his ownership of a copy of the New Testament (now in the Bodleian library), by writing his name in it at least seven times. While we may attribute the survival of his copy of the Gospels to the kind of artifact-hungry antiquarianism for which the dedication copies are a forerunner, the record of his encounter with the New Testament paints a picture of an actively engaged thinker and man of faith, far removed from the impulses of

xChap. numwꝏ x yeu ut ompetak piſh kenaomwꝏ
16.27. woſketomp wunnaumonuh apit menuhkeſue
1Theſſ. wuttinohkounit , kah peyont ut keſukque
4. 16. matokꝗſut.
Rom.
14. 10.   65 Neit negonne ſephauſuaen nehneguh-
kom wuthogkꝏunaſh, nꝏwau, wuſin blaſ-
phemiaonk, toh kuttin nano quenauwehik-
umun wauwacheg , kuſſeh, yenyeu kenꝏ-
tamumwꝏ upblaſphemiaonk.

   66 Toh kuttenantamwꝏ? kah nampꝏham-
wog nꝏwaog, keſohkꝏadtam nuppun.

y Iſai.   67 Neit y waſſuhquontamauouh wuſkeſuk,
30.6. kah wuttattagumouh, onkatogig wuſſoggoſ-
kinnumauouh , naſhpe wunnutcheganooaſh.

   68 Nꝏwaog kodneheantꝏaſh, ken chriſ-
tuean howan togkomukquean.

& Mark   69 z Onk Peter chippe appu miſhittau-
14. 66. komukqut, kah nunkſquau uppeyaonuh, nꝏ-
Luke wau, ken wonk kꝏwetomop Jeſus ut Gali-
22.55. le.
John
18. 25.   70 Qut ukquenꝏwontamun ut anaquab-
hettit wame, nꝏwau matta kꝏwautauunꝏh
toh anꝏwaen.

   71 Kah ſohhog petauukkomukqut, onka-
tuk nunkſquau wunnauꝏh, wuttinuh nahog
noh apinutcheh, yeuoh woſketomp mo wee-
tomau Jeſuſoh ut Nazareth.

   72 Kah wonk ukquenauwontamun naſhpe
chadchekeycuwaonk, matta nꝏwaheau woſketomp.

   63 Kah ompetaſik uppeyaonuh weethe-
kompaumoncheg , unaog Peteroh, wunna-
muhkut onk ken nag paſuk, newutche kut-
tinnontꝏwaonk kꝏwauſhanuk.

   74 Neit kitchu chadchekeyeuau , kah
mamatcheyeu, nꝏwau matta nꝏwaheau
woſketomp, kah teanuk manſh kuttꝏ-
wau.

   75 Kah peter mehquontam kuttꝏwong-
anath Jeſuſoh neanukuhp , monſh negonne
kuttꝏadt, woh kukkohkohnꝏwããnſoh niſh-
wudt nompe, kah ſohham, kah mau mꝏche-
ke.

CHAP. XXVII.

d Mark   Mohtompog, a wame negonne ſephau-
15.1.   uenuog kah miſſinninnue Elderſog
Luke   kenꝏnittuog, wutch Jeſus nuſhonat.
22.66.
John   2 Kah tohtogkupunáhettit, ummoncha-
18.28. nóuh, kah wuttiſſowunóuh Pontius Pilat ut
nanaánuwáen.

   3 Neit Judas noh wónaſſꝏmont, nauont
pakodchimau, aiukoiantam, kah uppaud-
taũn wonk ſhwincheg ompikot ſilver negonne ſephauſuenutu , kah nanaánuwuenu-
tu.

   4 Nꝏwau nummatcheſem, newutche nꝏ-
naſſꝏm matta keſontamꝏ ꝏſqheonk, kah
nꝏwaog, toh neentinukkongqunan , kena-
naeitaaſh.

b Acts   5 Onk pogketam teaguaſh ut Temple,
2.18.   b kah monchu, kah kechequaben...n hogkuh

   6 Onk negonne ſephauſuenuog neemun-
numwog teauguaſh , kah nꝏwaog, matta
wunnegeninno yeu ponamun moinnompeg-
anit, newutche yanóadtu wuſqueheonk.

   7 Kah kenꝏnittuog, kah tabbunwog
wutohke obkuhqueteaénin, ne naſhpe poſe-
kinónat penuwobteaog.

   8 Yowutche hettamun ne ohke, c mſque-   c Acts
heongane ohke, yeu pajeh.   1.19.

   9 Neit ne n oihyeup uttoh ánꝏwadt Je-
remias quoſhꝏdtumwaen , nꝏwau, kah
d neemunnum wog niſhwinchag ompikot ſil-   d Zech.
ver , wuttinn oadtuonk noh wonꝏhukup,   11.13.
yenoh wunnaumonuh Iſrael wanꝏwahetteu-
poh.

   10 Onk niſh ummagunaſh wutch wutohke
ohkuhqueteaénin, ne ahkehtimeup Lord.

   11 Kah Jeſus neepau anaquabit nanaánu-
waénin ; kah nanaánuwaen wunnatꝏtomau-
oh, nꝏwau, ken ketaſſꝏt ut Jewſe ut ? kah
Jeſus wuttinub, kuſſin .

   12 Kah negonne ſephauſuenuog, kah Elderſog adaſpunonáhettit , matta wunnam-
pꝏhamauoh.

   13 Neit Pilat wuttinub, ſun matta kenꝏ-
tamꝏh uttoh adtahſhu ayeuuhkonittúe
wauwoánnttedan ?

   14 Kah matta wunnampꝏhamau paſuk
kuttꝏwonk, yowutche nanaánuwaen mꝏ-
cheke monchanatam.

   15 Kah e ut miſhadtupwuñeat, nanaánuwaen as kodtumokiſh pohquoſhagkinnumau-   e Luke
au paſukꝏh , miſſinninnúog uttiyeu unnan-   23. 17.
tamhetticheh.

   16 Kah na mo woánumukquſu kuppiſhag-
kinauſuen uſſoweſu Barrabas.

   17 Yowutche moichetrit, Pilat wuttinuh
nahog , howan unnantamóg kuppohquoh-
ſhagkinnumáuouunneau, Barrabas aſuh Jeſus
uſſoweſu Ciriſt ?

   18 Newutche ꝏwahteauun uppaudtaóna-
óont newutche wuſſekeneauóuh.

   19 Onk apit wuliittumwåe ap ꝏnganit,
ummittamwu ioh annꝏtea nꝏnoh, nꝏwau,
toh neheongan noh ſanpweſeaénin , newutche yeu nohkog, uammꝏcheke wuttamhuk
nukkouéonk newutche yeuoh woſketomp.

   20 f Qut negonne ſephauſuenuog kah El-   f John
derſog ſ hhkouwaog mꝏanutcheh , ꝏwe-   18.40.
quetumunaóut Barrabaſoh,onk nuſhonat Je-   Acts 3.
ſus.   14.

   21 Nananuwaen nampꝏham kah wuttinuh, Yeug neeſwe uttiyeuwoh ahchewanum-
óg kutompeninámunaóut ? nꝏwáog, Barrabas.

   22 Newutche Pilat wuttinuh , neit toh
nuttinue Jeſus, noh aſꝏweſit Chriſt ? wame
wuttinóuh Pummetonkapunónaj.

   23 Kah nana inuwáen nꝏwau, tohwutch?
toh en matcheſu? qut nano mꝏcheké n ꝏ-
waog, Pummetonkapunonaj.

   24 Pilat nag matta wuſſohkauoh, qut tea-

Page from Samual Ponampam's 1661 New Testament, with his ownership
mark in the margin. Courtesy of the Bodleian Library, University of Oxford.
Shelfmark 4° L. 95. Th. Sig. E1 recto.

pristine preservation that make for good rare-book collections. The mission tracts record in great detail Ponampam's encounter with scripture, transcribing several of his conversion narratives. Taken together, the several accounts provide a traceable dialogue between Eliot and Ponampam. They represent the different configurations of colonial discourse that I have been examining, and yet they were unique individuals whose exchange of spiritual language and tropes is an extraordinary feature of New England contact literature.

Implicit in the tracts' early discussions of translation and Eliot's decision to avoid more difficult scriptures is the judgment of Indians as theologically childlike. Beverly Olson Flanigan claims, "Europeans . . . deliberately imposed their notions of 'contact talk' on the new people they encountered. . . . The transmission of a consciously simplified English was from the first under control of the newcomers."[64] Such strategies went both ways; Karen Kupperman suggests that Indians "deliberately fashioned" a simplified contact language "in order to shape what the newcomers learned about them."[65] Linguistic studies attending to American Indian Pidgin English and trade jargon offer another possibility: that what has appeared to be a "pidgin" reflecting Indian speech patterns literally translated into English might instead be a reflection of transdialect trade jargon.[66]

We might further speculate on the Indians' perception of the Puritans' simplified "trade language" of religion. In response to the "spiritual milk for babes" offered by Puritan preachers to potential converts, did Indians judge English theology as childishly simple? For instance, in *Tears of Repentance*, Ponampam suggests in a confession delivered to English elders that he may have initially questioned the English grasp of the facts of life:

> Gods free mercy shewed me in the Catechism, *That God made all the World*, yet my heart did not beleeve, because I knew I sprung from my Father and Mother. . . . I heard Gods promise to *Abraham*, *To increase his Children as the Stars for number*, but I beleeved not, because he had but one Son.[67]

Translation obviously had to improve if religious dialogue (or even effective monologue) was to take place. The tracts record the process by which missionaries and Praying Indians tried to understand one another. Most of that mutual learning occurred in conversation, in the oral traditions missionaries and Indians alike brought to the encounter. More tangible success—the approval of converts as church members and leaders—coincided with the printing of scriptural translations.

In 1659, a group of Indian converts came before Roxbury, Massachusetts church elders in hopes of forming their own church, to be led by Eliot. This was their second attempt to be approved as "pillars" of a new Indian church. The first trial, in 1652, was unsuccessful. The later trial—although they were finally approved, first for church membership and then for church leadership—must have been difficult for all concerned. The Praying Indians detailed their encounters with the Christian God, and Eliot translated their words to the English listeners, a tedious process. As the confessors concluded, some were questioned about specifics in their narratives. Issues of language, translation, and authentic expression led to some especially tense moments. One convert, Nishohkou, elsewhere described by Eliot as a "bashful man," was questioned by Samuel Danforth: "I ask you *Nishohkou* this question, and answer me in English, whether the same lusts which you have so much confessed, do not follow you still."[68]

The demand to speak in English suggests a degree of suspicion on the part of English observers of the missionary's ability to translate, the converts' sincerity, or both. Eliot's quick intervention shows that he felt the slight and felt Nishoukou's "bashfulness" deserved some consideration: "I said that a question to the like purpose was asked him, when he made Confession in private, to which he answered in broken English, if the Assembly pleased I would read that" (*Further Account*, 75). Eliot's suggestion was not accepted, and Nishohkou answers in language that recalls Thomas Shepard's metaphor for translation: "His answer was to this purpose; that the Word of God is all one like a sword: and he did with that, resist his temptations" (75). In the years since Eliot's first attempts to convert Indians, it would seem, he had "armed" them with the Word of God—a two-edged weapon, indeed.

At this point in the history of missionary–Indian encounter, the "Word of God" could refer to the oral transmission of Puritan beliefs as well as printed tracts and scriptures. And indeed, the confessions register the significance of both the Christian oral and print tradition. The confessions recorded in *Tears of Repentance* and *Further Account* show the converts using translated scripture to fashion a place for

themselves within the shifting boundaries of English-Indian relations. They register that those boundaries were defined in part by such
encounters as Eliot's sermon at the Merrimack River. Eliot's scriptural
paraphrase no doubt made a strong impression on those who heard it.
As we shall see, Praying Indians responded sharply to Eliot's sermon
and interpreted it knowingly from the perspective of a colonized people. In the 1652 confessions, printed in *Tears of Repentance,* three of
the five Indians who were allowed to speak before the elders, Nataôus,
Robin Speene, and Ponampam, report that they had been influenced
by Eliot's preaching on this verse.

Ponampam especially found Malachi 1:11 important, although
probably not in the way Eliot would have wished. Ponampam was a
lecturer at Natick in the Praying Indian community, and the tracts
record five versions of his confession. Three are from the first trial,
recorded in *Tears of Repentance,* and two are from the final, successful trial, published in *Further Account.* In each of the five confessions,
he refers to Malachi 1:11, paraphrasing it in the first three.[69] In the final transcribed confession, Ponampam reports that Eliot had preached
on this text on more than one occasion: "I heard the same word *again,*
to persuade us to pray to God; and I did so" (*Further Account,* 55; emphasis added). Ponampam seems to confirm Eliot's report on his original sermon, in which the Indian response to the sermon on Malachi
led the missionary to believe that "the sound of the Word is spread a
great way."[70]

However, as Ponampam continued to ponder the application of the
scripture to his own soul, he found reason to doubt its truth on a personal level. Although he says he was persuaded to pray, he registers
the coercive elements of Eliot's translation. Ponampam's initial decision "to pray," it seems, meant that he would conform outwardly to
Christian practices, but as for his inner self: "I considered whether I
should pray, but I found not in my heart that all should pray" (*Tears
of Repentance,* 242). Ponampam's accounts suggest he took away from
Eliot's preaching his message about the inevitability and totality of Indian Christianization (*all* shall pray) but doubted him.

Ponampam's dismissal of the translated message from Malachi is
matched by the other converts' responses, which are attenuated and
suggest that the verse had only a limited effect on them. Nataôus says
that "when I heard that word of God . . . I first understood it not"
(*Tears of Repentance,* 234). When Robin Speene heard Eliot preach on

Malachi, he "wondered at it, and thought, I being a great sinner, how shal I pray to God" (249). Ponampam himself at first welcomed the promise of the prophecy but then "lost that word, and sinned again" (241). Although the frequency of citation seems to support Eliot's contention that he preached to good—and immediate—effect, none of the men reports full conversion, and all report doubts. At best, Eliot's proclamation of universal conversion proved unsettling, as Ponampam reveals in his third recorded confession: on "considering of that word, that all shall pray, I was troubled" (242).

In Ponampam's 1659 confessions, we find an elaborate treatment of scripture and its application to his experiences. Whereas the bare bones of his later successful confessions are evident in the 1652 rehearsals, in the intervening years, he was able to flesh them out by attending Eliot's meetings and reading translated scripture. Scriptural literacy is even more important in the later confessions, and these accounts give us some sense of Ponampam as a reader and exegete. When Natick's leading Christians tried to form their own church in 1659, Eliot had translated more of the Bible. Although the Bible in full would not be printed until 1663, the New Testament was nearly complete. (It was published in 1660.) Ponampam seems to have received a copy in 1662, when he makes several ownership marks, but as a lecturer at Natick, he likely had access to manuscript materials. Moreover, Indian converts gave proof of their increased Christian understanding in sermons recorded in *A further Accompt of the Progresse of the Gospel*, which was published in 1659, the same year that Ponampam's confession, along with those of his fellows, finally met with the approval of English elders.

Thus it is unsurprising that in both of his 1659 confessions, his version of Malachi 1:11 more closely conforms to the King James Version rather than Eliot's paraphrase. He explicitly identifies it by chapter and verse in the second. As his quotation of Malachi comes closer to the standard English version, so too, in increasingly clear terms, his accounts depict his troubled sense of Christianity and conversion as inescapable. In the first confession recorded in 1659, he reports his response to Eliot's sermon:

> My heart did not desire [to pray], but to go away to some other place. But remembring the word of God, that all shall pray to God. Then I did not desire to go away, but to pray to God. But if I pray afore the Sachems pray [that is, before Indian leaders convert], I fear they will kill me, and there-

fore I will not pray. But yet when others prayed, I prayed with them; and I thought, if I run away to other places, they will pray too, therefore I will pray here. (*Further Account*, 20)

The confession painfully describes not a spontaneous conversion upon the hearing of the Word but the deliberations of a colonial subject with too few choices, in a world that Eliot's Malachi translation seems to fit all too well. The non-praying Indian literally has nowhere else to go—"from the rising to the setting Sun."

He is even more direct in his second confession: "Then I was troubled in my thoughts about running away, yet then I thought if I should go to another place, they must pray also, and therefore I cannot flie from praying to God, therefore I tarried" (*Further Account*, 55). Of course, Ponampam is confessing a great sin—the desire, however swiftly quashed, to hide from God. And he seems to be suppressing the desire because he foresees the fulfillment of Eliot's colonial prophecy that soon all Indians would "pray." Once again, his self-description reflects painful realities. Hemmed in by Christians, there is no escaping conversion.

Thus, we can see the influence of Eliot's translation of Malachi on Ponampam's decision to remain a part of the Praying Indian community. In this confession, as I have noted, Ponampam recognizes that Malachi 1 is being used to "perswade us to pray to God." However, it seems the verse had only qualified success as a tool of conversion, perhaps because Ponampam perceived Eliot's sermon as manipulative— if not at the time of delivery, then later when he had access to another version of the verse. He decided to pray, "but not for Gods sake, only it was before man." In other words, he turned to praying for political reasons, making an outward show "before man" in order to become a part of the Praying Indian community. However effective the verse had been in convincing him that he could not flee from God, it was not instrumental to his heartfelt conversion; he did not pray "for Gods sake." Moreover, Ponampam's words imply a connection between his understanding of the English settlers' use of this text for the work of colonization and conversion and his recognition of the consequent political utility of "praying before man."

This perceptive account of the motivations for Eliot's preaching on Malachi 1 and its limited effect on Ponampam appears in the mission record only after the convert reportedly leaves off the scriptural paraphrase, which he must have learned from Eliot and is described as accurately quoting from the King James Bible version. Now, on the one hand, Eliot may have had good reason for describing Ponampam's "mistakes" in interpreting God's word, even if initially Ponampam's encounter with scripture seems to have resulted in a confession of hypocrisy that ran counter to Eliot's many assurances of the Indians' true conversions. In other words, even as it seems to undercut Eliot's reputation as missionary, Ponampam's ability to work through his error and come to true faith certainly implies Ponampam's readiness for full church membership. It is a conventional confession of error, and so the confession survives in the mission literature. On the other hand, we might read this statement as a direct challenge to Eliot's accounts of his missionary successes and a testament to Ponampam's discernment of the coercive tactics of colonization and conversion. His testimony comes close to casting doubt on the missionary's ability to separate sincere conversion from dissembling. The seeming convert saw through the tactics of evangelism and initially rejected them.

Indeed, it is not until Ponampam applies a different scripture—of his own choosing—to his desire for escape that he can report a saving experience. His testimony on the effects of Matthew 4 exemplifies the potential for Puritan Indians to illuminate their experiences by reading the Bible and so to escape the control of colonial interpreters. Ponampam's confession describes a time when he considered moving to Connecticut to escape the rigors of the converted Indians' life. While debating the move, he finds a verse to guide him: "This merciful word of God I heard, That *Satan led Christ into the wilderness to tempt him*, and so I thought hee would do me" (*Further Account*, 22). He elaborates his reading in another confession, imagining Satan speaking directly to him: "You are a great sinner, and God will not pardon you, therefore cast off praying, and run away, it is a vain thing for you to pray. Here you want land, but in the Countrey there is land enough and riches abundance [*sic*], therefore pray no more" (56). This imagined offer strongly attracts Ponampam until he remembers a gospel lesson:

> My heart did almost like it, but I heard that word, *Mat. 4. Satan tempted Christ, and shewed him the Kingdoms of the world, and the glory therof, and promised to give them to him, if he would worship him.* Then my heart said, that even thus Satan tempteth me to cast off praying to God. (56)

Ponampam's confession of his temptation and triumph over it must have been accepted by the English who heard him, because it signaled to Puritan elders the successful repudiation of a traditional Indian lifestyle. Mission literature had impressed on its English readers that before colonization and evangelism, Indians were wandering in the wilderness, both spiritually in their ignorance of Christ and literally as a nomadic people. Ponampam's application of Matthew 4 to his own temptations demonstrates his internalization of that assessment, and the elders took it as proof that they could now trust him with church estate.

However, Ponampam's interpretation also illustrates once again that he recognized how few viable choices were available to him in 1659. He sees that from a Puritan perspective, the "Countrey" beyond English settlement is the site of the "wilderness" of sin. He is in the process of embracing Puritanism, so presumably he is prepared to accept that perspective. But reasons aside from the spiritual also explain why Ponampam considers and then rejects removing to Connecticut. The "Kingdoms of the world" with which Satan tempts Ponampam are Indian lands. In offering him such "kingdoms," Satan fails to register, like so many English colonists, either kinship ties or hostilities among various Indian peoples. Thus it is not surprising that this dialogue with Satan indicates Ponampam's separation from the English Puritans who seek to convert him while refusing to embrace him, who refuse his rights to Bay Colony land and tell him "you are a great sinner and God will not pardon you," while pushing him outside New England's bounds to lands that are already claimed and occupied. But the dialogue also underscores his alienation from non-Praying Indians and, possibly, his own earlier life. He recognizes clearly that Satan's alternative—to run away to "the country"—is not viable for him, although the English audience might see it as a real possibility for "heathens." The "wild Indian" identity, assumed to be his by English magistrates particularly fearful of Indian apostasy, in no way characterizes Ponampam, who was settled in a praying town and beginning to embrace a Christian identity.

The most striking aspect of this passage in Ponampam's confession is the way it seems to disturb the colonial mission's construction of the Christian Indian through, in Homi Bhabha's words, "colonial mimicry," that is, "the desire for a reformed, recognizable Other, *as a subject of a difference that is almost the same, but not quite.*"[71] New

England Puritans demanded that Praying Indians inhabit a Christian identity but one that kept them perpetually in between—almost regenerate, though never quite fully so—thereby necessitating continual infusions of money, goods, and missionaries from the metropolitan center (whether London or Boston). But as Ponampam inserts himself personally into scripture, he varies the pattern Puritan typology established for Praying Indians, reversing English colonial commonplaces and radically extending the message of Eliot's translation of Malachi 1:11.

In his confession, Ponampam creates his Puritan identity by casting his difficulties into recognizably Christian—and colonial—terms. In good Puritan fashion, he "mimics" the typological exegesis so central to New England's colonial articulations, asserting his centrality within a Christian belief system that, when translated by English settlers into the colonial register, marginalizes him. In this way, Ponampam in turn translates Matthew 4 into a colonial text, but his version reflects his displacement, both physical and spiritual. Ponampam sees his encounters with Satan and his temptations as taking place not in the "wilds" outside but within the bounds of colonial charters.[72] In his translation of Matthew 4, English "civilization" becomes his personal "wilderness," in which he encounters Satan and risks temptation.

Ponampam's appropriation to himself of Puritan tropes and genres disrupts the colonists' understanding of themselves as claiming either a vacant wilderness or the devil's territories. Ponampam so successfully adapts the conventions of the confession genre to his experiences that he and others like him threaten to displace the English elect as saintly colonists.[73] His decision not to run away seals his claim to a physical place in the colonies, to lands set aside for praying towns, even as his repudiation of Satan seals his claim to a Christian identity. As I discuss in chapter 6, the radical extension of the disturbance suggested by Ponampam's confession will be Indians' appropriation of prayer, psalm-singing, and scripture to their own ends as they fight English settlers during King Philip's War.

My claims for this moment of colonial encounter, however, are much more modest. In his essay "A Native American Perspective: Canaanites, Cowboys, and Indians," Robert Allen Warrior demonstrates how flawed a type "Israel in the Wilderness" is for Indians displaced by English settlers, as were Canaanites by Israelites.[74] And to be sure, Ponampam's reading of Matthew 4 is not, in Eric Cheyfitz's

terms, his "point of revolution," the moment "when the colonized begin to *read* the myth, begin, that is, to understand it as readable, or, to
put it another way, as charged with politics."[75] Nevertheless, with
such readings Praying Indians created Christian identities to serve
their needs, through which they performed a native Christianity unrecognizable to the Pauline orator at the Merrimack River, however
provisional such a misrecognition might have been or however temporary the disruption of the missionary's gaze. I have not been concerned in this chapter with interrogating the depth or quality of
Christian Indian knowledge and faith. I take Ponampam and others at
their word, mediated though it is, that they were Christians. My in-
tention has been to discover how their beliefs took shape and how the
representation of those beliefs developed in this record of an extended
moment of spiritual encounter. Such an approach can and should com-
plicate our notions about resistance and authenticity.

For his part, Ponampam created a narrative that called into question
English observers who doubted the Praying Indians' sincerity and
feared their "unsettled" lifestyle might tempt them to escape English
law and religion by running away to Connecticut or other "kingdoms
of the world." In Ponampam's interpretation of Matthew 4, only a Satan would see such an escape as possible for a Praying Indian. Through
this use of the Indian Bible, Ponampam has fully "translated" himself
into the gospel experience or, rather, translated the gospel into his own
experiences and appropriated one of the most cherished English Puritan tropes: New England as Israel in an American wilderness. Indeed,
he chooses the antitype itself for his own identity. Like Christ, he has
encountered Satan in the wilderness, and like Christ, he emerges triumphant. Ponampam thus finds strength in a reading of Matthew 4.
He wields the "Sword of Gods word" himself, the dangerous vernacular scripture, and so finds a place, however briefly, in colonial New
England.

4 Algonquians and Antinomians
"Spiritual Questions" and Dissent

In his *Key into the Language of America*, Roger Williams takes up the issue of religious exchange: "He that questions whether God made the world, the *Indians* will teach him."[1] Williams here refers to the prime thesis of his book: Indians "naturally" display religious affections that put the hypocrisies of English Christians to shame. Williams's work has been lauded as a remarkably sensitive portrayal of Indian-English relations, and it does stand apart from other colonial productions. But as a premillennialist, Williams could afford to be rather sanguine on the question of Indians' full regeneracy. He simply did not believe evangelism could take effect until after Christ's return and the establishment of the true church on earth. Without a true church, after all, to what would Indians convert? Thus, while his chapter "of Religion, the soule, &c." contains "implicit dialogues" on aspects of religious and especially Christian belief, he was not interested in imagining future directions to religious encounters.

Orthodox Puritan colonists, of course, urged on by millennialist beliefs, convinced of the spiritual and temporal necessity of a mission in New England, had to find ways to instruct. If they found a "natural" bent for Christianity among "lost and forlorn" Indians, so much the better. Regardless, colonists needed to find the means to mediate spiritual encounters between Indians and missionaries and so to "elevate" converts to the level of Christian understanding and expression of Ponampam's conversion narratives.

Catechism was the first, obvious step, and Puritan missionaries immediately began the ritual of questions and answers with Indian children.[2] Adults, however, needed more, and they would not accept passively the one-directional catechism. When asked whether they had questions for the missionaries, Praying Indians responded assertively, asking perceptive and wide-ranging questions about every aspect of Christian theology and practice. Their "spiritual questions" were codified in the mission tracts and became an early form of religious expression in the Indian church. They are generic predecessors of the conversion narratives, sermons, dialogues, and dying speeches that later appear in the tracts as evidence of converts' salvation.

Confession narratives have long been identified as *the* personal religious genre in Puritan New England. My identification of "questions" as a trope in the Praying Indians' religious practices may seem strained by comparison because questions appear so much less structured than the more rigorous confession. And the question is a common element of contact literature, a detail of quotidian interaction recorded from Columbus's journals on. In each of the six Puritan mission tracts published between 1647 and 1653, eyewitnesses refer to or transcribe questions asked by Indians of preachers at their meetings. From the seventeen questions listed in the first tract, *Day-Breaking, if not the Sun-Rising of the Gospell with the* Indians in New-England (1647), the record reaches a high point with seventy-six transcribed in the 1649 publication *Glorious Progress of the Gospel*. Questions often appear within narratives of encounter, but at times the tracts break off and the questions appear completely out of context in straightforward lists. In all, nearly two hundred questions are recorded in the eleven mission tracts published between 1647 and 1671.[3] They vary from inquiries about the natural world to minute examinations of scripture, to implicit criticism of both Indian and English behavior. Much of the descriptions of early meetings among missionaries and converts is devoted to the Indians' questions about Christianity, about the missionaries' motivations, or about the piety of the English settlers.

The necessity of questions in contact situations and the variability of their appearance in these tracts make them seem especially promising in terms of "unearthing" buried Native experiences. Indeed, James Ronda, Henry Von Lonkhuyzen, and others have found in the questions traces of Indian resistance to Christianization.[4] The give-and-take of these exchanges feels remarkably unscripted to the modern reader, as the textual appearance of questions seems less contained than the narrated encounters. Here, it seems, we are much closer to hearing the words of new converts than in other records of Praying Indian speech.

And perhaps we are. John Eliot was surprised and discomfited by some questions put to him by Indian listeners. Thereafter, a ritual of questions and answers seems to have evolved as a response to the need of convert and missionary alike to understand one another's experience of faith. We can see in the tracts that the practice of asking questions after the sermon was improvised out of early exchanges between Indians and missionaries and became an orthodox form of Praying Indian religious instruction in the early years of the New England mission.

Yet, while the ritual of asking questions after the sermon does seem to have been largely invented by the Indians and responsive to their needs, the *record* of these exchanges was carefully shaped to meet the needs of a distant English audience as well as an immediate Praying Indian congregation. By tracing the shape and genealogy of the form as an important part of Praying Indians' "morphology of conversion," we can see how the colonial encounter met the early modern print industry. In particular, the oral ritual of asking questions—derived from traditional Indian as well as Puritan practices—was filtered through Calvinist theology and entered the transatlantic pamphlet wars of the civil war period, contributing to colonial and English nationalist identity construction.

To understand spiritual questions, it is necessary to contextualize them with the information flowing from New England to Old more generally. The publication of Indian questions coincided with the publication of New England's Antinomian controversy, reports that were being used in high-level debates between English Presbyterians intent on discrediting their opponents, whom they identified with New Englanders, and Congregationalists who were mustering alliances to modify if not defeat Presbyterianism at the national level. Even though missionary-Indian encounters appear far removed from the "internal" disputes between Anne Hutchinson and colonial authorities, a close look at the mission tracts reveals the extent to which the various colonial discourses in which they participate are inseparable. Against a range of charges that, on the one hand, New England Puritanism engendered dangerous heresies and, on the other, that New England Puritans harshly punished people for their private beliefs, the reports of Indians questioning Puritan ministers reassure English readers that the New England Way created orderly communities of faith.

The "Fourth Exercise"

For this discussion of questions and the Praying Indian community, we must turn once again to that "true relation" of mission beginnings, the mission tract *Day-Breaking* and its account of a brief religious encounter. The anonymous author begins by describing a meeting with a group of Indians interested in Christianity. The English preacher, unnamed, but most certainly John Eliot, had been apprised aforetimes of the powwows (i.e., religious leaders) in his congregation. After the sermon, Eliot questioned one so identified:

> and propounded these questions, viz. 1. Whether doe you thinke that God or *Chepian* is the author of all good? he answered, God. 2. If God bee the author of all good, why doe you pray to *Chepian* the devill? The *Pawwaw* perceiving him to propound the last question with a sterne countenance and unaccustomed terrour, hee gave him no answer, but spake to other *Indians* that hee did never hurt any body by his *Pawwawing,* and could not bee got by all the meanes and turnings of questions that might bee, to give the least word of answer againe.[5]

My sympathies are entirely with this unnamed man. There he is, listening to this English preacher, perhaps a bit disquieted by the changes in his community—other powwows had taken to the English ways and given up older practices—but confident in his own position. Not disruptive, back of the crowd, then suddenly he becomes the preacher's object lesson in Christian power.

Maybe his answers reflect his long-standing belief in Manitou and Chepien. Manitou (a word that the English glibly translated as "God") "authors" good, but Chepien is just as important to life's processes and balances.[6] Or maybe he responds to the first question as he does in hopes of placating the preacher and ending this uncomfortable exchange. Regardless, he does not get the chance to finish his discussion, and he turns to his fellows in a plea for support or sympathy, ending the "dialogue" with the preacher entirely. Despite his withdrawal from the debate, the man is still hounded by "all the meanes and turnings of questions that might be." And although those "meanes and turnings" are likely put to him by the preacher, there is a sense in this passage that he stands alone, that the "other *Indians*" side with Eliot and urge him to further answer.

In any event, the powwow is clearly set apart from the community of Praying Indians being created here, and the man ends his silence only in a more private setting:

> A little after the conference was ended, [Eliot] met with this *Pawwaw* alone and spake more lovingly and curteously to him, and askt him why hee would not answer, he then told him that his last question struck a terrour into him and made him afraid, and promised that at the next meeting hee would propound some question to him as others did.[7]

This story is included in a section added because the "Ship lingers in the Harbour," affording the writer more time to complete his letter. Both the belated addition of the anecdote to the letter and the powwow's response strike me as curious. Why is this story of a powwow's resistance added to the letter, and why would "propounding" a question be the resolution of the conflict between Indian and missionary?

The first question is perhaps easier to answer than the second. The contest with the powwow almost immediately follows the tracts' description of two "young lusty men who offered themselves voluntarily to the service of the English" so they might become Christian. The juxtaposition is surely meant to showcase the colonists' abilities to conquer as well as to convert, to deal with the recalcitrant powwow as well as the willing proselyte. And the claim that the episode is an afterthought, included because the ship's delay afforded the author unexpected time to write, adds to the texts' verisimilitude with its unplanned, "from-the-front" effect. Colonial missionaries appear to be resilient, improvisational crusaders for Christ.

But the end of the story, the powwow's promise to ask a question at the next meeting, "as others did," seems at once banal and bizarre. The two young men, when confronted by the Christian message of personal sin and redemption, display an affective response. They "fell a weeping and lamenting bitterly" and "burst out . . . into a great mourning" (18). The powwow's response, by contrast, signals not a personal spiritual sensibility but rather a communal, even secular need. Others ask questions of the preacher after a sermon, and so he indicates his willingness to continue with the Praying Indian community by conforming his behavior to theirs. Originally opposed to the mission message (it seems), the man decides to ask a question as "others did" not because he has an eager interest in Christ but because he recognized his isolation from the newly formed Christian Indian community. To rejoin them, he must adapt his speech to the new patterns of religious expression, in this case, to ask a question after a sermon.

As this story illustrates, New England evangelism from the start addressed the need for discursive forms that would allow Indians to participate in Protestant identity formation, whether such participation was enthusiastic or painfully acquiescent. Many observers of Puritan missionizing—both witnesses in New England and readers in Old England—were highly skeptical that Indians, whom they castigated as degenerate and savage, could become regenerate Christians, pious, spiritually knowledgeable, modest and industrious. The outward traits of a Christian—modesty and industry—were relatively easy to achieve: they could be legislated by the "praying-town" laws and the Bay Colony's justice system. The first set of laws that Indians adopted at Noonatomen (a praying town), for example, imposed fines if "any woman shall goe with naked breasts" or "if any man be idle a weeke."[8] Christian virtues might also be encouraged by wages and gifts of clothing and tools. The "invisible" qualities of piety and spiritual knowledge, however, were attributes difficult enough to inculcate in English churchgoers, and the means by which these qualities were cultivated in the English community—catechisms, printed scriptures, and devotionals—were not available to Eliot's converts until much later.

Praying Indians needed alternative ways to express their commitment to their new faith and to identify one another as members of the fledgling religious community. Moreover, critical English observers, who demanded proof that every potential communicant experienced true reformation, raised their expectations for Indian converts, linking the spiritual and material support of the mission effort to proofs of conversion even before Praying Indians sought church communion.[9] To meet these demands, mission tracts offered descriptions of the converts' altered lifestyles and appearances as the first tangible sign of conversion. Such evidence ran the risk, however, of making Indian conversions seem superficial or hypocritical, or worse yet, made the food, clothing, and tools offered to potential converts appear to be bribes. Observers worried lest Indians were converting "for loaves," that is, for food and other goods, rather than out of spiritual conviction.[10]

Of course, mission tracts did use physical evidence to prove that Praying Indians were really being saved. For instance, they described Indians who wept in response to the Word, a reaction that Puritan writers praised. But even tears, no matter how heartfelt, did not prove to English observers that converts understood Christianity, nor did they demonstrate an experience of full conversion.[11] Moreover, as an intensely personal expression of "holy desperation," tears could not forge a Puritan community based on shared religious convictions and experiences. The Praying Indians and their religious leaders needed to find a form of religious expression that would identify regenerate Indians to one another and to outside observers.

In English congregations in New England in this period, the publicly related conversion narrative was a highly visible means not only of disciplining the individual believer, but also, by allowing members of a congregation to witness narratives and to absorb the form of the recitation, of forging a Christian community.[12] However, Indian hopefuls, separated by geography, language, and social standing from English churches, did not witness public confessions in the early years of their meetings and thus were not regularly exposed to the generic exemplars and inspiration available to English congregants.

Praying Indians would eventually use conversion narratives quite adeptly. As they learned the elements of the genre, they internalized and successfully reproduced it, forming their own church in 1660. Nonetheless, theirs was a distinct form of Puritanism. James Holstun observes that "the preaching, catechism, encouragement of questioning, and admonition and censure combined to create the melancholic Praying Indian."[13] Holstun's careful articulation of the Praying Indian is persuasive, as is his understanding of the theological forces shaping the construction of the figure. I would emphasize more than he does, however, the attributes other than confession and weeping. The Praying Indian could not move from tears to acceptable confession without intermediary steps, for both pedagogic and political reasons. It would be some seven years from the first missionary description of a weeping Indian to the first transcription of a Praying Indian confession. In the intervening years, Eliot and other mission writers document the spiritual questions as a form of religious speech with meaning for the community as a whole. This first mode of adult Praying Indian religious expression was developed and enjoyed widespread approval from 1646 to 1652, anticipating the enlarged confessions of faith that would begin to appear in print in 1653.

The mission tracts published in this period describe Indian meetings that began with three conventional oral exercises: catechism of children, preaching on scripture, finishing with admonition and censure.[14] Eliot reports that in meetings of potential converts, the presentation of his message was designed to compensate for his weakness in the Indian language, the exigencies of teaching Puritanism to a people with a radically different religious framework than his own, and the Praying Indian community's lack of translated scripture. In *A further Accompt of the Progresse of the Gospel*, Eliot notes that not until 1659 could he draw on his translation of the entire Bible; only Genesis, Matthew, and a few psalms had been printed to that point.[15] The lack of translated and printed scriptures during the early years of the Puritan mission meant that most Indian converts could not study the written gospels for themselves (as behooved good Protestants). They could, however, examine the preachers who sought to convey the Christian message to them. To the first three more conventional exercises, the Praying Indians added a time for asking questions.[16]

The tradition of asking questions following the sermon was not planned as an ongoing exercise by English missionaries, and judging from the written record, terse as it is, the Indians' "fourth exercise" did not always accomplish what the missionaries desired. In *Day-Breaking*, the author describes the meeting that four English ministers conducted at Waban's house. English missionaries prayed and preached a sermon.[17] Then, the tract reports, they intended to interrogate their audience so that they "might skrue by variety of meanes something or other of God" into the gathered Indians.[18]

Before they progressed to such a violent-sounding task, they inquired, almost as an afterthought, if those in attendance had any questions about what the English had prayed and preached. Not surprisingly, the Indians did, asking six questions that probed the limits of the Puritan God and seeming inconsistencies in the sermon's message.[19] They even questioned the Christian commitment of the English themselves, asking "Whether English men were ever at any time so ignorant of God and Jesus Christ as themselves." Despite the marginalia's seamless notation identifying *"Quest."* and *"Answ.,"* it seems that here the record elides considerable dialogue. The tract notes that the import of the question was not self-evident; the missionaries took some time to understand "the root and reach of this question," which apparently responds to the Indians' immediate observation of sinful English behavior. The evangelists concede that some Englishmen are "bad and naught," but the rest of their answer refocuses the discussion from the bad example of the English (thereby suppressing the suggestion of Indian criticism) to the Indians' understanding of their own lost state. Though some Englishmen may be ignorant of God, the answer reassures, others repent and come to know God and Jesus Christ. Likewise, even though Indians know they are "bad," they can follow the good Englishman's example and "so seeke him also" (6).

Note that according to this report, the question period had been imagined by the missionaries as a kind of advanced catechism to screw God into potential converts, not as a rigorous interrogation by Indians of the Christian message. From one perspective, the exchange might be interpreted as the Indians' unseemly attempt to take charge of the meeting. Certainly, they seem to be approaching the ministers in the spirit of real, give-and-take dialogue. As in any such discussion, the Indians assume the right, even the responsibility to question the speaker closely. Whatever the relation of this exchange to Indian customs and commonplaces, the tract takes care to place the question firmly in the realm of successful religious pedagogy, translating it from a moment of mutual encounter into an orthodox, Calvinist dialogue by detailing the specific questions asked in the meeting.

Even more importantly, the account contrasts this mission moment with an earlier English attempt to preach to the sachem Cutshamekin's men at Dorchester Mill. Unlike the positive—or at least interested—reception at Waban's home, Eliot reports later that the Dorchester Mill listeners did not welcome him. They "were weary, and rather despised what I said."[20] On the surface, the comparison of the two groups in *Day-Breaking* serves simply to emphasize the acceptability of Waban and his guests as proselytes versus that of the men at Dorchester Mill. But the textual appearance of that encounter in a curiously extended parenthetical aside may point to a real discomfort with this new religious ritual that seems to have been initiated by or at least insisted upon by Indians hostile to Christian evangelism. In the midst of detailing the interest of Waban and his men to the mission message, a reference to the failed mission to Cutshamekin's men erupts into the narrative:

> We then desired to know of them, if they would propound any question to us for more cleare understanding of what was delivered; whereupon severall of [Waban's men] propounded presently severall questions (far different from what some other *Indians* under *Kitshomakin* in the like meeting about six weekes before had done, *viz.* 1. What was the cause of Thunder. 2. Of the Ebbing and Flowing of the Sea. 3. Of the wind) but

the questions (which wee thinke some speciall wisedome of God directed these unto) (which these propounded) were in number six.[21]

The narrative is almost incoherent in its attempt to contrast Cutshamekin's men from those being described at greater length in the tract.[22] The poor reception Eliot received at Dorchester Mill seems still to rankle. The second and third parenthetical insertions are an attempt to clear up the first, poorly handled aside. We read that Waban's men asked several questions at the October meeting. Some weeks earlier, Cutshamekin's men had likewise asked questions. But the grammatical weight is not on the ostensible main idea—that Waban's men asked six good questions. Rather, the sentence dwells at length on the bad questions that Cutshamekin's men asked earlier.

The reasons for including this challenge in the tract are obvious in one sense: Waban contrasts positively with Cutshamekin. However, the moment also suggests the dangers of engaging in open dialogue and hints at the ways Eliot worked to control the exchange. In the first, unsuccessful meeting, Eliot may have been surprised by the inquiries and their challenges to the English understanding of the natural world.[23] Although the tracts do not mention whether Cutshamekin's men volunteered questions or posed them in response to a carefully worded invitation, as Waban's followers did, Eliot learned from the first encounter that he could not turn the meeting over to open dialogue. The Indians were well prepared for and expected debate. By contrast, the opportunity to question that he presents to the audience at Waban's house closes off the conversation. From that time on, the "fourth exercise" offered his listeners a chance to probe only those issues on which he had preached or about which he had prayed.

The Call to the Unconverted

This channeling of questions toward "what was delivered" in the sermon is one way Eliot and other English writers make Indian questions seem quite orthodox. Although it is difficult fully to evaluate the report from the scant information provided, it is reasonable to surmise that this fourth exercise was suggested by the Indians' practices rather than by the missionaries' determination to invite challenge and initiate cross-cultural dialogue. However, Eliot's belief system afforded him the means by which even the most difficult questions fit perfectly well in a Christian conversion experience. As Calvinists, Eliot and other missionaries understood "the unconverted" as an inclusive, multinational category; Indians may have needed more "civilizing" than English sinners, but Puritans believed all unconverted must "turn" or be damned. Moreover, all of the chosen trod a common path on their journey from sinner to saint. In evangelical writings, the unrepentant, whether English or Indian, discover the same objections to conversion and ask the same questions of God.[24]

Eliot's later choices of English texts for translation for his converts illustrate the role Puritans understood such questions to play in all conversions—English as well as Indian. In 1663, Eliot wrote to his friend Richard Baxter, planning to translate Baxter's *The Call to the Unconverted to Turn and Live* into Wôpanâak.[25] Although Baxter urged Eliot to turn his attention to works "more worthy of your labours, Eliot published his translation, *Wehkomaonganoo asquam peantogig,* in 1664.[26] In the English original, Baxter presents his sixth doctrine, "The Lord condescendeth to reason the case with unconverted sinners," and then "transcribes" a question-and-answer dialogue between God and a sinner. In it, the English sinner objects that he does "not see that it goes any better with those that are so godly, than with other men; they are as poor and in as much trouble as others."[27]

Praying Indians discover the very same objection in the mission tract *Clear Sun-shine.* They ask Eliot how they are to reply to unconverted Indians who inquire "What get you . . . by praying to God, and beleeving in Jesus Christ? you goe naked still, and you are as poore as wee, and our Corne is as good as yours."[28] The tract ascribes the question to those who "oppose their praying to God," but the Praying Indians want an answer "for their own information also," and Eliot takes pains to answer the objection as if it were their own. Salisbury discusses Eliot's choice of Baxter's *Call to the Unconverted* and the later translation of Lewis Bayly's *Practice of Piety,* concluding that "the works translated for the Indians were those encouraging an inward, socially passive piety."[29] I agree. Missionaries certainly attempted to channel Praying Indian piety into "safe" expressions. The question quoted in *Clear Sun-shine* about Praying Indians' poverty, for instance, displaces any doubt onto distant, non-Praying Indians rather than on the converts. Nevertheless, the traces of Indian resistance described in the mission tracts are both contained *and* made possible by these English exemplars. If Eliot had not taken challenging questions as signs that Indians were converting, these questions would not have survived in his accounts.

Eliot also discounted as weak or impertinent Indian questions that did not meet his expectations for piety or seriousness. The only way Praying Indians could enter the dialogue was by clothing their participation in safe conventions. That they recognized and made use of even "passive" models to oppose or simply question the mission message is a testament to their energy and engagement with Puritan doctrine.

Then again, Puritan missionaries had the ability to assimilate even the most potent challenges into orthodox encounter. Any questioning of Christian doctrine—unlike observations of the natural world or comparisons of traditional Indian beliefs to those of the English—was recognized as a failure of human reasoning common to all sinners, rather than as effective resistance to Puritan evangelism. Although thorny theological questions such as "why did not God give all men good hearts that they might be good?" or "why did not God kill the Devill that made all men so bad, God having all power?"[30] might indicate a fundamental hesitancy about the mission message or a skepticism about a "benevolent" God who allows evil to exist, readers familiar with Protestant evangelical literature would have recognized these as perennial and generic questions. Eliot presents such inquiries as an indication of the Indians' seriousness about the Christian message, not as worrisome challenges.

This either/or reading of Indian questions may seem perversely ambivalent. But in examining these materials for early modern subjectivity, whether English or Indian, the best we can do is to hold alternate, even contradictory readings in productive tension and to examine the ways that, on the one hand, the missionary insistence on orthodox forms created a rigid Praying Indian identity "reduced" to Christianity and, on the other, how Native Americans changed Puritan religious discourse, if only by forcing colonial writers to deal with their presence. For instance, the question from *Clear Sun-shine*— "what get you . . . by praying to God"—is a canny presentation of Indian concerns. It certainly reflects plausible caution on the part of potential converts who were seeking a solution to economic and political disruptions as they asked what material good would come of the Puritans' new way.

It is entirely likely that such a question was posed, not once but many times, as Indians and English negotiated their material as well as spiritual co-existence in the colonies. But the question must also be understood discursively as a particularly New English translation of Baxter's work. While in *The Call to the Unconverted,* the English sinner notes that Christians are poor and "in as much trouble as others," the similar question as put by Indian sinners emphasizes the (to the English) "exotic": nakedness and corn as wealth. The passage registers a double translation, the Americanization of the universal objections posed by all sinners to the Christian way, and the translation of the mission encounter itself for an English audience. The tract thereby reverses the flow of evangelical ideas. Rather than a westward migration, now the Christian message moves from New to Old England.

The tracts thus shape English readers' perception by describing American versions of established forms and conventions. Even so, some questions seem more vexing or confrontational than others, as when potential converts query the sinful actions of biblical figures and of the neighboring English: "Did not Abraham sin in saying she is my sister?" and "Doe not Englishmen spoile their soules, to say a thing cost them more then it did? and is it not all one as to steale?"[31] Eliot uses a different representational strategy to contain the threat of such questions and to defuse any challenge to his message. He carefully suppresses the appearance of an equal exchange in his presentation of Indian questions and erases the dialogue between preacher and listener. Although the answers to such questions as *"What Countrey man Christ was, and where he was borne"* should have been obvious to English audiences, it is striking that answers to even the most complex questions go unrecorded.[32]

Of the two hundred Indian questions set down, only around ten percent of the answers are recorded. More than half of the questions appear without any context whatsoever. Not only does Eliot leave out his answers, he does not describe how or when Indians made specific inquiries or even identify individual speakers. At times, we get massed lists of as many as forty or fifty questions. By placing such questions in long lists, Eliot defuses the negative impact of even the most difficult questions, encouraging passive reception. Readers are not required to judge either the question or the response but simply to note inquiry itself as evidence of the conversion process.

The questions themselves—not the answers they elicited, not the dialogue they might have engendered—signify the Indians' status as potential converts. Since Indian questions measured converts' "wisdom," the questions vary and change as they increase in knowledge. Some questions were, as the tracts note, "weaker"; some were more "spirituall." By contrast, the answers to those questions were, missionaries believed, Truth, culled by the godly from scripture with the assistance of God. These tracts were concerned with the Indians' response to grace; therefore the answers did not need to appear in the tracts.

When Cutshamekin's people in the first, unsuccessful mission meeting asked questions, they focused on the natural world, asking after the causes of thunder, the tides, and the wind, marked by the tract as "far different" questions than those asked by Waban's men. The tract insists that good Praying Indians ask more sophisticated questions, or "sundry philosophicall questions, which some knowledge of the arts must helpe to give answer to."[33] Even though Praying Indians did ask questions about the natural world ("How it comes to passe that the Sea water was salt, and the Land water fresh"), they first made "higher" inquiries. Once Waban's men are distinguished from Cutshamekin's followers, then all other kinds of questions are assumed to be part of a Christian dialogue. The missionaries answer questions about the natural world on two levels, giving them the "reason of it from naturall causes," but emphasizing that the first cause was "no reason but the wonderfull worke of God." Such discussions aimed "to make [Indians] acknowledge God in his workes," an acknowledgment Waban and his followers seemed prepared to make.[34]

Cutshamekin's men at Dorchester Mill apparently intended no such thing, and their questions, although similar to some Waban's people asked, were "far different" not because they had a different content but because they did not signal a desire to enter into Christian dialogue. Thus the tract interprets the Indians' question as conforming to orthodox conversion patterns, and as we have seen, it goes on to attribute the probing quality of this and other Indian questions to divine inspiration: "Wee thinke some speciall wisedome of God directed these unto [their questions]" (4).

Of course, as the example of the unnamed powwow discussed at the beginning of this chapter suggests, not all questions asked by Praying Indians were spiritually inspired. Some were politically motivated, and others, as even Eliot admits, were simply "weaker."[35] These latter, however, are not recorded. Rather, as Indians move from the initial encounter with Puritanism to—in Eliot's view—a state of grace, the lists of questions that are transcribed in the tracts characterize Praying Indians as sincere, intelligent, and increasingly knowledge-able about scripture and Puritan doctrine. Eliot offers transcriptions of selected questions in order to refine the Praying Indians' image for an English audience: "good" Indian questions gave immediate hearers, correspondents, and readers of the tracts evidence that the Praying Indians were truly preparing to convert. Eliot evaluates these questions with the same metaphors others used to assess English confession narratives. Like confessions in English religious communities, questions are performances of faith; they make grace visible and allow others to "savor" the state of the inquirer's soul. Thus, Eliot offers his correspondents a "taste" of Praying Indians' knowledge "by their Questions."[36]

Moreover, Eliot savors the Indians' faith as a sign of radical, world-wide Christian movements. And here we see the homely lists of Indian questions taken to new interpretive heights by English commentators, the "raw data" of mission contact translated into prophecy. As I discuss in chapter 2, mission writers connect Indian questions to millennial prophesies, including them in letters to England so that readers there could see "how these dry bones begin to gather flesh and sinnews."[37] Even Thomas Shepard, who as we have seen was less sanguine about such millennial identities, nevertheless viewed Indian questions positively: "I have heard few Christians when they begin to looke toward God, make more searching questions that they might see things really."[38] Such comparisons between Indians and other Christians indicate the significance of the questions. They link the Indians' experiences to a "universal" if not a millennial plot of conversion and identify Indians as truly "coming in" to the faith. Spiritual questions, simply put, are a means of identifying the saints, wherever they may be found.

Indeed, the Indians' habit of asking questions is understood typo-logically by some English observers. The postscript by John Dury to *Glorious Progress of the Gospel* likens some Indian questions to those which Paul answers in his letters to the Corinthians, terming them "of great and weighty concernment."[39] And in *Clear Sun-shine*, Shep-ard goes on to treat the practice of questioning as a positive marker of Indians' praying identity: "by these [questions] you may perceive in what streame their minds are carried, and that the Lord Jesus hath at last an enquiring people among these poor naked men, that formerly never so much as thought of him."[40] The label "enquiring people" may be drawn from Psalms 27:4, a verse Joseph Caryl paraphrases in his preface to another mission tract:

> *Beloved Brethren,* As, The *One thing* which ye have desired of the Lord, and which yee have sought after, is, that your selves might dwell in the house of the Lord all the dayes of your lives, to behold the beauty of the Lord, and to enquire in his Temple: So, I am much assured that the next thing which yee have desired of the Lord . . . is, that they who have hitherto been strangers to, might dwell also in the house of the Lord all the dayes of their lives, to behold the beauty of the Lord, and to enquire in his Temple.[41]

Shepard may also have intended his phrase to modify the notion of God's "peculiar people," especially as it is used in 1 Peter 2:9–10, which lays out the relationship of God and humanity within covenant theology: "But ye are a chosen generation, a royal priesthood, an holy nation, a peculiar people . . . which in time past were not a people, but are now the people of God."

From the beginning of colonial contact, some English settlers identified Indians as those who "were not a people." When Praying Indians became "enquiring people," the tracts present them as moving away from their state of complete degeneracy and toward the higher state enjoyed by the English, who were understood to be the "peculiar people," God's chosen. The identity stops short, however, of signifying full salvation, full regeneracy. The continuing ontological difference between the converts and English Christians allows writers such as Shepard to endorse the process of evangelism but to reserve judgment about whether God's time had come for the Indians.

Antinomians and Indians

But of course, in the late 1640s and 1650s, many people had cast off their skepticism and embraced the idea that indeed God's time had come, at least for the English. And so, because these questions and the encounters they register were published to an English audience, they must be understood within the theological and political contexts of the tracts. For, as much as the presentation of Indian questions works to contain and make orthodox the Indian experience of Christianity, the tracts also comment on the state of English Puritanism. While historians have seized on Indian questions as evidence of intercultural dialogue or as windows on the Indian reception (or rejection) of Eliot's evangelical message, they have not considered the extent to which the tracts' construction of Christian Indians was engaged with other debates then making their way into print. It is a mistake to sift through the tracts for moments of Indian expression in order to reconstruct a scene of cultural reciprocity without understanding that Eliot and other English writers who recorded Indian questions presented them to their readers in order to raise funds, pass bills supporting New England in Parliament, and involve themselves—through the representation of the Indian engagement with Reformed Christianity—in the most contentious issues of the day.

Although I place these questions in a transatlantic context, other possible reasons for the tracts' seeming indulgence of Indian challenges have less to do with Old England than with a purely colonial construction of events and Native peoples. The record of questions is not meaningless to such investigations. Perhaps, as Myra Jehlen argues about John Smith's writings, colonial literature such as the mission tracts records "history before the fact." They are not retrospective analyses of Indian evangelism but hastily written missives from the front lines of English-Indian encounters.[42] Their authors may not have had the leisure to ponder every question they recorded; they may not have even known at the time of composition which questions were truly unsettling or which would become so. Readers today have the advantage of hindsight, and we are (possibly) more attuned to the nuances of Indian critiques in these reports. And, as Holstun persuasively argues, the challenging questions show that the missionaries can "contain and rationalize Indian resistances" and "catch the Indians in the process of transformation."[43] These possibilities offer plausible explanations for the record of questions, and each has a part in answering the question of representation here.

Such explanations, however, do not entirely suffice for this moment in the mission discourse, or at least, other possibilities suggest themselves when we take the transatlantic production of the tracts into account. In 1647, when Indian questions first appear in mission publications, English Puritans had been embroiled in theological debates of their own for some time. Their debates were first published when the "*de facto* breakdown of censorship" during and after the English civil wars gave rise to the "pamphlet wars."[44] Answers to every conceivable theological and political question were published on all sides. The colonies entered the fray when the so-called New England Way was introduced to a wide readership in England as a model, or at least as an example for Parliamentarians debating the shape of English Christianity and English nationalism.

In particular, transatlantic debate focused on the Antinomian controversy, the colonial crisis that several years earlier had made New England Puritans aware of the dangers of unregulated public questioning of religious authorities. The practice of allowing lay questions following sermons and lectures became suspect during the late 1630s, when laywoman Anne Hutchinson proved herself a potent rival of clerical influence. Not only did she lead meetings in her home in which she critiqued the sermons of her Boston minister John Wilson and criticized New England ministers in general, but her supporters also used the time set aside for questions during worship to interrogate preachers. Their questions seemed so threatening that in his contribution to *A Short Story of the Rise, reign, and ruine of the Antinomians, Familists, and Libertines*, Thomas Weld describes them as guns shot off in the face of the preacher. In response, the practice of questioning the sermon was disallowed by the synod of 1637.[45] The record of so many Indian questions and the widespread approval of them needs to be understood within this context, unless we are to assume that the colonial Indian discourse was completely insulated from other aspects of English national and colonial identities.

And it is tempting to think of the mission work as set apart. Because these tracts seem to have been so universally well received—and perhaps because some of the "apostle" Eliot's saintly glow still emanates from them—the mission tracts have not been read as a part of the pamphlet war waged at mid-century. Francis Bremer, James Holstun, and others have noted that the signatories of the tract's prefaces and dedications came primarily from the ranks of the "Dissenting Brethren" and other Congregationalists at odds with the Presbyterian majority of the Westminster Assembly. Yet some Presbyterians also signed the tracts, and so critics tend to take the tracts' appearance of consensus at face value; this was "a noncontroversial cause," which both Congregationalists and Presbyterians could "unquestioningly" support.[46]

As I show in chapter 2, however, considerable differences did exist among mission supporters, and it is important to recognize the partisan politics being waged within and by these publications. One of the most significant tensions of Eliot's career is in the contrast between the radical import of his millennialist missionizing and his whole-hearted persecution of Anne Hutchinson during the Antinomian controversy. Richard Cogley's account of Eliot's development as a missionary suggests that his intimate experience with Indians forced a change, turning the conservative young minister of the controversy into the radical of the 1640s and 1650s.[47] And, certainly, I have been arguing for this kind of mutuality within the mission discourse. But, as Jim Egan claims, colonial "experience" is not a natural existential category. It must be put into historical context and carefully interrogated.[48] We must take heed as well of the publication history of these hastily improvised reports; they appeared when other publications—such as *The Bloody Tenent of Persecution, A Short Story,* and *Mercurius Americanus*—were arguing the case for or against the value of the colonial "experience" in the Bay Colony.

At about the same time that New England began publicizing its mission to the Indians, writers in both Old and New England began producing and publishing the debates over the New England Way and the Antinomian controversy. Stephen Foster notes that "between 1642 and 1645, the correspondence begun with New England in the late 1630s suddenly and conveniently appeared in print."[49] The timing can in part be explained by the easing of censorship, but it is also due to increased interest and attention to New England at a time of looming schism in Old England. The Aldermanbury accord of 1641, in which leading Congregationalists and Presbyterians agreed not to attack one another in print, forced English Congregationalists to rely "on New Englanders' surrogates to spread the message for them."[50]

As we have seen, the Puritan mission first found its way into print with the 1643 tract *New Englands First Fruits.* And at just this moment, English presses erupted with competing colonial accounts of the New England Way. Richard Mather's treatises, *An Apologie of the Churches in* New-England *for* Church-Covenant, as well as *Church-Government and Church-Covenant Discussed In an Answer of the Elders of the severall Churches in* New-England, were also printed in 1643 to describe and defend New England polity. Just a year later, in 1644, we find Thomas Shepard and John Allen's *A Defense of the Answer made unto the Nine Questions or Positions sent from New-England,* and a response to a tract by John Ball, Thomas Weld's *An answer to* W.R. *His Narration of the Opinions and Practices of the Churches lately erected in New-England,* all of which defended the colonial Puritan model. Roger Williams's first salvos against colonial clergy, *Mr. Cotton's Letter* and *The Bloody Tenent*, appeared in the same year as did Thomas Lechford's *New-Englands advice to Old-England*, which was "written by one that hath liv'd there, and seene the devision and danger that followeth upon the obtruding a different Government to that of Old England."[51]

As Francis Bremer and Stephen Foster both point out, the 1640s saw a turn to New England in the debates among members of the Assembly and of Parliament, charged with constructing new civil and ecclesiastical polities in England. On the one hand, Congregationalists and Independents had recourse to New England's example as a corrective—and perhaps because it was a distant example, a less incendiary one—to the errors of Presbyterianism, and on the other, Presbyterian authors "cite[d] the early history of New England as proof that Congregationalism bred error," in works such as Robert Baillie's *A Dissuasive from the Errours of the Time* (1645).[52] "By discrediting the New Englanders," Bremer argues, "Presbyterians hoped to defeat the English members of the [Congregationalist-Independent] network. The result was to draw New Englanders and their experience ever more deeply into the English struggle."[53]

As Bremer demonstrates, New Englanders had close ties with the most influential English divines, who used their sympathies with the colonies in support of their own efforts to influence the possibility and definition of an English national church. Perhaps the most important of their publications was *An Apologetical Narration*, a tract that laid out clearly the limits to Congregationalists' accommodations with Presbyterians. It was penned by the "Dissenting Brethren," five Congregationalists who were firm supporters of the New England Way, calling colonists "godly men of our own Nation . . . whose sincerity in their way hath been testified before all the world."[54] Although the mission tracts are not considered with these more obviously polemical works, they are just as decisively engaged with issues of church authority, lay power, and toleration. All the mission texts are written, edited, prefaced, or championed by the very same people in the thick of sectarian battles, and all aim for the same readers. In particular, the tracts, like other polemical pamphlets, attempt to influence parliamentary debate, succeeding with the 1649 Act for the Propagation of the Gospel. Supporters willing to subscribe their names to the mission tracts during this turbulent period were drawn from the ranks of Congregationalists and Presbyterians alike. Significantly, all five Dissenting Brethren took an interest in the mission publications:

Thomas Goodwin, Philip Nye, Sydrach Simpson, Jeremiah Burroughs, and William Bridge signed the prefaces to *Clear Sun-shine of the Gospel* (1648) and *Strength out of Weaknesse* (1652). Indeed, the list of Englishmen who lent their names to the London publication of mission reports between 1648 and 1655 reads like a mid-century "who's who."[55]

The tracts supported by these English signatories explicitly contrast the efforts of New England missionaries with the "brangles" in which so many in Old England were caught. In the dedications, prefaces, and appendixes to mission reports, added in London before publication, New England is presented as a safe haven from the errors and schisms of Old England. Indians, as I discuss in chapters 1 and 2, are "sermons" for English backsliders, preached by radical English divines to warn readers that their Christian identity was not essentially theirs. In such Indian sermons published in London, men such as the Dissenting Brethren, along with Henry Whitfield, John Owen, and Joseph Caryl, urged reform. They used Christian Indians as exemplars to illustrate the danger to the nation brought about by the hypocrisy of English "professors." In these writings, Christian Indians do more than call England to repent and purify itself. They trouble the status of English Puritans as a chosen people and England as a chosen nation. "Indians" and "English" become floating signifiers that retain a relative valence, negative and positive, respectively, but which can be attached to individuals or nations as evaluative terms of another kind. The prefacers of *Clear Sun-shine* bluntly warn that England's identity could be given to others:

> God may wel seek out for other ground to sow the seed of his Ordinances upon, seeing the ground where it hath been sown hath brought forth no better fruit to him. . . . if he cannot have an England here, he can have an England there.[56]

Mission literature is thus enlisted in the pamphlet wars, offering New England and, even more surprisingly, the Praying Indians as positive examples to Old England but cloaking the more polemical statements as simple stories of evangelism, an enterprise that would redound on all the English, to their credit.

Direct commentary on England's controversies is largely confined to those parts of the tracts added in London. Again, the New England reports appear mostly as eyewitness letters detailing facts and transcribing conversations. But a close look at those letters reveals the ways they respond to a subgenre of writings concerning New England—reports of the Antinomian controversy. The events surrounding the controversy occurred in 1636–37, but the texts through which English readers (and readers today) learned about it were not published until the 1640s. Winthrop's *Short Story* was published in 1644; the accused Antinomian John Wheelwright's self-defensive critique of colonial authorities, *Mercurius Americanus*, appeared in 1645. The publication of these texts was bracketed by the printing of *New Englands First Fruits* (1643) and *Day-Breaking* (1647). Thus, when *Day-Breaking* presented the phenomenon of lay questions during meetings or debates with traditional Indian religious leaders, it was addressing an audience already worried about issues of authority, conscience and church practice, and significantly, already familiar with the contours of Anne Hutchinson's challenge to New England's order.

Winthrop's tract circulated in manuscript until publication and was intent on demonstrating the English rather than New English origins of error. The recent editor of *A Short Story* notes that "from the colonists' point of view, the *Short Story* testified to the triumph of Congregationalism over the dangers of Antinomianism."[57] Or as Francis Bremer has it, "The message was clear: New England Congregationalism did not breed error but could control it as efficiently as any Presbyterian system could."[58] Opponents disagreed, naturally, and *Short Story* provided them with evidence that New England was on the one hand heretical and on the other intolerant.[59] This latter charge was an acutely embarrassing one for New England's Congregationalist allies who were trying to forge partnerships with Independents (157).

Against this context of charge and countercharge, of debate over toleration and the formation of a new national identity, the tracts present the colonial handling of dissent by way of Indian questions, and they use evangelism to justify and promote other colonial practices. By publishing the mission tracts in London, colonists and their supporters offered English readers another window onto the New England Way. We can see in the tract's presentation of spiritual questions—which could be considered generically as acts of dissent—New England's grappling with cases of individual conscience, issues of secular and ecclesiastical authority, and, strikingly, given the prominence of Anne Hutchinson to the Antinomian debates, with gender roles.

Consider the example of "George," who learned the forms of Puritanism and Eliot's four exercises well enough to parody and disrupt them. We learn of George when Thomas Shepard inserts his story into a description of Indian questions in the tract *Clear Sun-shine*. Shepard first lists thirteen questions, such as "How long it is before men beleeve that have the Word of God made known to them?" and "How they should know when their faith is good, and their prayers good prayers?" Then, as if to give a negative object lesson, Shepard follows the list with the story of how George disrupted the time for asking questions at a Praying Indian meeting. George "boldly propounded this question, Mr. *Eliot* (said he), *Who made Sack? who made Sack?*"[60] George's question about the creation of alcohol obviously parodies the standard catechism question "Who made you?" Shepard inserts the disruption into his narrative immediately following his treatment of worthy questions, and he interprets the interruption as intended "to cast some reproach, as we feared, upon this way."

George's story contains an appealing wit (who made sack, indeed?) as well as an illustration of the Praying Indians' colonized subjectivity. Despite George's obvious rejection of Eliot and his message, the interruption becomes a demonstration of how well converts had internalized Christian teachings. Before Eliot can reply to George, the Indians themselves rebuke him, defending the sanctity of the fourth exercise by disciplining an unruly speaker: "He was soon snib'd by the other *Indians*, calling it a *Papoose* question" (47). These elements of colonial contact are certainly important here, but once George is placed within the context of transatlantic dissent, another layer of meaning can be added. Like Anne Hutchinson's followers, George disrupts a meeting with his questions. Shepard's fear, that George spoke up in order "to cast some reproach upon this way," links this moment to the many attacks on the New England Way being circulated and printed in the 1640s and 1650s.

Unlike Williams, Lechford, or the Antinomians, however, George clearly presents no real threat to the minister he questions. The anecdote defuses his dissent by belittling the dissenter. New England writers maintained that Hutchinson and her followers had been tried and banished not for reasons of "conscience" but because they disrupted civil order. Similarly, this account implies, George disrupts the meeting, not because he is prompted by the "light and checks of [his] own conscience," as one tract in favor of toleration calls the dissenting impulse,[61] but because, in Shepard's words, George is a "malignant drunken *Indian.*" Eliot elaborates on this description in a letter to Thomas Shepard, published in the same tract:

> It was *George* that wicked *Indian,* who as you know, at our first beginnings sought to cast aspersions upon Religion by laying slanderous accusations against godly men, and who asked the captious question, *who made Sack?*[62]

Note that Eliot's characterization of George changes Shepard's description of a drunken Indian who hoped to cast "some reproach . . . upon this way," to one who, as Hutchinson was accused of doing, sought to attack "godly men" personally. Nothing in Shepard's account of George's "captious question" indicated that he attacked ministers or missionaries, or any other "godly men." Perhaps the more intense description reflects Eliot's sense of personal injury or reflects discussions between Shepard and Eliot about George's case. Regardless, this characterization of his dissent should be read through the lens of the pamphlet wars, which reflected the spiritual and political-theological disputes in which England was enmeshed. Eliot's turn to George in this letter likewise denigrates him and downplays his significance. He disrupts New England's order, according to this report, not because he is a man of conscience but because he is a criminal: "This fellow having kild a young Cow at your Towne, and sold it at the Colledge instead of *Moose,* covered it with many lies" (55).

The criminalization of dissent is one side of the representational coin. The Praying Indians' chastisement of George is the other, because it suggests that dissent is treated calmly and easily, that the rejection of challenges such as George's mocking question is natural to native-grown American Puritanism. Supporters of the New England Way were at pains to apologize for their harsh treatment of dissenters such as Hutchinson, and also to defend against charges that their civil and ecclesiastical organization bred heresy. The treatment of Indian questions provides a counterexample to the Hutchinson trials.

The representation of spiritual questions also affords us one of the few sustained accounts of women in mission reports. Again, new light is shed on these accounts if we consider them in conjunction with colonial authorities' treatment of Hutchinson. Earlier, in *Clear Sunshine,* Shepard describes a visit he made to an Indian meeting in 1647. He was struck by the presence of women among the new converts:

Perceiving divers of the *Indian* women well affected, and considering that their soules might stand in need of answer to their scruples as well as the mens; & yet because we knew how unfit it was for women so much as to aske questions publiquely immediatly by themselves; wee did therefore desire them to propound any questions they would bee resolved about by first acquainting either their Husbands, or the Interpreter privately therewith: whereupon we heard two questions thus orderly propounded. (41)

The two questions asked by women (neither of whom is named, except through her husband) provide exemplary models for the fulfillment of conventional gender roles. The first woman asks whether her silent assent to her husband's voiced prayer was sufficient: "Shee therefore fearing lest prayer should onely be an externall action of the lips, enquired if it might not be also an inward action of the heart" (41). Shepard offers little comment on the question; the circumstances themselves suffice for an answer. Just as in the meeting her question could be acceptably voiced by her husband, so too could the heartfelt prayer of a wife be voiced properly by her mate. The couple in this way becomes emblematic of the Reformation church and its relationship with God. Not incidentally, the couple also reaffirms proper gender roles in the colony; wives submit to husbands just as Christian souls submit to Christ.

The import of the next question is not so clear cut, but read within the context of the Antinomian crisis, it too reaffirms conservative gender roles, especially as they serve as the basis for other kinds of social hierarchies. The "Wife of one *Totherswampe*" asked a question that, the tract explains, had a hidden significance: "her meaning in her question (as wee all perceived) was this, *viz.* 'Whether a husband should do well to pray with his wife, and yet continue in his passions, & be angry with his wife?[']" (42). Shepard first provides this interpretation and, only then, her words: "Before my husband did pray hee was much angry and froward [*sic*], but since hee hath begun to pray hee was not angry so much, but little angry." One can only imagine the reaction of Totherswamp, who is asked to voice this question and then listen to the interpretation put on it by the missionaries:

Wherein first shee gave an honorable testimony of her husband and commended him for the abatement of his passion; secondly, shee gave implicitly a secret reproofe for what was past, and for somewhat at present that was amisse; and thirdly, it was intended by her as a question whether her husband should pray to God, and yet continue in some unruly passions; but she wisely avoyded that, lest it might reflect too much upon him, although wee desired her to expresse if that was not her meaning. (42)

The meaning the English ministers give to this moment is in perfect accord with orthodox ideals of gendered behavior. As they listen to her question, they hear an appropriate negotiation of what Mary Beth Norton has identified as the "Filmerian" social order, which "assumed the necessity of hierarchy in family, polity, and society at large." Unruly challenges to a husband's "natural" authority could lead to civil disorder, as the "[Filmerian] outlook saw family and state as analogous institutions."[63] Here, the husband's putative abuse of authority is properly and effectively dealt with (from the ministers' point of view) by an indirect appeal to church hierarchy, yet not (the Puritan commentators insist) in a way calculated to defame or even embarrass the husband.

The mission tracts are primarily concerned with describing Praying Indian men as leaders of church and town. The description of these pious women, and in particular the association of them with the fourth exercise of spiritual questions, is all the more striking for their absence in other contexts.[64] Their appearance here is important because they demonstrate how colonial Puritans presented themselves as promulgating an orthodox system in which women know their proper place. Whereas, as Norton argues, "The Antinomian controversy was above all a crisis in the system of gendered power," this scene publicizes New England's ability to wield that "gendered power" without challenge.[65] Such descriptions of gendered control are important because, as Philip Round points out, opponents of the New England Way "leaped at the chance to use the example of Anne Hutchinson's 'abominable errours' as evidence of 'the fruits of their [Congregational] Church-way.'"[66] Round calls the attacks and counterattacks that responded to the Antinomian controversy "discursive performances [that] eventually served as the foundation for a broader relationship between the New England and metropolitan cultural fields" (142).

Read in conjunction with the tracts and letters discussing Anne Hutchinson, this mission tract becomes a subtle defense of colonial methods. Indian women appear in public but act under their husbands' cover and approval. Any abuse of power on the part of a husband (and so, by extension, the abuse of power by any authority) is handled easily within established church rituals. By contrast, colonial writers and observers suggested, Hutchinson's heresies and her challenge to gender norms were imported metropolitan "infections" rather than malignant colonial growths.[67]

Praying Indian Christianity and culture are presented as metonymic of colonial Christian and gender practice; a "native" New England faith is proffered as proof of the efficacy of the New England Way. If Anne Hutchinson's irrepressible speech was a sign of her severely disordered beliefs, Christian Indian women guarded their public speech with care. As Shepard noted in his 1648 account of their questions, "We knew how unfit it was" for women to speak in public. Therefore, Indian women are represented as easily accepting the suggestion that they propound questions through their husbands, and these reports argue that Praying Indian women, converted and instructed solely by New England Puritans, inhabit proper gender norms. The publicly silent yet privately pious Praying Indian woman thus illustrates to a skeptical English audience the sanctified nature of colonial as opposed to metropolitan forms of Christianity.

The tactics of mission writers in presenting Indians' questions—references to a universal conversion process, a decontextualized presentation, and the converts' own adherence to English gender norms—cast Indians' regeneracy in the best possible light and invite widespread endorsement of missionaries' diligence and efficacy. The tracts anticipate outside criticism by offering the diversity and seriousness of Indian questions as proof of authentic Indian conversion. Eliot faced opponents who were suspicious of Indians' motivation for converting, and even well-wishers doubted Indians' ability to understand Christianity fully. Puritans had a horror of hypocrisy; for them, true evangelism contrasted favorably with Catholic tactics, "that art of coyning Christians."[68] English observers needed to be convinced that Indians who initially heard the Word through translators were really learning and internalizing God's truths, not simply memorizing and parroting catchphrases in the manner of the hated papists. To allay such fears, Eliot reported questions with an eye to representation of unfeigned faith.

We find an important example of such representation in Eliot's treatment of the sachem Cutshamekin's conversion. That this prominent leader "came in" to the Praying Indian community was a considerable achievement for Eliot, who believed converted sachems would draw in their followers to Christianity.[69] Moreover, it must have afforded the missionary personal satisfaction to see the leader of the recalcitrant questioners at Dorchester Mill "reduced" to Christianity and to posing acceptable spiritual questions. But whatever the political or private reasons for Cutshamekin's conversion, Eliot must fold him into the mission narrative of Indian regeneracy. To that end, Eliot recounts one of Cutshamekin's questions at the end of the sachem's self-assessment:

> Before I knew God . . . I thought I was well, but since I have known God and sin, I find my heart full of sin, and more sinfull then ever it was before, and this hath been a great trouble to mee; and at this day my heart is but very little better then it was, and I am afraid it will be as bad againe as it was before, and therefore I sometime wish I might die before I before I be so bad again as I have been. Now my question is, whether is this a sin or not?[70]

This speech is the epitome of Puritan conversion, and Eliot regards it as truly indicative of an inner state of grace. It testifies to Cutshamekin's knowledge of the sin of despair, his increasingly sensitive and deepening recognition of his own sinful nature, and his "holy desperation." As a good question should, it gives the listener a "taste" of Cutshamekin's private experience with God. The question, Eliot asserts, "could not be learned from the English, nor did it seem a coyned feigned thing, but as reall matter gathered from the experience of his own heart, and from an inward observation of himself."

Eliot to the contrary, Cutshamekin's question *is* learned from the English. If not stamped on an adamant heart as a "coyned feigned thing," it is certainly inspired and shaped by missionary preachers and Puritan doctrine as they understood, preached, and recorded it. And it illustrates how Indians conformed their speech to patterns accepted by the missionary and Praying Indian communities. My point is not that Cutshamekin's question is inauthentic or even opportunistic. Rather, the record of his question exists because Eliot took the ongoing encounter of Indians and missionaries and constructed a narrative for English consumption. Nonetheless, his work allowed Indians to take part in a dialogue that made possible their religious and political affiliation with Puritans in New England, albeit only for a short time.

5 Kinfolk and Penitents

"Indian Dialogues" as American Fiction

As sallies in the "pamphlet wars" of the Civil War and Interregnum periods, mission tracts were published regularly, even rapidly, between 1647 and 1660. The reports made their way into print at the rate of about one per year between 1647 and 1655. In all, nine tracts appeared during these first thirteen years of systematic evangelical effort. The rate of publication slowed after 1660. It became much more politically risky to publish such reports in the years following the Restoration, and colonial writers contented themselves with more ambitious but safer publications, such as the Indian Bible. As I discuss in chapter 2, colonial authorities even expunged John Eliot's name as dangerously radical from copies of the Bible sent to England. Thus, while Eliot's enduring reputation has been built on the translations produced and published in the 1660s, after the Restoration, his views on political events and his reports on continuing Indian evangelism were not circulated publicly. This quiet period came to an end in 1671, when Eliot published *A Brief Narrative of the Progress of the Gospel amongst the* Indians *in* New England, a straightforward report detailing conversion successes and numbers, as well as the more surprising *Indian Dialogues*. Although the latter work appears to have had only a limited readership, it is an extraordinary production, one that suggests the stresses on Indian-English relations in New England and contains what we might classify as the earliest fictional representation of Indians in British-American literature.

If in early tracts Indians' questions are presented as real speech, as unmediated, transparent transcriptions, in *Indian Dialogues* Eliot shows that he was also interested in staging more elaborate representations of his converts' faithfulness. Unlike the Indians questions or confessions published in earlier tracts, Eliot does not represent these conversations among friends and relations as real speech acts. As he writes in the preface, these imagined conversations, "partly historical . . . partly instructive," were intended to model for Indian missionaries "what might or should have been said, or that may be . . . hereafter done and said, upon the like occasion."[1] His text is a series of religious dialogues in which Christian Indians preach, question, and answer the concerns of non-Christian friends, kinfolk, and sachems. Amazingly, a character obviously meant to represent the man who would be known to the English as "King Philip," is in Dialogue III a central character, called "Philip Keitasscot."

The "partly historical" form and extraordinary content of the dialogues have made them difficult to place in the English-Indian discourse and may explain why so little critical attention has been paid to them. Among the few scholarly treatments of the text, Thomas Scanlan provides a powerful analysis of the dialogues as a "colonial allegory" of Protestantism. He sees *Indian Dialogues* as "suggesting that the real future of English Protestant identity lay not in England but in the colonies" and as linking all English Protestants to Eliot's mission.[2] I associate this task of forging transatlantic unity primarily with earlier mission publications, a task made possible by the millennial enthusiasm and antimonarchism of the 1640s and 1650s; *Indian Dialogues* is a careful revision of those earlier reports. By the 1670s, successful mission propaganda was more difficult to create than ever before, and *Indian Dialogues* registers the strain. Underneath the perhaps allegorical elements of the mission tracts lies a grounded, pragmatic response to the mission's loss of both discursive and economic power that is purely colonial.[3] More so than any other mission report, *Indian Dialogues* had to respond to immediate local realities as well as to far-flung evangelical hopes. *Dialogues* thus takes up two difficult tasks at once, that of affirming Eliot's placement of the Praying Indians in worldwide Christendom and, most urgently, of convincing New England authorities that the converts had a tangible role to play in local concerns, whatever their divine signification.

To accomplish this latter goal, the *Dialogues* promises that Praying Indians will, of their own accord, mediate both physically and spiritually between the English colonial settlers and "wild," potentially violent, unconverted Indians. Specifically, it promises to convert the Wampanoag sachem Metacom (called "Philip" by the English) and make him accountable to New England authorities. Such political control had, of course, long been one aim of colonial evangelism. But the mission publications of the 1640s and 1650s, as I have discussed, were primarily directed toward events in England rather than the colonies. The authors and audiences of those earlier works were drawn from both Old and New England. While the tracts certainly discussed colonial situations, they did so in service to the national, eschatological identity of England. The result, as we have seen, was a political-theological description of Indian Christianity meant for a world stage. Christian Indians, in this earlier construction, were caught up in a cosmic crisis, their conversion fortunate but fairly incidental to events happening elsewhere.

In contrast, *Indian Dialogues* is, above all, an intervention in local affairs. The text does not include any voices from Old England. Eliot is the sole author of the dedication, the preface, and the main text, which is made up of four dialogues (although only three have individual titles). Written in English, in the subjunctive mood, and dedicated to the Commissioners of the United Colonies rather than to parliament or king, the dialogues model for New England authorities an approach to subjecting Indians to the rule of Christ and king that is meant to be both plausible and physically nonviolent.

In addition to promising the conversion of prominent Indians, *Indian Dialogues* addresses colonial concerns by redefining Boston's place on British imperial margins. In representing Praying Indians as go-betweens, stand-ins for colonial English agents among Native communities, the book constructs for colonial authorities a safe and comfortable position in a newly defined metropolitan center. In the imagined landscape of the dialogues, Boston and London seem equally distant, equally potent centers of power; thus Indians rather than English settlers occupy a colonial periphery. The book gives over the anxious assertions of English identity that characterized earlier mission publications. English identity is fixed, no longer improvised in a colonial contact zone, no longer forced to respond and adapt to an Indian presence. Rather, the Indians continue to improvise, continue to negotiate their colonized and colonial identities.

In this renegotiation of Praying Indian and English identities, *Indian Dialogues* suggests to colonists a "means of healing and overcoming their divisions."[4] Moreover, it does so in a way that requires its readers to radically reinvent themselves. Nancy Armstrong and Leonard Tennenhouse examine a similar effect in later captivity narratives, arguing that captivities "required readers to change the way they imagined being English, because they had to imagine being English in America."[5] Along these same lines, *Indian Dialogues,* building on earlier mission reports, requires an equally profound reconstruction. The dialogues require readers to change the way they imagine being Christian, because they must detach "Christian" from "English," and even from "European." Eliot asks them to do so through particular and creative revisions of the earlier, improvised mission reports, which create Indian speakers and characters with kinship ties, histories that encompass their precontact lives and affective interior existences, even senses of humor.

When we look closely at *Indian Dialogues* as a revision of previous mission representations, we find that the earlier "Indian sermons," preached by metropolitan observers about Praying Indians to English readers, are now being delivered directly by fictional "Indian" characters. Whereas before, the English alone could see Ezekiel's promise of resurrection fulfilled by Indian conversions, *Indian Dialogues* creates Indian characters who themselves comment on European and "Christian" foibles.

Indian Dialogues thus suggests the direction mission discourse might have gone were its energies not sapped by the Restoration and cut off completely by King Philip's War. Increasingly stylized, intentionally distant from the "intercultural" forces that shaped earlier mission publications, the mission discourse as exemplified by *Indian Dialogues* may be seen as an antecedent to later fictional and even satiric representations of Indians written by white authors far removed from actual Indian contact.

Rising Tensions

The early 1670s saw escalating tensions between the Wampanoag Indians and the Plymouth colonists, who had formal ties dating back decades. The sachem Massasoit and his sons Wamsutta and Metacom had made treaties with Plymouth Colony and sold land to the English. The two brothers had even petitioned the Plymouth Court for new English names—Alexander and Philip, respectively.[6] Following Massasoit's death in 1661, Alexander led for three years, during which time English-Wampanoag relations deteriorated. Plymouth officials haled Alexander to a colonial court in 1664 because they were not pleased with his style of leadership nor with the land sales he conducted. His death immediately following that incarceration raised suspicions of foul play as Metacom-Philip took his place.[7]

If the English assassinated Alexander in hopes of eliminating a troublesome Indian leader, Plymouth did not find Philip a more accommodating successor. Even before Alexander died, Philip had been embroiled in land-use fights in the English courts. As a sachem, he watched his Wampanoag followers become increasingly pressed for land, especially in 1667, when Plymouth established Swansea on territory that his people had occupied. The likelihood of war increased in 1671, when the Wampanoags made a show of force at Swansea. Violence seemed sure, and Plymouth officials scurried to defuse the situation by treaty or control it by force. On April 10, 1671, Plymouth forced Philip to sign the disastrous treaty of Taunton, in which he retroactively submitted himself, and his brother and father before him, to Plymouth's authority.[8] Plymouth was not long satisfied with Philip's compliance, however. On August 23, 1671, the colony charged Philip with violations of the treaty, and a colonial Council of War ordered him to appear at Plymouth.

During this critical period of negotiations and preparations for war, Eliot aggressively championed the Praying Indians, the fruits of his long mission years, as mediators between the English and non-Praying Indians. In the years prior to the treaty at Taunton, the Praying Indians had expanded their lands and increased their numbers. Finally, in 1669 and 1670, Eliot wrote letters to his supporters in England and to the Commissioners in New England describing the nine existing praying towns and their leaders. These were published in his *Brief Narrative* (1671). Although he admits to some backsliding and alcohol abuse among the converts and to some conflict between English and Indian settlements, he positions the Praying Indians in these towns as literal and spiritual hedges between the English and hostile Indians. They are described as good Christians who love the English and, more pragmatically, who build and maintain garrisons against the Mohawks.[9]

In this period, Praying Indians proselytized their neighbors, confirming Eliot's long-held belief that the most effective Indian evangelism would be performed by Indians' "fellow countrymen." Although he had desired that more Englishmen join him in the mission field, few did, and his hopes that John Eliot, Jr. would be his successor were dashed when his son died in 1668. Early on in *A Brief Narrative*, he finds it "hopeless to expect *English* Officers in our *Indian* Churches. . . . [Indians] must be trained up to be able to live of themselves in the ways of the Gospel of Christ."[10]

It is evident even from Eliot's terse descriptions in *A Brief Narrative* that the Praying Indians' "frontier" lives were not easy ones. On the one hand, their defenses against other Indians were regularly breached. He says of Nashope, "This place lying in the Road-way which the *Mauquaogs* [Mohawks] haunted, was much molested by them, and was one year wholly deserted" (7), and of Wamusut, "This place is very much annoyed by the *Mauquaogs,* and have much ado to stand their ground" (7). On the other hand, these settlements were being squeezed by the English. Eliot's description of the rivalry between the praying town of Okommakamesit and Marlborough is especially revealing for his cautious criticism of the English and for his continued reading of the colonial situation through biblical typology:

> *Ogquonikongquamesut* is the next Town; where, how we have been af-
> flicted, I may not say. The *English* Town called *Marlborough* doth bor-
> der upon them, as did the lines of the Tribes of *Judah* and *Benjamin;* the
> English Meeting-house standeth within the line of the *Indian* Town, al-
> though the contiguity and co-habitation is not barren in producing mat-
> ters of interfering; yet our godly *Indians* do obtain a good report of the
> godly *English,* which is an argument that bringeth light and evidence to
> my heart, that our *Indians* are really godly. (6)

The rising tensions between Philip and the colonists may have suggested to Eliot that he could defuse antagonisms, or at least divert the attention of near neighbors such as Marlborough from the Praying Indians, by aggressively publicizing the converts' role as political and spiritual mediators between New England colonists and non-praying Indians. His other 1671 publication, *Indian Dialogues,* offers a blueprint for colonial Indian diplomacy, featuring Praying Indians as English agents. In *A Brief Narrative,* he imagined the ring of praying towns that surrounded English settlements, detailing their numbers, resources, and their commitment to Christian rule. In *Indian Dialogues,* he describes Praying Indians as Native missionaries who issue from that protective ring to convert their unregenerate brethren to civil and religious alliance with the English, just as they themselves had been converted.

The publication of *Indian Dialogues* could not have been better timed to address immediate colonial concerns. It appeared just as the dispute between the United Colonies and the sachem Philip seemed about to erupt into violence. Eliot presented his *Dialogues* to the Commissioners of the United Colonies on September 4, 1671, less than a month after the Plymouth Council of War had summoned the real Philip to answer charges of treaty violations.[11] Eliot was obviously working on the leading edge of events, hoping to position his mission at the heart of the most important of the colonies' hopes and cares. Into the midst of the English settlers' fears of imminent attack, Eliot inserted the Praying Indian as a diplomatic go-between, able to work at the limits of white settlement and society.[12]

Ideal Sachems

A key strategy in *Indian Dialogues* is the conversion of Indian leaders. Each of the dialogues describes the converts' ready access to sachems: when Praying Indians who are loyal to the English preach, they convert Indian leaders, who in turn bring their people securely under the authority of both Christ and the Bay Colony government. In Dialogue I, Piumbukhou, a Praying Indian, encounters an unnamed kinsman in his travels. The kinsman is interested in praying but dares not unless his friends join him. So Piumbukhou proposes that they persuade the others to pray as well. The dialogue ends with the "sontim" (ruler) assenting to their suggestion that the church at Natick send "a wise man to teach" the community. Although the ruler and his people promise only to "come together on the Sabbaths, as you have done this day, and hear the Word of God,"[13] a Puritan reader would assume that once they have inclined their ear to the Lord, these Indians, if they have been called by God, cannot help but hear and be converted.

Dialogue II presents a much more elaborated encounter between an Indian ruler and a Praying Indian and clearly illustrates Eliot's willingness to fictionalize the history of the praying movement. In the dialogue, Eliot's first and best-known convert, Waban, effectively preaches to Peneovot, a fictional character. Once Peneovot is persuaded to pray, they both appeal to Nishohkou, a character who is a shrewd blend of fact and fiction. The Nishohkou in this dialogue is an elderly, unconverted sachem, but Eliot's regular readers would have known him as a Praying Indian from *Tears of Repentance* and *A Fur-*

ther Account, which make no mention of any sachem status. By returning Nishohkou to an unconverted state in this dialogue, Eliot asserts the mission's ability to influence sachems with reference to a known convert. By extension, we may assume that the sachem "Nishohkou" will convert as well, offstage as it were, and, like the real Nishohkou, become a pillar of the Indian church. The dialogue implies that Praying Indian missionaries will bring Indian political leaders—and all their followers—into the faith and into allegiance with the English. Eliot speaks here to a colonial audience concerned about the outbreak of violence with coastal Algonquians. Unlike his previous writings, his attention is focused almost entirely on the local readership, with barely a nod to an English audience.

Although characters' names and settings are familiar to regular readers of mission literature, it is impossible to place the dialogues in the history of the mission movement. Judging by the character Nishohkou's unconverted status, we might assume that Dialogue II is meant to take place before the real Nishohkou's conversion, sometime before 1652. But if we take the character Waban as an historical figure, we must reassess that date; in 1652, Eliot presented Waban as inexperienced and, in his first printed confessions, nearly inarticulate about Christian spirituality.[14] If the dialogue is meant to demonstrate Waban's increased powers of persuasion in 1671, then the still-unconverted Nishohkou figure is completely fabricated. The continuous blend of real and imagined elements assures readers that the Praying Indians they have come to know through the mission tracts are boundlessly influential preachers and teachers of the Word. The blurring of real and fantastic elements creates a Waban who is, always has been, and promises to continue as an articulate, knowledgeable, and skillful evangelist. Unconverted Indians like Nishohkou are themselves always on the verge of conversion.

Eliot's tactics in Dialogue II, especially the intermixing of historical elements (such as the characters based on real people and representations of real questions, concerns, and discussion) with imaginary characters and conversations, allows him to project an outcome of the dialogue that the colonies would find politically desirable. Unlike the policies of colonial authorities, which provoked high passions and misunderstandings and, in 1671, threatened to erupt into warfare, the mission strategy sketched by this "instructive" conversation produces sachems who are gracious, reasonable agents of Christ's rule—administered, of course, by colonial authorities.

Dialogue II also provides the foundation for the much grander claims of Dialogue III. Significantly, this third dialogue does not represent a stage of conversion distinct from the previous one. Rather than moving to the next level, it explores and expands on a sachem's early interest in the Christian faith. This pause in the morphology of conversion sketched by the tract as a whole allows Eliot to elaborate the "proven" possibilities of Dialogue II. This third dialogue makes even grander promises of the Indians' political and religious submission to the English, directly tying the conversion of sachems to colonial interests.

Whereas the first two dialogues are extraordinary pieces of mission propaganda, this "explosive" third dialogue seems to strain "poetic license to a painful degree."[15] "Philip Keitasscot of Paganoehket" appears in this dialogue as a major character and a potential convert. Bowden and Ronda identify him as the sachem Philip for whom the 1675–76 war is named. They also note, however, that this is the only time he is called "Keitasscot," an innovation that underscores Eliot's blending of fiction and fact in these "partly historical" dialogues.[16] It is our retrospective knowledge that this "hopeful" sachem will lead his followers against the English that makes the representation seem naïvely optimistic and the Keitasscot character so distant from the "Philip" of later colonial writings.

In 1671, however, the outcome of the dispute between the Wampanoags and Plymouth was by no means certain. Eliot had converted other sachems in the past, and the Praying Indians had a means of reaching the Indian leader. By representing Philip as a reasonable ruler interested in Christianity rather than a lawless violator of treaties (as later English writers would), Eliot promises that extended missionary work will make English settlements more secure and English rule more sure.

As outlandish as the prospect of a safely Christianized King Philip might seem in hindsight, the premise of Dialogue III, if not its conclusion, is not so far-fetched. In 1664, the Natick church had sent some of its members to meet with Philip, ostensibly at his request, to teach him to read.[17] When Plymouth and the Wampanoags began to provoke one another in 1671, Praying Indians acted as go-betweens, just as Eliot describes in this dialogue. On August 1, the Natick church directed William Nahauton and Anthony (in a letter signed by Eliot) to broker peace between Plymouth colony and the Indians at Missogkonnog.[18] In that letter, Eliot urges the emissaries to suggest both to Plymouth and to the Indians that the "rulers of Massachusetts" would be good arbiters of their disagreements. His message seems to have made sense to Philip. In a letter dated September 1, James Walker writes to Governor Prince of Plymouth that Philip refused to report to Plymouth: "They could get no positive answer about Philip's coming to Plymouth, because Mr. Eliot had sent for him to Boston."[19]

The connection between the Natick church's commission of Anthony and William and Philip's decision to go to Boston rather than Plymouth is not necessarily direct. Philip may not have met with William and Anthony, and the treaty of Taunton (April 10, 1671), in which Philip became a subject of Plymouth Colony, did allow for the Massachusetts colony to act as arbiter. So Philip's decision may initially have been suggested by the terms of the treaty itself. But Walker's letter makes it clear that Eliot is somehow advising Philip— or, at least, that he is perceived to be doing so. And then, a few days later, on September 4, Eliot writes to the Commissioners of the United Colonies and presents them with a copy of his Indian dialogues. Although Eliot had been composing the dialogues at least as early as June, the timing of their presentation to the Commissioners seems designed to remind them of his influence both in the Praying Indian community and, through them, on non-Praying Indians, especially Philip.[20] The events of Dialogue III thus parallel the diplomatic steps that Praying Indians took in the summer of 1671. The proselytizing characters are named Anthony and William Abahton; they tell Philip that they have been sent to him by the church at Natick, just as the real Anthony and William were sent by their church to Missogkonnog in August. Eliot makes the characters and events of Dialogue III seem credible by mirroring historical events.

Eliot also makes his Philip seem real by modeling him after a sachem well known to mission readers and by revising encounters reported in earlier mission tracts. William and Anthony's conversation with Philip Keitasscot can be read as an idealized retelling of Eliot's engagement with the sachem Cutshamekin in the tract *Light Appearing*. Cutshamekin was the sachem whose men had given Eliot such a difficult time during their first encounter, asking what seemed to the Puritan missionary inappropriate or challenging questions.[21] Since that time, Cutshamekin had "come in" and become the ruler at Natick, albeit with some reservations. In 1651, however, Eliot suddenly records the apparently systemic opposition of Indian leaders to Christianity, including that of Cutshamekin:

> This businesse of praying to God . . . hath hitherto found opposition only
> from the *Pawwawes* and profane spirits; but now the Lord hath exer-
> cised us with another and a greater opposition; for the *Sachems* of the
> Country are generally set against us, and counter-work the Lord by keep-
> ing off their men from praying to God as much as they can.[22]

The reason they are so set against the mission? "They plainly see that
Religion will make a great change among them, and cut them off from
their former tyranny."

Eliot goes on to describe Cutshamekin's particular opposition, re-
casting his once more cordial relationship with Cutshamekin and ex-
plaining their personal encounter as a dispute about paying tribute.
Cutshamekin, that erstwhile heckler turned hopeful sachem, now becomes a peevish and unreasonable ruler:

> This temptation [losing power and tribute] hath much troubled *Cut-
> shamoquin* our *Sachem*, and he was raised in his spirit to such an height,
> that at a meeting after Lecture, he openly contested with me against our
> proceeding to make a Town; and plainly told me that all the *Sachems* in
> the Countrey were against it. (Whitfield, 140)

Eliot here describes the influence sachems can have on those he calls
"the lesser sort": "When he did so carry himself, all the Indians were
filled with fear, their countenances grew pale, and most of them slunk
away, a few stayed, and I was alone, not any English man with me"
(140). Such imperious behavior could not be countenanced. Just as English Puritans defeated the tyrant Charles, Eliot conquers this king in
a direct display of personal authority, demonstrating the force of
church discipline. Eliot is also "raised" but, he argues, by a very different spirit:

> It pleased God . . . to raise up my spirit, not to passion, but to a bold res-
> olution, telling him it was Gods work I was about, and he was with me,
> and I feared not him, nor all the *Sachems* in the Country, and I was re-
> solved to go on do what they can, and they nor he should hinder that
> which I had begun, &c. And it pleased God that his spirit shrunk and
> fell before me. (140)

Eliot later learned the cultural significance of Cutshamekin's public loss of puissance: "And since I understand that in such conflicts
their manner is, that they account him that shrinks to be conquered,

and the other to conquer; which alas I knew not, nor did I aime at such a matter" (140). Eliot's humiliation of Cutshamekin destroys his tyrannical passions and empowers his "oppressed" subjects: "When those Indians that tarried saw, they smiled as they durst, out of his sight, and have been much strengthned ever since" (140). Eliot duly marks the differences between his passion and Cutshamekin's. Even though both are "raised" in spirit, Cutshamekin is inflated with passion, whereas Eliot is "carried beyond my thoughts and wont" by the Lord to conquer Cutshamekin and champion ordinary Indian converts.

Later, in *Light Appearing,* Eliot explains that the main problem for Cutshamekin is that of tribute: the sachem has complained that he is not receiving it from converts. Eliot investigates the matter, finally determining that the sachem was receiving his due but not as much as he had received previously. Eliot finds the reduction appropriate, although he sympathizes with Cutshamekin's frustration:

> He formerly had all or what he would; now he hath but what they [Praying Indians] will; and admonitions also to rule better, and he is provoked by other *Sachems,* and ill counsel, not to suffer this, and yet doth not know how to help it; hence arise his tentations, in which I do very much pity him. (141)

Eventually, according to Eliot, Cutshamekin comes around, reconciling himself to the new situation, and "he hath carried all things fairly ever since" (141).

As Eliot turns to the same set of concerns in his *Indian Dialogues,* he implies that Philip will take a comparable path to acceptance. He will "progress," like Cutshamekin, from early resistance to full participation in the community. In Dialogue III, William and Anthony use the example of Cutshamekin to reassure Philip when he objects that "you praying Indians do reject your sachems, and refuse to pay them tribute, in so much that if any of my people turn to pray unto God, I do reckon that I have lost him" (121). In reply, William describes his peoples' relationship with Cutshamekin and his successors, concluding that Philip's conversion would bind his people closer: "This I know by experience, for the more beneficent you are unto them, the more obligation you lay upon them. And what greater beneficence can you do unto them than to further them in religion?" (122).

Despite some similarities, in *Indian Dialogues* Eliot radically revises his earlier encounters with Cutshamekin, defusing the previous hostile treatment and promising the New England Commissioners tractable, nonviolent Indian leaders. The Cutshamekin episode is rewritten without the personal antagonism that characterized Eliot's earlier treatment of a sachem. As missionaries, Anthony and William follow Eliot's example but only as detailed *after* the passionate encounter with Cutshamekin. In 1671, when tensions were clearly high, Eliot may not have wanted to present Praying Indians at odds with their unconverted brethren. After all, he not only claimed that indigenous teachers would be more effective than English ones (and, presumably, would better understand the implications of such public encounters than Eliot himself did at the time), but he also would not have wanted to imply to an anxious English audience that Indian missionaries from Natick would antagonize such a powerful Indian sachem as Philip.[23] In *Light Appearing*, Eliot proved that he could personally control hostile sachems by meeting high spirits with higher yet, whereas in the dialogues, he depicts an autonomous Indian mission effort, absent the violent conflict that New England's Indian policies threatened to unleash.

In Thomas Scanlan's reading of Dialogue III, Philip's resistance to Christianity and the language concerning the rights of rulers and the responsibilities of "common" people invoke religious and political affairs in England, in particular, "the Restoration subtext of a veiled Catholic threat." The Philip of *Indian Dialogues*, then, is "a politically repressive monarch, who refuses to accept Christianity."[24] I agree that this context makes Eliot's presentation of kingly anxiety intelligible. But if we consider *Indian Dialogues* as a careful revision of earlier mission writings, especially earlier descriptions of Cutshamekin, we can see that it stops short of advocating, as Scanlan puts it, "the establishment of a democratic commonwealth among the Indians" (169). In this 1671 version of a missionary's encounter with a sachem, Eliot erases the antimonarchism implicit in his defeat of Cutshamekin, when the sachem's people had "smiled as they durst" at his humiliation. However acceptable the encounter was in 1647, such political sentiments were much more dangerous post-Restoration, as Eliot well knew.[25]

In *Light Appearing*, Cutshamekin is represented as angry, deceptive, and sullen: "We found him very full of discontent, sighing, sower looks, &c. but we took no notice of it."[26] Philip, by contrast, is presented as a misguided but indulgent ruler. He is easy to persuade, quickly acceding to points made by William and Anthony. And even when he does not acquiesce, he promises that their arguments "lie soaking in my heart and mind."[27] When he asks his people whether they will allow Praying Indians to follow Christian practices while visiting them, their eager assent to that and more surprises Philip. But his response is positively avuncular:

> You go too fast. Your answer goes beyond my proposal or their request. We spake only of private conversation. I said nothing of the Sabbath, nor of their public teaching. This is a greater matter. But go to, seeing you have made the motion. I will not refuse it. What say you my friends? (131)

Despite this wishful presentation of Philip's goodwill, the dialogues make clear that evangelism does not shirk conflict but remains potentially a potent, dangerous stratagem. Rather than describing the mission encounter as a direct and personal exchange of (verbal) blows, however, violence and conquest are couched in metaphor. In Dialogue II, Peneovot echoes the Gospel descriptions of the apostles as "fishers of men" when he exclaims to Waban, "You have dealt with me like as the fishers do by the fish. You laid a bait for me to make me desire it, and bite at it. But I saw not your hook, until you had catch'd my soul" (97). Later, on learning about sin and hellfire, he exclaims, "Oh you have killed me again. By the first light you showed me, I thought you had made me alive, and I joyed in the light. But I understood it not. Now your light is become a sword. It hath pierced through my heart" (98). In Dialogue III, Philip describes William's words to him as arrows: "I feel your words sink into my heart and stick there. You speak arrows" (130). His metaphor is ironically effective because of the iconographic linking of arrows to Indian warfare, even though Indians regularly used guns both for hunting and for waging war. Eliot thus attributes evangelistic conquest to Waban and William, a tactic that is especially significant in the 1670s, when the colonies were on the brink of outright war with the real Philip.

An Indian Errand into the Wilderness

Although in *Indian Dialogues* Eliot's presentation of Cutshamekin revises previous mission accounts, the work as a whole continues themes from earlier tracts, in particular the rewriting of New England's "beginnings" and the purposes of migration. In Dialogue I, Piumbukhou describes his missionary task in terms especially resonant with New England colonialism. In reply to his kinsman's welcome and questions about the Praying Indian way of life, he says, "I am glad that you are so desirous to speak with me about our religion, and praying to God, for that is the very errand I come upon, that I might persuade you to do as we do" (64). Again, it seems that Eliot is attempting to place his mission at the heart of colonial concerns. He writes of Piumbukhou's "errand" into what would have seemed to his readers the definitive wilderness of outlying Indian communities just a year after his friend and Roxbury Church colleague Samuel Danforth preached his famous election-day sermon, "A Brief Recognition of New England's Errand into the Wilderness," which famously decries Puritan New England's declension from founding piety and purpose.[28] Both Eliot's *Indian Dialogues* and Danforth's sermon were published in the same year.

Piumbukhou goes on to summarize the godly errand of New England's first generation:

> we have great cause to be thankful to the English, and to thank God for them. For they had a good country of their own, but by ships sailing into these parts of the world, they heard of us. . . . God put it into their hearts to desire to come hither, and teach us the good knowledge of God. (72)

The errand represented here, as focused totally on Indians and their conversion, is the one delineated in many mission writings (though not described by Danforth in his sermon). Puritans emigrated because they had heard of Indians and knew they needed to hear the gospel message. Only after this description do we read briefly about the errand's original articulation: "Their King gave them leave [to plant in New England], and in our country to have their liberty to serve God according to the word of God."[29] Piumbukhou's purpose in visiting his friend is thus modeled after his English friends' re-envisioned errand; both Piumbukhou and the English wish to speak to Indians about praying to God.

This moment in Dialogue I would seem to support Scanlan's assertion that "the narrative of the conversion of the Indians . . . functions for Eliot as an allegorical one that will reinvigorate Protestantism and give it a new sense of purpose."[30] By making the Praying Indian responsive to an evangelical errand, Eliot draws attention to the colonists' shocking lapses in spreading the gospel to the "heathen." This moment, however, is less allegory and more a real shift of the mission onto the shoulders of Praying Indians. The vision of Indian evangelism that Eliot presents is autonomous. The English had been the spark, but this movement rightly (he suggests) continues without their active presence, led only by the word of God:

> God put it into the heart of one of their ministers (as you all know) to teach us the knowledge of God, by the word of God, and hath translated the holy Book of God into our language, so that we can perfectly know the mind, and course of God. And out of this book have I learned all that I say unto you.[31]

Although Eliot takes credit for translating the Bible, his actions serve finally to remove him from the conversion process. Indians, empowered by the bible to know Christ (and by Christ to understand scripture), will convert themselves: "So we read with our own eyes these things which I speak of, to be written in God's own book, and we feel the truth thereof in our own hearts" (72). And rather than seeking to infuse English readers with a new desire to emulate or even simply to facilitate the conversion of Indians, this tract seems quite comfortable with imagining spiritual struggle to take place "out there," beyond the limits of English concerns.

By displacing the errand onto the likes of Piumbukhou, William, and Anthony, Eliot constructs a new colonial relationship for English settlers and Indian converts. Earlier tracts were addressed to England in hopes of garnering support; they were colonial petitions to the metropole for money and goods to support English endeavors in America. English settlers and Indian converts were surely presented in a hierarchical relationship, but both groups were comparably placed on the edges of the English empire. Here, however, Boston is described as the center, and the various Indian communities and homes are clearly peripheral. Conversion wins the support of and ties converts politically to the English colonies, whose residents and governors are depicted as powerful and imperially distant. William and Anthony repeatedly respond to Philip's concerns in terms that stress the political advantages of the potential alliance between Philip and colonial forces. Consider the hierarchy of allegiances promised him here: "It will be a joy to all the English magistrates, and ministers, and churches, and good people of the land, to hear that Philip and all his

people are turned to God, and become praying Indians" (120). Philip
clearly senses the reciprocal advantages of converting: "I am ready to
think that the Governor and Magistrates of the Massachusetts would
as well oblige you to him [the converted sachem], as him to you" (123).

The Bay Colony—both its people and rulers—are in the same position vis-à-vis these Indian missionaries as the Society for the Propagation of the Gospel in London had been to Eliot's mission. Indeed,
even other English colonies are subordinated to Massachusetts.
William reminds Philip of old alliances between his father and Plymouth colony, promising that the people of Plymouth will "embrace
[him] as a brother in Jesus Christ" (126). But the Bay Colony will have
a quite different relationship with him, one akin to that of the king to
his colonies. The equivalence is underscored by William's litany of the
English allies Philip would gain by converting, though he would lose
some of his own subjects:

> the Governor and Magistrates of the Massachusetts will own you, and
> be fatherly and friendly to you. The commissioners of the United
> Colonies will own you. Yea more, the King of England, and the great
> peers who are heads of the Corporation there, who yearly send over
> means to encourage and promote our praying to God, they will take no-
> tice of you. And what are a few of your subjects that hate praying to God,
> in comparison of all these?[32]

This is the imagined fulfillment of the "farther Arrand" described
in the earlier mission tracts—still a focus, although events had voided
the errand's millennial promise. The Great Migration that had
brought the English to America is represented as finished, a task accomplished. Whereas earlier authors described the continuing labors
and risks of the colonial enterprise for English settlers, here there is
no such discussion. Governor, king, magistrate, peer: they are all one
from the perspective of Indians discussing a new religion on the periphery of the colonies. The English are an unseen presence in *Indian
Dialogues;* they offer a distant, "fatherly" approval of Christian Indians. But the text is no longer concerned with the working out of English colonial identities by posing Praying Indians as pious Christians,
whose examples should shame English sinners, or with frantically
convincing an English readership of New England's importance to the
endeavors of the saints in England.

Rather, it is the Indians who self-interrogate, who fear, who despair.

It is they who strive to negotiate their place in Christ's kingdom as established by the colonies. We are given a glimpse of Philip's inner workings as he "pours out" his thoughts and feelings to Anthony and William: "Know this, that in the rowlings of my thoughts, the disquiet turnings and tumblings of my mind, so oft times molest me with variety of passions" (132). He goes on at some length, so much so that we see him caught in the process of conversion. His speech exhibits him not as a static character but represents the inner workings of a sinner becoming a "new creature": "I have quite lost my self. I did not intend to open and pour out my mind and thoughts about these matters; but full vessels are ready to run over."[33]

Godly Speech

Such speeches by Philip help explain why Dialogue III is usually considered the most significant exchange in the book. Post–King Philip's War, it is an especially shocking representation of the sachem. But given the real negotiations conducted by Eliot and the Praying Indians, perhaps we should be less taken aback by Philip's characterization here. Nevertheless, *Indian Dialogues* is a thoroughly surprising text. Read carefully, each dialogue should startle, and other moments in the text deserve more attention for the ways they thoroughly revise earlier mission accounts and create protofictional representations of Indians. Like Dialogue III, other sections of the tract blend fact and fiction. Of the unconverted characters participating in the dialogues, some are named; others have generic identifications, such as "kinsman" or "sachem." The Praying Indians who exhort others are all named after historical persons and members of the Natick Indian church. In addition to William and Anthony, we find Piumbukhou and Waban, among others.[34] The figure of the Praying Indian throughout these dialogues, then, is built on earlier reports, uses familiar names, and completes the description of cultural and spiritual conversion begun in the tracts. Idealized agents and substitutes for English missionaries, they occupy a discursive and physical middle ground between the English religious or civil authorities and the unconverted Indians, using kinship ties to move safely from one side to the other. None of these elements are especially surprising for this type of missionary propaganda. What deserves attention, however, is the detailed and sympathetic attention paid to unconverted Indians in order to present them as worthy of evangelism and to imagine Indian friendships and family life (always through the mediating mission lens, of course).

What do the "instructive," often unnamed characters talk about with the more familiar historical personages? They discuss their families, local news, their travels, rituals of hospitality, and, of course, religion. All of these topics are plausible, for the dialogues present traces of real encounters and actual speech. But *Indian Dialogues* is not merely reporting or transcribing actual encounters, and an understanding of the text requires close reading for its calculated literary effects. Consider the difference between Roger Williams's phrasebook dialogue "On Religion," in *Key Into the Language of America*, and Eliot's dialogues. Williams's speakers get right to the point. The dialogue is always focused on the subject at hand:

Nétop Kunnatótemous.	*Friend, I will aske you a Question.*
Natótema.	*Speake on.*
Tocketunnántum?	*What thinke you?*
Awaun Keesiteoûwin Kéesuck?	*Who made the Heavens?*
Aûke Wechékom?	*The Earth, the Sea?*
Míttauke.	*The World.*[35]

By contrast, Eliot's Indians engage in small talk, joke, eat together, *and* proselytize. Relationships are presumed and embroidered upon, as when Piumbukhou's kinswoman in Dialogue I asks, "How doth your wife, my loving kinswoman, is she yet living?" and receives a message from her in return.[36]

Both Christian and non-Christian characters engage in such pleasantries. But when it comes to God talk, it seems reasonable to expect the characters to exhibit their greatest differences. Indeed, David Murray argues of the main characters in *Indian Dialogues:* "There is little to distinguish them from whites or from each other. Where the distinction is really made is between Christian and pagan."[37] Most of the players in the dialogues *are* undifferentiated, but even the distinction between Christian and pagan is subsumed by Eliot's desire to project *all* Indians as worthy—or perhaps susceptible—to Christianity. As the dialogues present them, non-praying Indians "naturally" respond to Christian truths; Praying Indians consciously conform their utterances to scripture and to Puritan homiletics. The difference between these "instructive" Praying and non-Praying Indians, then, is that the former consciously allude to scripture whereas the latter do so unintentionally.

As missionaries, the Praying Indian characters demonstrate above all their abilities to preach and to persuade as orthodox Puritans. Conversant with their old community's values and habits, they lay out the principles of Christianity and open scriptural texts in the plain style. Piumbukhou answers one of his kinsman's later inquiries, "What are those heavenly riches of which you speak so highly," with a numbered list of six kinds of spiritual "knowledge."[38] In the meetings he leads on the Sabbath, he puts aside catechisms and psalm singing, because like Eliot in an earlier stage of his work, he believes that these unconverted Indians "are not yet fitted and prepared for" such forms of education or worship. Nevertheless, he follows other Puritan sermon conventions, addressing the text, doctrine and reasons, and uses in turn. He begins with a reading of Matthew 7:13–14, opens it in an orderly, subdivided explanation, and concludes with a two-part exhortation. Likewise, in Dialogues II and III, Waban and Anthony open texts by enumerating their points. Christian messages clothed in the plain style are presented as almost immediately effective. The kinsman in Dialogue I meets Piumbukhou's narrative descriptions of the praying life with skepticism and questions until the Praying Indian lists the "true riches" of spiritual knowledge. The kinsman replies, "These are great and strange things you speak of. I understand them not. But yet methinks there is a majesty and glory in them" (68).

Just as Praying Indian missionaries learned the proper hortatory style from Eliot, so Eliot argues that each generation of Indian converts bequeaths the plain style to the next, propagating the Christian message exponentially and quickly reaching Indians who live outside the sphere of direct English influence. In Dialogue II, after Waban spends an afternoon and night praying with and teaching Peneovot, the new convert is able to imitate his teacher.[39] He unfolds the chief tenets of Puritanism to his sachem Nishohkou, repeating four points drawn from Matthew 11:28–29 (114–17).

The Praying Indians' new lives mark not only their formal exhortations but also their more informal conversation, further elaborating the imagined thoroughness and naturalness of their acculturation. Hearkening back to Eliot's assertion made more than twenty years earlier, that Indians "use and delight in demonstrations,"[40] the Praying Indians teach, persuade, and cajole their listeners with a series of metaphors influenced by scriptures. Dialogue I is particularly rich in

metaphors and similes, perhaps because it is meant to represent a people's first encounter with the praying life, and Piumbukhou cannot yet
rely heavily on direct scriptural proofs or illustrations. When he first
chances on his kinsman, Piumbukhou describes his conversion and
his desire to convert others: "I am like a friend that has found honey,
and plenty of food, and I come to call my friends to partake with me"
(64).

Henry Bowden and James Ronda note that the first dialogue "begins
with a proclamation of the gospel incorporating native idioms" (43).
Perhaps the honey simile was chosen to reflect a hunter-gatherer existence and connote a celebration of a traditional and earthly sort
(against which Piumbukhou shortly rails). Nevertheless, the word
"honey" is heavy with scriptural allusion. When Piumbukhou next
uses it, the biblical connections are more explicit. On finding more
friends and relatives gathered at his kinsman's house, he again describes his new life: "Our joys in the knowledge of God, and of Jesus
Christ, which we are taught in the Book of God, and feel in our heart,
is sweeter to our soul, than honey is unto the mouth and taste" (69).
Piumbukhou's illustration echoes a variety of texts, most closely
Psalm 119:103—"How sweet are your words to my taste, Sweeter
than honey to my mouth!"[41]

In describing the growth of the Praying movement, Piumbukhou
also makes use of a weather metaphor: "At first this matter of praying
to God was a little thing, like a cloud in the west of the bigness of a
man's hand. But now the cloud is great and wide, and spreadeth over
all the country" (80). This illustration, like that of the honey-eater, describes a quotidian experience, a weather pattern moving across the
sky, appearing small at first, but gaining strength. Yet Piumbukhou's
metaphoric expression is, like his use of "honey," biblical. It draws on
scripture, I Kings 18:44: "Behold, there ariseth a little cloud out of the
sea, like a man's hand."

Such allusive language contrasts with the occasional incomprehensible utterances by unconverted Indian characters. In Dialogue I, immediately after Piumbukhou asks his kinsman to partake of his
new-found spiritual riches, he asks, "What noise is that I hear?" (64).
Piumbukhou hears the sounds of a celebration, described as "great
dancing, and sacrifice, and play." His kinsman responds by noting that
as a Praying Indian, Piumbukhou no longer participates in such activities and therefore, "You have forgot the meaning of such noises."

Piumbukhou has completely replaced his old language with that of Christian catechism and scripture. Once his kinsman reacquaints him with the meaning of those sounds, Piumbukhou further demonstrates his new Praying Indian sensibilities, declaring the celebration a sign of the "deep pit" in which unconverted sinners were sunk (65).

When Piumbukhou and his kinsmen are joined by others, the larger audience continues to exemplify the antithesis of godly speech. They accompany the dialogue with an ubiquitous "Ha, ha, he" that is part refrain, part frivolous discourse, and part guttural babble.[42] Puritans disapproved of frivolous laughter, and the abandon these unconverted Indians exhibit is in keeping with their unregenerate state—a condition the kinsman recognizes only when he begins to be affected by Piumbukhou's message. In addition to laughter, Eliot assigns the larger crowd an instance of untranslated speech. After Piumbukhou prays, the company responds in Wôpanâak: "Tabat, tabat, tabat" (77). Presumably, the entire dialogue is "actually" conducted in Wôpanâak, so this "transcription" intrudes into the flow of the language as foreign, nonsensical, akin to the noisy laughter. We have no way of knowing whether his English readers would have readily recognized the word, which Roger Williams translated in *Key* as "I am glad."[43] Eliot does not gloss it. Whatever the English reader's understanding, the untranslaed words interjcct a "foreign" element in an otherwise "domestic" linguistic representation.

Were Eliot consistently to represent Praying Indians as speakers of an allusive language and non-Praying Indians as noise-makers, true dialogue among those characters would be impossible, and I would agree with David Murray that Eliot seems to mark a strong difference between Christian and pagan characters. However, even though non-Praying Indians are made to seem debased by their frivolity, they also speak in metaphor, at times unconsciously echoing scripture. This linguistic commonality implies the missionaries' ultimate success. Although Eliot does not invoke his earlier millennialism and identify these Indians as parable-speaking remnants of the tribes of Israel, the descriptions do reflect those older representations.[44] If they are not Jewish remnants, the characters' allusive language at least signals their responsiveness to the Word, an expected and necessary quality in those capable of conversion. Ethnicity, class, gender—all such categories are submerged in what was for Eliot the much more fundamental classification of "sinner," an identity that includes his Praying and non-Praying characters alike. In these dialogues, the pattern of unredeemed human speech is inscribed in scripture and followed by unconverted speakers.

The sachem in Dialogue I couches his objections to Christianity in metaphoric language:

> If any man bring us a precious jewel, which will make us rich and happy, everybody will make that man welcome, and if this friend of ours do that, who more welcome? But if by receiving his jewel, we must part with a better jewel for it, then wise men should do well to consider, before they accept his offer (86).

If not an exact match for the "pearl of great price" parable of Matthew 13:45, the sachem's "parable" certainly fits the pattern and illustrates his lost state. He cannot see the superior value of the "jewel" that Piumbukhou offers him and his people.

New converts also make use of such patterns for their religious speech. Peneovot, whom Waban converts in Dialogue II, matches scripture more exactly when he reaches a state of despair and fear as he learns about the commandments, sin, and hellfire. He cries, "Oh, that the rocks and mountains would fall upon me, and hide me from the stroke of his wrathful hand!" In his desperation, he echoes Revelation 6:16: on the opening of the sixth seal, the people of the earth begin "calling to the mountains and rocks, 'Fall on us and hide us from the face of the one seated on the throne and from the wrath of the Lamb.'" After only one night of teaching and prayer, when his despair has turned to joy, Peneovot begins an exhortation to his sachem Nishohkou:

> I will declare unto you strange news, to which I entreat your attendance a little while, and all the people here present. I am like a man that was looking for a shell and found a pearl of inestimable value. . . . My blind eyes are opened, my dead heart is made alive, my lame legs are enabled to walk in the way to heaven, where I shall enjoy an eternal kingdom. (*Indian Dialogues*, 113)

Here Peneovot does adapt the "pearl of great price" parable to his own experience and proclaims that he lives the gospel promise of Matthew 11:5: "The blind receive their sight, and the lame walk, the lepers are cleansed, and the deaf hear, the dead are raised up, and the poor have the gospel preached to them." These speech patterns provide a careful presentation of Indians, whether converted or not, as naturally inclined toward Puritan ways of organizing thought and of speaking.

So far, I have focused on fairly general characteristics to describe the case *Indian Dialogues* makes for continuing colonial support of Eliot's mission. I turn now to a character even more surprising than the Philip of Dialogue III—the unnamed "kinswoman" of Dialogue I, who synthesizes Eliot's past presentations of evangelism and gender. She is perhaps the most winning character in the dialogues. From her first appearance, we see her provoke and challenge Piumbukhou, the Praying Indian who has come to convert her, yet the dialogue presents her as a likable character. She begins by making a rather formal welcome to Piumbukhou, adding, "I wish you had come a little earlier, that you might have taken part with us in the joys of this day, wherein we have had all the delights that could be desired, in our merry meeting, and dancing" (69). Piumbukhou responds in proper Puritan form, perhaps, but with a shockingly poor return for her graciousness:

> And whereas you wish I had come sooner, to have shared with you in
> your delights of this day. Alas, they are no delights, but griefs to me, to
> see that you do still delight in them. . . . I abhor to taste of your sinful
> and foolish pleasures, as the mouth doth abhor to taste the most filthy
> and stinking dung, the most sour grapes, or most bitter gall. (69)

The kinswoman's response, though obviously meant to anticipate Piumbukhou's subsequent arguments against her way of life, is nonetheless engaging and recognizably human:

> We have all the delights that the flesh and blood of man can devise and
> delight in, and we taste and feel the delights of them, and would you
> make us believe that you have found out new joys and delights, in com-
> parison of which all our delights do stink like dung? Would you make
> us believe that we have neither eyes to see, nor ears to hear, nor mouth
> to taste? Ha, ha, he! I appeal to the sense and sight and feeling of the
> company present, whether this be so. (70).

Puritan readers, alert to biblical allusions, would have seen in her incredulous reply the foreshadowing of her subsequent conversion. She alludes not only to the promises in Matthew 11 that the blind will see but also to Philippians 3:7: "Yea doubtless, and I count all things but loss for the excelling of the knowledge of Christ Jesus my Lord: for whom I have suffered the loss of all things, and do count them but dung, that I may win Christ."

Tellingly, it is not the kinswoman but her husband who is persuaded by Piumbukhou: "If these things be so, we had need to cease laughing, and fall to weeping" (71). He and Piumbukhou conduct the next exchange concerning the provenance of the Bible ("May we not rather think that *English* men have invented these stories to amaze us and fear us") and the Puritans' migration to America on an evangelical errand. So the dialogue reflects the conventional gender roles laid out in earlier mission tracts. Although women are present, serious theological discussion occurs between men.

Indeed, the kinswoman comes back into the conversation only to put an end to it with a joke:

> You make long and learned discourses to us which we do not well understand. I think our best answer is to stop your mouth, and fill your belly with a good supper, and when your belly is full you will be content to take rest yourself, and give us leave to be at rest from these gastering and heart-trembling discourses. We are well as we are, and desire not to be troubled with these new wise sayings. (73)

Here, the kinswoman echoes English evangelism literature. Her request is similar to one raised by Baxter's nonbeliever in *Call to the Unconverted:* "There are so many ways and religions, that we know not which to be of, and therefore we will be even as we are."[45] This dialogue not only models the ideal speech of the instructor, but the kinswoman also illustrates the response any sinner would (or should) make.[46] Eliot thereby strikes a balance in his representation of the Indian woman. On the one hand, she is carefully subordinated to her husband. She makes the meals, tends to the physical needs of her guests, and is largely absent from the most serious religious instruction. Like Totherswamp's good wife in Shepard's *Clear Sun-shine of the Gospel,* she follows her husband into the praying life: "I shall gladly join with my husband in this change."[47] Moreover, when the dialogue switches from a family gathering to a discussion with a sachem and a powwow, she drops out entirely.

And yet, in her huswifely duties and even in her frivolity, Eliot gives her some of the dialogue's sharpest criticism of missionary ways, and her speeches even approximate an individual voice. She scolds her husband for taking advantage of their guest: "Husband, what do you mean to withhold our friend from rest so long, so late? Alas cousin, you had need to be at rest. I pray tire not yourself with these long discourses" (81). And as Piumbukhou talks of the Praying Indians' recent sufferings, she remarks, "These are but cold and weak arguments to persuade us to take up the English fashion, and to serve their God, when you tell us how sharply he dealt with his servants" (75). And even after she has started to accept Piumbukhou's teaching by asking him to pray before their meal, "according as you wisely discourse" (84), she gently mocks Piumbukhou's pretensions: "Cousin, I am glad to see you eat so heartily. You are very welcome to it. And I see that praying to God doth not fill your bellies. You need food for all that" (84).

Clearly, Eliot is interested in using this character to illustrate proper gender roles and as a dialogic foil for his mouthpiece, Piumbukhou. The effect is a strong characterization, and yet she is a figure of whom Eliot obviously approves. Piumbukhou responds to her jokes and wit very genially throughout. She is not meant to be a figure of sin but rather of weak womanhood, "corrected" by her husband's decision to convert. Read in conjunction with Eliot's earlier descriptions of godly Indian women, the effect here is of a lively character, flawed but appealing, providing ample reason for continuing evangelism.[48]

Noble Savages

As the kinswoman's character shows, we can see in these dialogues the history of mission contact not only idealized but also very close to being fictionalized. Nancy Armstrong and Leonard Tennenhouse have recently made the case for the American captivity narrative, particularly Mary Rowlandson's well-known and popular account, as a genre from which early novelists derived at least some of the key elements of the novel in English.[49] Armstrong also suggests that the American captivity narrative is the "principle of continuity" that has created the tradition of the English novel.[50] Tennenhouse and Armstrong's arguments are helpful to any consideration of American fiction in English. Whatever the strength of their views in terms of describing the English novel, they articulate the difficult relations between New England and Old England, and they bridge the chasm between American and British literary studies that often unthinkingly reinforces problematic theories of origins and exceptionalism.[51] Rowlandson's narrative in particular exemplifies this push-pull relationship.

Before there was Mary Rowlandson, however, or even "Mary Rowlandson," there were Piumbukhou and John Speene, Anthony, William, and Ponampam. As I discuss in the next chapter, Rowlandson's text made room for the valuation of her body in captivity and her voice in redemption by displacing the bodies and voices of Praying Indians in the English colonies. Before the war, however, Eliot's *Indian Dialogues*, a carefully shaped revision of early mission reports, was meant to continue the presence of Praying Indians not only in mission literature but in colonial discourse more broadly. It should be seen as belonging to an alternative literary history violently cut off by the war in which Mary Rowlandson's voice drowns theirs out. In mission literature, including *Indian Dialogues*, the English colonial enterprise depends on the correcting gaze and active presence of Praying Indians in America, not on the passively chaste captive woman.

Here, then, is a "literary thought experiment": Where might *Indian Dialogues'* representation of Indians have taken colonial literature if the war and captivity narratives had not directed the discourse so completely toward vilification? If Mary Rowlandson's representation of Philip had not intervened, to what formulations might Eliot's "Philip Keitasscot" have pointed? By placing *Indian Dialogues* at the start of an alternate literary history, I do not mean to suggest that it is a benign or benevolent—or even a more desirable—representation of colonial relations. It is different, however, from the rhetoric of extinction that came to the fore during King Philip's war, and it marks a radical discursive shift in colonial Indian writings from 1671 to 1676.

In Dialogue III, another sachem, unnamed, joins Philip Keitasscot's discussion with William and Anthony. Clearly meant to offer a contrast to Philip's reasonable and inquisitive attitude, this sachem suggests that ordinary people should not "meddle" with reading the Bible. Such a comment quickly gives rise to an anti-Catholic discussion of European religion and politics. William says,

> I have heard that in the other part of the world there be a certain people
> who are called Papists, whose ministers and teachers live in all manner
> of wickedness and lewdness, and permit and teach the people so to do.
> And these wicked ministers will not suffer the people to read the Word
> of God.[52]

Thomas Scanlan provides a careful analysis of this moment, concluding that Eliot is "linking the political structures of Indian culture with those of Catholicism. Thus, by converting Indians, the Puritans can, by analogy, be participating in the destruction of Romanism."[53] This reading seems clear from the text, but equally important is the tone and form of Philip's response:

> What you have said hath fully settled and satisfied my heart in this point. I will never hinder my people from the knowledge of the Word of God, and I wonder at those vile ministers that do so wickedly abuse the people. And I wonder at the sachems, that they will suffer such vile ministers to abuse their people in that manner, why do they not suppress them? (137)

Philip's attitude is, of course, the right Protestant one. And his question, couched in exotic diction, offers a challenge to European rulers. It is jarring (or would have been to seventeenth-century readers) to hear European kings called "sachems" and held to such a question. In effect, Philip's speech here translates Old World concerns into New World terms, making them available for colonial consideration and judgment.

Philip next questions the clergy. William provides the standard Protestant vilification of the priesthood: they are rich, they are powerful, they do not marry but have illegitimate children so as to pass on their wealth and power within the church. And if anyone objects, William reports, "they will kill him presently, so that partly by their wealth, and partly by their cruelty, they keep everybody in fear of them" (138). Philip's response turns the gaze of the New World back on the Old: "O strange!"

William goes on to complete this reversal of the colonial gaze as he recounts Catholic hierarchies and names, always returning to Indian touchstones of familiarity:

> They choose one chief, and call him a Pope, and say that he has power to pardon men's sins and will sell pardons, for money, and by that means they get a great deal of wealth. For people are such fools as to think that he can pardon them, when as the Popes be as vile sinners as anybody, and keep whores, and get bastards. Other of these ministers they call Cardinals; others Lord Archbishop; others Lord Bishop; other, Lord Abbot, others, Lord Friar, and I cannot tell how many more. And many of these as rich as sachems. (138)

This sequence seems remarkably like the skeptical, superior descriptions of indigenous traditions and religions recorded by early European explorers of America. Philip's response to such descriptions is decisive: "Here be ministers with all my heart! Are these men that manage their religion? These are worse than our pauwaus. If any pauwau in my dominions should be half this vile, I would scourge him" (139). Here we see the earlier "Indian sermons" put into the mouths of Indian characters. To be sure, times had changed; now it is European Catholics rather than English Protestants who are chastised. Despite this difference—though it is significant—*Indian Dialogues* builds on the earlier mission examples and creates in Philip an "innocent" character or at least a naïf, as he holds up Old World ways to criticism with that earlier, Miranda-like exclamation, "Oh strange!"

In such moments, *Indian Dialogues* can be seen as introducing an approach to Indian representation more fully realized in eighteenth-century satirical writings: the savage innocent commenting on the foibles of the civilized European. Indeed, part of the problem of reading *Indian Dialogues* for such challenges to staid identity formation is that its most important rhetorical tactics are familiar to us through later literature. The passage translates English to Indian concepts— "kings" are termed "sachems," and "priests" are "powwows"; biblical types "naturally" arise in non-Christian Indian conversation; and Indians become individuals who are learning about and passing judgment on the English. Scholars of American literature most often associate such tactics with Enlightenment representations, as in Thomas Jefferson's Logan from his *Notes on the State of Virginia*, or Benjamin Franklin's "Savages in America." Perhaps this familiarity is why the mere appearance of Philip in Dialogue III shocks, although the rest of the work seems relatively tame. Reading backward from the eighteenth century, we have difficulty recognizing *Indian Dialogues'* other surprises.

As an early example of the kind of Enlightenment representations that echo *Indian Dialogues,* consider the 1710 visit to London of four Iroquois men. Their embassy was a response to a failed military maneuver: the attempt in 1709 by British forces to wrest Canada from France. Although colonial forces had been prepared to move against the French, Queen Anne failed to send promised naval support. Colonial authorities, still invested in the Canadian conquest, sent representatives to London to ask again for the crown's support, and they also recruited four Iroquois in order, as Eric Hinderaker notes, "to dramatize their case and to impress the Iroquois with Britain's power."[54]

As contemporary records of the visit make clear, the London public was fascinated. The men were mobbed whenever they left their rooms at the Two Crowns and Cushion Inn on King Street to attend official functions or entertainment. British artists painted their likenesses. British authors memorialized them in ballads and, significantly, imagined their thoughts in fictional journals.

The transatlantic nature of such representations is significant. These men were not acting as mediators of Iroquois-British relations, or at least this was not their primary function. Rather, they had been recruited to mediate the British colonies' relations with the crown. Their representation had more to do with the construction of British colonial and metropolitan identities than with faithfully recording the agency or identity of the Iroquois. Thus, these mediated and fantastic materials function in much the same way as earlier Puritan mission tracts: they present an Indian figure working across an Atlantic rather than western American frontier.

The Iroquois's behavior and appearance reflect their specific use as symbols of imperial power. Like Praying Indians before them, these colonized subjects are made to register their willing acceptance of British rule and the colonial administration with the regard they have for English religion and goods. In a set of paintings commissioned by Queen Anne and executed by John Verelst, the Indians wear a mixture of English and Indian clothing.[55] All four men betray some mixedness of dress, but that of "Tee Yee Neen Ho Ga Row," the so-called Emperor of the Six Nations, is most striking. He is pictured in a forest setting, standing with a wolflike dog behind him. He wears English buckled shoes, black hose, and a tunic unbuttoned to his waist, with a white English shirt beneath it. Over his shoulders is draped a rich-looking blanket. He wears a small belt of wampum and holds a larger one out as a gift. It is important, both politically and discursively, that his appearance mixes domestic and exotic elements, thus signaling his tractability—he values and adopts English ways for his own—and also the continued necessity for direct British rule in America. Partly "civilized," he has a long way to go. It should come as no surprise to careful readers of earlier English mission literature that the four kings end their visit, as do those being proselytized in *Indian Dialogues*, with a request (granted, of course) for Christian missionaries to live and work among their people.

The reported speech of the Iroquois visitors exhibits the same approach to Indian representation as does *Indian Dialogues,* especially because their words appear only in translation or are wholly imagined. In his 1757 history of New York, William Smith records an address supposedly delivered through interpreters to Queen Anne. In it, the men explain their visit as informative. They will "relate to her those Things, which we thought absolutely necessary for the Good of her, and us her Allies."[56] Remembering the preparations for the Canadian invasion, they explain, "We were mightily rejoiced, when we heard our great Queen had resolved to send an Army to reduce *Canada,* and immediately, in Token of Friendship, we hung up the Kettle and took up the Hatchet" (136).

The concluding picturesque speech—"kettle" and "hatchet" represent peace and war—lends this speech verisimilitude for British readers, who would have expected to hear marked differences between their own and the Indians' expressions. This pattern of metaphoric speech set within an otherwise conventional and proper address to the queen parallels the mix of "domestic" and "foreign" elements not only in *Indian Dialogues* but in earlier tracts as well.

Joseph Addison's *Spectator* essay of a year later (April 27, 1711) illustrates another element of this "noble savage" representation, one that seems quite a clear parallel to the representation of *Indian Dialogues:* the "innocent" observations of *his* imagined Indian king are used to criticize English behavior quite explicitly. Addison notes that his great interest in what the Indian kings thought about their stay in London leads him to discover the "journal" of "King *Sa Ga Yean Qua Rash Tow,*" retained by his upholsterer-landlord and now translated into English. The journal records the king's astonishment at seeing St. Paul's, which he assumes was originally a "huge misshapen Rock" worked into its current form. That observation is followed by a comment on the inattentive worshipers (the "Natives of this Country")— "a considerable Number of them fast asleep."[57] The fictional journal continues with a lengthy discussion of "Native" dress and appearance. In particular, the king comments on "the Women of the Country" who

look like Angels, and would be more beautiful than the Sun, were it not for little black Spots that are apt to break out in their Faces, and sometimes rise in very odd Figures. I have observed that those little Blemishes wear off very soon; but when they disappear in one Part of the Face, they are very apt to break out in another, insomuch that I have seen a Spot upon the Forehead in the Afternoon, which was upon the Chin in the Morning. (100)

The comments work as satire because the speaker has an air of naïve attentiveness—he takes women's beauty patches at face value, so to speak, as occurring naturally. But rather than perceiving a pleasing contrast between patch and skin, he sees only blemishes. His observations, moreover, get an additional edge from his unaffected admiration for English women's beauty—any ironical effect is subdued and belongs wholly to Addison—which he expresses in mixed "Indian" and "English" terms. He relies on a biblical comparison: "They look like angels." But the comparison of English women's beauty to the sun suggests a native-sounding, metaphoric linguistic pattern. There is just enough exotic difference in his speech to underscore the fiction of a wide-eyed noble savage in London.

The point of Addison's essay is made clear in the concluding comments:

The Author [the Indian king] then proceeds to shew the Absurdity of Breeches and Petticoats . . . which I shall reserve for another Occasion. I cannot however conclude this Paper without taking Notice, That amidst these wild Remarks there now and then appears something very reasonable. (100)

Wild and reasonable; noble and savage: throughout this fictional journal, what makes the Indian king a valuable observer of English mores is his colonial identity. He is in London but not of London, literate but inexperienced. His "natural" observations rebuke English sophistication.

I have only suggested here a parallel between seventeenth-century mission literature and later satiric or fictional works. In my imagined literary history, I would go on to include the nineteenth-century Pequot writer William Apess's knowing description of himself as a "son of the Forest." Of course, many other influences can be found for such patterns, particularly for the British tradition; one might discuss the myth of Eden, Ovid's golden age, or Columbus's letters. Yet mission literature and *Indian Dialogues* in particular should be useful in bridging the gap between scholars of early American and early modern English writings, for Eliot imagines colonists as occupying a metropolitan center just as surely as Addison imagines himself as far distant from Iroquois lands. Yet, too often, historians and scholars of early American literature sum up colonial English discourse as moving directly from narratives of exploration and settlement to prerevolutionary formations, as if Bradford's Squanto led directly to Jefferson's Logan. If such scholars admit Puritan representations as significant, they often point to King Philip's war writings as a contrast to later, romantic portrayals. It is as if those wartime representations erased the earlier and quite serious efforts to fix Indian identity within a Christian rather than a military conquest.

Eric Hinderaker, for instance, compares the image of the four Indian kings to the "older idea that Indians were simple and savage."[58] Hinderaker also includes William Hubbard's and Increase Mather's accounts of King Philip's War as contributing to the older view. This literary history presumes a kind of colonial stasis that ignores forty years of evangelical rhetoric. To be sure, Hinderaker focuses on eighteenth-century representations, and he rightly sees the descriptions of the Iroquois men's visit to London as decidedly different from these colonial accounts. But by eliding the mission literature and their transatlantic significance, the representation of Indians as "ambiguous, contradictory, and half realized" (488) may seem sui generis or at least purely metropolitan, when in fact such a representation is also colonial.

There is no doubt that King Philip's War had a profound effect on the Indian discourse, as inscribed in continuing American literature. But later representations also drew on and revised earlier mission forms.

One can only speculate on the effect that Eliot's *Indian Dialogues* would have had on Commissioners who read it in 1671. Surely, agents for Plymouth Colony would not have been pleased to see Philip's submission to Massachusetts, even in an instructional dialogue, because they were attempting to bring him under their control. Many New England readers must have been incredulous about Eliot's representations when the threatened war did erupt in 1675. Certainly, they reacted violently against Christian Indians. Between 1643 and 1671, Eliot had made a space for converts in the colonies by representing Praying Indians as a hedge between English and non-Praying Indians, placing them firmly in the Bay Colony's jurisdiction and imagining them as fully engaged with Christian conversion.

When, in 1675, Philip's forces attacked Swansea, proving that the hedge could be breached, Praying Indians lost their protected status. Nevertheless, Eliot's construction of the Praying Indian figure in his missionary writings profoundly influenced the English perception of Indians. As we shall see, King Philip's War chroniclers make full use of the figure, even as the colonies blast the hopes and lives of real converts.

6 Satan's Captives, "Preying" Indians, and Mary Rowlandson
Revising the American Captivity Narrative

As *Indian Dialogues* makes clear, however improvised the rituals of encounter recorded in mission tracts such as *The Day-Breaking, if not the Sun-Rising of the Gospell,* however hastily drawn the picture of evangelism sent back to England in *Tears of Repentance,* by 1671 an elaborate representation of Indian converts had been created and a standardized "plot" of Indian salvation had been constructed from these from-the-front reports. *Indian Dialogues* represents non-Christian Indians for the most part as well-intentioned but desperately ignorant of the means to their salvation. As John Eliot presents the evangelical encounter, English and Indian missionaries bring the blessing of God's word to an eager people who readily seize upon it and are convinced of its truth. These missionaries are the heroic rescuers of Indians, who were imprisoned, as the opening of *Indian Dialogues* declares, in "the dark dungeon of their lost and ruined condition."[1] These roles withstood upheavals of Old English rule and New English economy alike. They were part of an American drama that insisted on a heroic, emphatically English role for settlers and a helpless, benighted, necessarily colonized role for Indians.

By the early 1670s, the picture of the individual Praying Indian had also been drawn. As James Axtell observes, "The infallible mark of a Protestant 'praying Indian' was his English appearance: short hair, cobbled shoes, and working-class suit. . . . In the eastern woodlands you could often tell a convert by his cover."[2] To Axtell's Praying Indian, we can add more detail. English descriptions of converts stressed their mixed appearance; converts often blended Indian and English clothing. Sensible of their inner state, Praying Indians wept. They spoke English (even if imperfectly) and expressed themselves in metaphors and "parables." In addition, Praying Indians, settled in praying towns at the border of English colonies, served as a physical and spiritual hedge between English settlements and "Satan's dominions" outside of English control. Although converted Indians faced racial prejudice, political rivalries, and competition even for their small landholdings, their transculturated[3] physical appearance and settled praying towns did offer them a measure of physical security and the promise of a place within New England, albeit on the margins of English society.

In 1675, the possibilities of the Praying Indian figure for negotiating the Indians' role in Puritan New England came to an end with the outbreak of war between the colonists and an alliance of Native Americans. While the racial stereotyping and demonization of Wampanoag and other coastal Indians by white writers during and after King Philip's War is well documented, this period witnessed a more startling discursive transformation—the vilification of the Christian Indian convert.[4]

In wartime literature written between 1675 and 1677, the conventions of mission literature, and the descriptions of Praying Indians written by Eliot and his fellow evangelists in the 1640s and 1650s, were appropriated by anti-Indian writers and used to articulate virulent racism.[5] Despite this reversal of representation, the Praying Indian as an actor on the colonial stage did not vanish. Rather, when the figure appeared, the audience was expected to hiss rather than to cheer. The traits missionaries identified as characteristic of their converts were wholly appropriated by wartime writers, such as William Hubbard, Mary Rowlandson, Benjamin Tompson, and Thomas Wheeler. In earlier accounts, missionaries had noted bobbed hair, psalm singing, and broken English as evidence of the Praying Indians' redemption from Satan and transformation into Christians. But war chroniclers cite these same signs as evidence of intrinsic deception, blasphemy, and stupidity made all the more despicable by evangelists' earlier promises of acculturation.

As all Indians were cast as villains by wartime writers, the American drama of rescue moved from the evangelical stage to the theater of war. Rather than "poor prisoners," Christian Indians became Satan's instruments. Captives, especially white women, took their places as emblems of suffering souls rescued by God through the heroic efforts of Englishmen. The Praying Indian, as we shall see, continued to play a part in these new captivity narratives, but the figure was detached from mission writings and set loose in American literature, to be appropriated by writers with motivations far different from the Praying Indians' original champions. Thus the early American captivity narrative was transformed from a mission genre detailing the spiritual redemption of Indians into a frontier genre of white women menaced by those same Indians. In particular, Mary Rowlandson's 1682 narrative turned American literature and Indian representation firmly in the direction of racist exclusion or extermination.

Satan's Captives

Consider first this discussion of New England's military security:

> It behoveth us not to be secure, and regardlesse of our safety; for if the Adversary should discerne us naked and weak, and see an opportunity, who knoweth what their rage and Sathans malice may stirre them up unto to work us a mischief? Nay, it is our duty to be vigilant, and fortifie our selves the best we can, thereby to put the enemy out of hope to hurt us, and to prevent them from attempting any evill against us.

This pragmatic military statement could have been written at any period of early English settlement in America, penned by John Smith, William Bradford or John Winthrop. With the word "adversary," it neatly conflates the external enemies who threaten violence with Satan. And, of course, it was a colonial commonplace to associate Indians with evil.

But this call to self-defense was written by John Eliot in 1650 and published in Henry Whitfield's *The Light appearing more and more towards the perfect Day*. The "us" of the statement includes both missionaries and Praying Indians. And the "adversary"? The previous few paragraphs describe the enemy as anyone from non-Christian sachems and powwows to the English themselves, who "hinder charity from hoping that there is grace in [the Praying Indians'] hearts."[6] With hindsight, we can identify the slippage between this evangelical rhetoric and postwar anti-Indian diatribes in which "Satan" and "Indian" mean virtually the same thing. But at this point, the spiritual and physical safety of Praying Indians—not English colonists—is at stake. Vigilance was all the more important because Indian converts had a recent history of fallen defenses. Before the coming of the English, or so the tracts assure readers, Indians had been Satan's captives. And now that the English had delivered some from this devilish bondage, those who remained under Satan's control could be expected to vent their "rage" on them.

From the first attempts at evangelical salvation until the eve of King Philip's War, mission writers repeatedly rehearsed the plot of their converts' captivity and rescue in gothic terms that anticipate later captivity narratives. In his introduction to *Strength out of Weaknesse*, Whitfield likens Indian evangelism to "the rescuing of deluded Soules out of the snares of the Devill." In the preface to *Light appearing*, he assures readers,

> Truly the work [of evangelism] is honorable . . . it tending so much to
> the good of the souls of these poor wild creatures, multitudes of them
> being under the power of Satan, and going up and downe with the chains
> of darknesse ratling at their heels.[7]

To Thomas Mayhew, working on present-day Martha's Vineyard, Indians were "miserable Captives," "slaves to the devil from their birth," and "poor captivated men (bondslaves to sin and Satan)." Daniel Gookin, in his prewar *Historical Collections of the Indians of New England*, talks of the "strong bands" that held these captives fast "under Satan's Dominions."[8] English writers picked up the trope as well. In his appendix to Edward Winslow's *Glorious Progress of the Gospel*, John Dury pities the "poor soules who had been *Captives to Satan.*" And the preface to *Strength out of Weaknesse* commends "this work of Christ" (that is, New England missions), because "*hereby the soules of men are rescued out of the snare of the Devill*, in which they were before held captive at his will."[9]

English missionaries understood themselves to be part of a divine effort to rescue Indians from this captivity. Eliot's *A Late and Further Manifestation of the Progress of the Gospel* allusively trumpets New England's missionary success in like terms: "Christ hath there led captivity captive." The preface to *Strength out of Weaknesse* claimed that Christ's presence in America was as a military leader, riding out "Conquering and to Conquer."[10] And although missionaries were most often represented (by themselves and others) as pacific benefactors, at times they saw themselves as soldiers of Christ, enduring hardship and danger as they sought to redeem these captives' souls.[11]

If Praying Indians were captives and English missionaries their rescuers, who (besides Satan, of course) held them? Mission writers found
"adversaries" who, not surprisingly, offered resistance to the English
colonization of Indian souls and Indian lands. The most obvious villains were political and religious leaders. Missionaries insisted that
converts were grateful to the English for rescuing them from im-
placable sachems, who "used to hold their people in absolute servitude.[12] In a letter printed in *Light appearing*, Thomas Mayhew calls
powwows a "yoke" from which God would free those who converted.
The particular danger the powwows offered was their link to the Indians' past ways of worship. Their continuing practice of traditional
"meetings," "wayes," and "customes" is called "the strongest cord
that binds them to their own way, for the Pawwawes by their witchcraft keep them in feare." He describes a dozen people interested in
Christianity but unwilling to convert: "Such was their unspeakable
darknesse, their captivity in sin and bondage to the Pawwawes, that
they hardly durst for feare take the best way."[13]

Such a discussion of wicked Indian leaders and saintly English missionaries might suggest that the captivity motif is most readily found
in "frontier" mission literature in which English and Indians face off
against one another. But the missionary captivity story belongs fully
to the colonial contact zone, with its multiplicity of actors. Redemption was national as well as individual, for the English came to rescue
Indians not only from powwows and sachems but also from those familiar adversaries, the Spanish:

> Other Nations . . . have onely sought their owne advantage to possesse
> their Land, Transport their gold, and that with so much covetousnesse
> and cruelty, that they have made the name of Christianitie and of Christ
> an abomination, that the Lord should be pleased to make use of our
> Brethren that went forth from us to make manifest *the savour of Christ*
> among the people.[14]

The passage is a classic illustration of the English "Black Legend,"
the vilification of Catholic Spain as a New World tyrant. It also is an
expression of the English imperial rivalry that gave impetus to
Cromwell's Western Design. The translation of Las Casas's *Tears of
the Indians*, one of the key pieces of propaganda used to justify Anglo-
Spanish aggression, cited the Indians' "Tormenting Captivity" at the
hands of Spanish conquistadores, "by many degrees worse than that

of Algier or the Turkish Galleys."[15] Fear and tyranny, powwows and Catholics: America becomes in the mission descriptions a dark and fearsome place, a wilderness of sin that is very familiar to readers of later American literature, from Mary Rowlandson's narrative to Nathaniel Hawthorne's "Young Goodman Brown." But at this point, the Indians rather than the English are threatened.

This story of captive Indians and English redeemers can only work if all traces of Indian suffering or displacement at the hands of the English are suppressed. English colonists must be understood as standing in stark contrast to bad kings, whether Indian or Spanish. Judging from their confession narratives, however, Praying Indians do not understand their experiences as figuring in this colonizing narrative. We might expect to see the captivity trope appear in *Tears of Repentance* or *A further Account of the progress of the* Gospel, tracts that transcribe the confessions of faith Indians delivered before English church elders in hopes of founding their own church. After all, the rhetoric of captivity and redemption is a commonplace in Puritan salvation theology.[16] During King Philip's War, captivity narratives produced by white authors are easily and generically connected to the confession narrative through the trope of Babylonian captivity. The generic connections are direct. White authors' captivity narratives are formally linked to New England confession narratives; the spiritual journey to God was mirrored physically by captives' journey into the wilderness and their return—a doubled "redemption."[17] So we might expect that transcriptions of Indian confessions register a similar notion of their "captivity" to Satan and rescue by the English, especially since the idea was being circulated among English observers of the Puritan mission. And indeed, when William Leverich began preaching to Indians in New Plymouth during 1650 or 1651, he found at least one Indian convert who understood his spiritual state as captivity: "Another laying his hands upon his knees and hams, complains he was a man tyed in Cords, and prayes to God to be unloosed."[18]

Such a usage was rare, however. Christian Indians understandably did not see themselves as captives. They were hardly likely to view their former lives as captivity, and their preconversion state as Puritans defined it did not fit indigenous models of captivity.[19] Rather, in *Tears of Repentance*, the first tract to transcribe Indian confessions, the clearest reference to captivity comes not from the confessors but from Eliot. He likens the Indians' state in 1650 to a biblical type: "*When* Israel *was to return from* Babylon, *the Spirit by the word of*

Prophesie, raised up such actings of Faith."[20] In other words, the Indians' confessions on which he reports are signs that indicate, spiritually speaking, the return from heathen captivity typified by Israel's bondage in Babylon.

The terrible irony is that the English use of spiritual captivity to characterize Indian conversions completely overwrites Indian experiences.[21] For if Praying Indians were drawn to the theme of captivity, they would have been as likely to cast the English themselves as the adversary, a perspective that could not have met with approval from the English elders sitting in judgment of Indian confessors. Rather than make use of a captivity trope in their confessions, the Praying Indians concentrate on other personal afflictions. Family deaths, illness, deprivation—like the captivity described by later, more familiar colonial authors, these sufferings are brought on by sin, but the instrument is internal rather than external. There can be no sense of the confessors' present state as "captive." Instead, the narratives recount an orthodox denigration of the preconversion self.

Nevertheless, the speakers' descriptions of their earlier lives at times does mark their colonized state as a captivity—just not in the sense assumed by mission writers in previous publications. Rather than being subject to Satan, Indian speakers report that they felt hemmed in by Christians. For many, the decision to pray was reached when they realized that the only way to avoid giving up their lands was to convert to Christianity. Monequassun (who eventually became a schoolteacher at Natick) at first "scorned praying to God." When Christian evangelists came to his home he reports, "I still hated praying, and I did think of running away." But he stays and decides to pray "because I loved to dwell at that place."[22] Another confessor, Magus, feels similarly caught: "I could not find how to pray to God, and therefore I thought of going away; yet I also thought if I do go away, I shall lose my ground" (252). In his confession, recorded in *Further Account,* John Speen makes the link between colonization and conversion most directly: "And because I saw the *English* took much ground, and I thought if I prayed, the *English* would not take away my ground, for these causes I prayed."[23]

The confession of Nishohkou, also published in *Further Account,* provides especially eloquent testimony to the sacrifices of converts living within English bounds. He remembers a time when he and his family

prayed to many Gods, and many other sins we did, and all the people did
the same, both men and women, they lived in all lusts, they prayed to
every creature; the Sun, Moon, Stars, Sea, Earth, Fishes, Fowl, Beasts,
Trees, &c. all these things I saw when I was a youth, and all these things
I liked and loved to do, and was delighted with these things. (38)

Despite terming his past practices "sins" and "lusts," some sense of
previous happiness comes through in Nishohkou's litany of "every
creature" and his "delight" in them. He remembers that these ways
"were in my bones, and there grew." Despite his affection for these
ways, he decides to join the Praying Indian community, but his confession reveals the checks to his faith when the English colonists exercised their authority. He remembers the English coming one Sunday
to disarm Cutshamekin and his men—and wonders why they would
profane the Sabbath in this way (40). Later, he explains how he was
"troubled about our wants, poverty, and nakedness" (41).

Of course, he does find scripture comfort for such concerns: "Also I
heard that riches were the root of all evil, and *Dives* with his fine apparel and dainty fair, was in hell, and poor *Lazarus* was in heaven[24]:
When my heart is troubled about our Land and about riches, I quiet
my heart with these meditations" (41). On the one hand, this passage
illustrates a passivity that mission theology encouraged: he is com-
forted for his material poverty by the promise of a heavenly reward.
But, on the other hand, Nishohkou is recording colonial injustices. He
is often troubled about "our Land," that is, the rapidly eroding holdings of Algonquians or, perhaps even more specifically, that of the
Praying Indians with whom he identifies. His self-portrait is of a man
who finds his previous way of life untenable but who is also barred
from full enjoyment of the colonial economic and political order. He
is caught between the two possibilities and uses Christianity in an attempt to define a third way.

Reading against the grain, we can see that Praying Indian confessions indict the colonial order. Praying Indians are trapped by a new
colonial landscape. On the surface, however, these confessions are
quite orthodox, and English mission writers presented their testimony
simply as evidence of Indians' "unsettled" lifestyle, not of the Puritans' own encroachment. And so mission writers ignore even as they
record the converts' sense of the English rather than Satan as the cause
of misery.

Though a direct inscription of Indian captivity by the English is not found in the mission annals, one cannot avoid the connection of violence with the spiritual captivity and redemption so important to mission authors. In 1636–37, New England colonists fought a brief, bloody, total war against the Pequot people. When they won, the English colonial government tried to extinguish the Pequots entirely, by forbidding any individual to identify himself or herself as a Pequot and by enslaving any Pequot—man, woman, or child—captured during the conflict.[25] A great many of these people were transported to the West Indies or put into service in the colonies. Among those who were kept in service in New England was a man who became John Eliot's tutor and translator of Indian languages.[26]

It is tempting to speculate on the tutor's feelings about his work. Did he welcome it as relief from more strenuous labor? Was he simply happy to have remained in New England rather than being transported? Did working with a minister afford him any status in the colonies? Was this the only opportunity he had to speak his language, or had the years since the war lessened English fears of new Indian "conspiracies"? The mission tract that records his efforts gives us no clues. He is described as

> an *Indian* living with Mr. *Richard Calicott* of *Dorchester*, who was taken in the *Pequott* Warres, though belonging to *Long* Island; this *Indian* is ingenious, can read; and I taught him to write, which he quickly learnt, though I know not what use he now maketh of it: He was the first that I made use of to teach me words, and to be my Interpreter. Now of late, the Lord hath stirred up his heart to joyn unto the Church at *Dorchester*, and this day I am going to the Elders, meeting, to the examination and Tryall of this young man, in preparation for his admission into the Church.[27]

And so we learn the English master's name but not his own. We learn nothing of his present situation, whether he continues to translate, or of what his current duties consist. We learn nothing of his church examination, although we might imagine the connections he made between his servitude to Richard Calicott and his Christian faith. We learn nothing in this or subsequent tracts of his "trial" in a Puritan church. All we do learn is that he has decided to join that church. And from the point of view of colonial writers and readers, that is all that counts: this Pequot War prisoner had been rescued from the only captivity that mattered.

Doings and Sufferings

Although the missionary construction of Indians as Satan's captives left little room for converts to explore the relationship of their faith experiences to their political or even physical situation in the colonies, their spiritual confessions did create for the redeemed Praying Indian a place within in the colonial order. Praying towns were set aside for the use of converts, an Indian church was established, and mixed groups of Indians and English even observed some fast-days.[28] But in 1675, war broke out and such activities came to an end. The sachem Metacom, who had been so troublesome to the English in the early 1670s, yet who was recognized as the gracious, hopeful Philip in Eliot's *Indian Dialogues*, became the focus of New England's renewed anger. Although some historians have suggested that his leadership was not as complete as contemporary English observers thought,[29] hostile encounters between Plymouth colonists and Philip's Wampanoag followers seem to have touched off the wider violence. The Puritans perceived Philip as the leader of all their enemies. In January 1675, Sassamon, a Praying Indian who had been living with Philip as a scribe, preacher, and perhaps as a spy, died. In the spring, when Sassamon's body was found, English authorities concluded he had been murdered. In response, they arrested and executed three of Philip's men for the crime.[30]

Near the end of June 1675, Wampanoags attacked the town of Swansea in Plymouth. It is unclear who fired the first shot or who suffered the first fatality. But the violence quickly escalated when the colonies began to rally their forces, and Indians attacked remote settlers and burned outlying towns in Plymouth and Massachusetts. As the bloody war progressed, the colonists feared that they could not trust any Indian. By February 1676, the English believed that "all the praying Indians, except those secured on the islands, [were] with the enemy."[31] Despite some Indians' demonstrations of loyalty to the English, many colonists assumed that the entire Indian population, regardless of prior allegiances or protestations of friendship, had risen against the colonies. Some Praying Indians clearly took part in the war against the English. Not only do survivors of the attacks on Brookfield and Springfield testify that Praying Indians fought against them, but individuals also brought their mission training to Philip's service in other capacities.[32]

The supporters of Praying Indians recognized that colonists, enraged by what they saw as Christian Indians' treachery, would turn their anger on those Indians who remained within English bounds. These supporters warned converts to abandon the identity they had spent years constructing and learning to occupy, lest they become identified with enemy Indians and fall victims to the English. The term "Praying Indian" became a liability for a beleaguered people, who were incarcerated, attacked, and killed by white New Englanders who, a few years before, had benefitted from the image's ability to focus their colonial identities. As Daniel Gookin notes,

> The animosity and rage of the common people increased against them, that the very name of a praying Indian was spoken against, in so much, that some wise and principal men did advise some that were concerned with them, to forbear giving that epithet of praying.[33]

John Eliot, Daniel Gookin, and other interested New Englanders, as well as the faithful Praying Indians themselves, quickly understood that the undifferentiated hatred many colonists felt for all Indians could prove fatal not only to individual converts but to the missionary enterprise as a whole.

One of the saddest human consequences of the war was this wholesale persecution of converts by angry and fearful white colonists, which was accompanied by the rejection of the mission's earlier model of Indian captivity and Christian redemption. The Praying Indians' compromises, accommodations, and collaborations counted for little as garrisons were burnt and frontier settlers removed to better-protected Boston. The always precarious middle ground between settler-colonists and indigenous people that had been occupied by the Praying Indians, eroded completely. In *An Historical Account of the Doings and Sufferings of the Christian Indians,* Gookin quotes Joseph Tuckapawillin of Hassanamesit, a praying town:

> The English have taken away some of my estate, my corn, cattle, my plough, cart, chain and other goods. The enemy Indians have also taken a part of what I had; and the wicked Indians mock and scoff at me, say-

ing "Now what is become of your praying to God?" The English also censure me, and say I am a hypocrite. (504)

For faithful Praying Indians who allied themselves with English colonists, the war initially meant that popular white suspicion was to be accompanied by official colonial legislation restricting the Indians' movements. A few months after the start of the war, it meant the exile of men, women, and children to Deer Island in the Boston harbor, a place destitute of adequate food or shelter, as the Indians were enjoined from cutting live wood or killing any sheep in the island's herds. Even then, relocated and incarcerated as they were, Praying Indians were subject to both "vulgar" and official threats. Gookin reports that after the enemy burned the town of Medfield, Massachusetts, some colonists called for mob vengeance: "Oh come, let us go down to Deer Island, and kill all the praying Indians" (494). Colonial authorities took the feelings of the general populace seriously. In February, the General Court considered what measures they should take against the new residents of Deer Island. Gookin reports that they included in their deliberations the possibilities of destroying or enslaving them.[34]

Eventually, colonial authorities realized that Praying Indians could be usefully integrated into their war effort. Converts Tom Dublett and Peter Conway negotiated Mary Rowlandson's release from captivity.[35] Job Kattenanit and James Quamapokit served as spies among the enemy. Other converts acted as scouts or fought alongside English troops. Their service did something to blunt English rage against them.[36] But this recovery of a few individuals' reputations did not translate into a more general rehabilitation of the Praying Indians' image. Rather, from the loose collection of animosities set free by wartime violence, a counterimage emerged that turned the figure of the Praying Indian on its head and discredited the characteristics that missionaries had identified as belonging to their converts.

Gookin's writings can serve as a window on this discursive shift in pre- and postwar literature. An official of the General Court, a member of the Massachusetts militia, and an Indian superintendent, Gookin wrote two histories of the Praying Indians. The differences in his accounts reflect the abrupt reversal of colonial public sentiment toward Indian converts during the war.[37] His first account, *Historical Collections of the Indians of New England* (1674), documents missionaries' success and promises further achievement. The second, *An Historical Account of the Doings and Sufferings of the Christian In-*

dians (1677), was written for the New England Company, the society charged with overseeing new England missions. In it, Gookin attempts to counter the vilification of Praying Indians fed by rumors and by the stories of returning English captives. His accounts can be used to measure just how thoroughly the image was discredited by literature created during and just after the war.

Virtually until the first shots were fired in June 1675, missionaries confidently described the figure of the Praying Indian as valuable and important. As late as 1674, Gookin had no qualms about writing a report praising the thousand or so converts living in praying towns and asserting the importance of the Praying Indian to New England. Although it remained unpublished in his lifetime, his *Historical Collections*, like earlier mission tracts, was an attempt to publicize evangelism to an English audience and to win continuing support for the effort. Gookin addressed the tract to Robert Boyle and the New England Company, and he dedicated it to Charles II.

Nearly thirty years after New England first encouraged systematic evangelism, proselytizing remained, in Gookin's view, a promising means of transforming Indian rulers into amenable English subjects. Gookin supports Eliot's fictionalized portrait of the sachem Philip in *Indian Dialogues* with his own hopeful description:

> There are some that have hopes of their greatest and chiefest sachem, named Philip, living at Pawkunnawkutt. . . . [He] is a person of good understanding and knowledge in the best things. I have heard him speak very good words, arguing that his conscience is convicted: but yet though his will is bowed to embrace Jesus Christ, his sensual and carnal lusts are strong bands to hold him fast under Satan's dominions.[38]

Satan's dominions may be vast and his bands strong, but Gookin believed that even the most recalcitrant Indians could be rescued by Christianity. The Mohawks, for instance, are "a stout, yet cruel people; much addicted to bloodshed and cruelty." And so, "It were a most desirable thing, to put forth our utmost endeavours to civilize, and convert these Indians to the knowledge of the gospel: which is the only means to turn this curse into a blessing."[39] Rather than violently subduing the Mohawks, Gookin advocates bringing them within the sphere of English influence by Christianizing them. Conversion rescues them from their violent "addictions" and is more to be desired than a conquest that kills the captives, but leaves the real enemy—Satan—unscathed. Once converted, the Mohawks would be subject to English rule no less than to the English God. Like Philip in *Indian Dialogues,* even if they only become knowledgeable of the Gospel rather than experiencing a full conversion, they would be more "inclined" to the English and their ways. In 1674, the political as well as the spiritual and political possibilities of conversion remained open.

Gookin has good news to report to metropolitan supporters: he describes a successful mission, arguing that converted Indians are easily distinguished from those who had not yet embraced English ways and faith. As a group, Gookin reports, converts have a clear-cut identity. They are "the civilized and religious Indians, which I shall denominate by the name of Praying Indians." This name is "a title generally understood."[40] Unconverted Indians, he insists, abuse alcohol, and they dress only in a blanket and loincloth.[41]

Indeed, he reports, the physical appearance of Praying Indians is so consistently anglicized that it can be used to distinguish them from other Indians and to protect them. He includes an account of the arrest in 1665 of several Mohawks who had been harassing Praying Indians living in Massachusetts. The court releases the Mohawks with the injunction not "to kill and destroy any of the Indians under our protection, that lived about forty miles from us on every side: which they might distinguish from other Indians, by their short hair, and wearing English fashioned apparel."[42] Clearly, Gookin and the Court do not hesitate as late as 1674 to assert an absolute, recognizable difference between Praying and unconverted Indians. Throughout *Historical Collections,* Gookin cheerfully details the accomplishments of New England evangelists since 1646, apparently little anticipating the violence that was shortly to engulf not only the praying towns under his supervision but all of New England as well.

Sometime between 1674 and 1677, when Gookin wrote his two accounts, he lost this confidence in the ability of outsiders—whether Indian or English—to judge converts by their appearances. During the war, Gookin witnessed the rise of anti-Indian sentiments among English colonists and was aware of the English publication of a counter-image of the converts as perfidious hypocrites. In his account, he enters a transatlantic discussion of Indians and the war, offering a more positive account of the mission and the Praying Indian image. His work is remarkable among reports of the war because it purports to chronicle an Indian perspective on the conflict, albeit that of a safely subject Indian population. Gookin attempts a defense of the Indians who have been under his watch, both those who have remained unquestionably faithful and those who joined their kinfolk among Philip's forces, such as the Indians from the praying town of Hassanemesit.[43]

Gookin's strategy is twofold. First, he relies on a distinction between Praying Indians and the enemy. This war, he reminds his readers, began between the "barbarous heathen" and the English and should not reflect on "the poor Christian Indians" who have "acquitted themselves courageously and faithfully," as their English military commanders attest.[44] By insisting that, while some are barbarians, other Indians are in fact valuable English allies, Gookin returns to mission arguments that good or evil does not exclusively characterize any one people; the English themselves are capable of passionate and sinful acts. In a striking reversal of English charges against Indians, Gookin accuses Dedham residents of treachery against their Natick Indian neighbors. An abandoned house on the outskirts of Dedham was burned, supposedly by apostate Praying Indians. Gookin doubts their agency:

> This house, in all probability, was set on fire a purpose by some that were back friends to those poor Indians; thereby to take an occasion to procure the removal of all those Indians from Natick; the contrivers whereof well knew that the magistrates generally were very slow to distrust those poor Christians, this artifice was therefore used to provoke them. (472)

The burnt house is a calculated move in the old Dedham-Natick land dispute.[45] Incidents such as these "infect" the "common people" with what he terms a "spirit of enmity" against all Indians.[46] Moreover, the actions of the Dedhamites are paralleled by the efforts of enemy Indians who hope to divide Christian Indians and the English in order to gain allies.[47] In this context of mounting English suspicion toward Praying Indians, the defection of a few converts "had a tendency to exasperate the English against all Indians, that they would admit no distinction between one Indian and another." Worse yet, "They accounted it a crime in any man to say that they hoped some of those Indians were pious persons."[48]

Gookin's second line of defense flatly contradicts his prewar belief that Praying Indians and unconverted Indians could easily be judged by their appearance. Most damning to the reputation and treatment of

Praying Indians during the war is the eyewitness testimony of redeemed or escaped captives. Gookin does not wish to discredit the captives' reports, but he does suggest that they may have been mistaken:

> Accusations came against some of them by English captives escaped,
> that some of them were in arms against the English, (how true those
> charges were God only knows, for 'tis very difficult, unless upon long
> knowledge, to distinguish Indians from one another). (492)

This suggestion of indistinguishability among Indians directly coun-
ters a long-standing mission rhetoric of difference. Gookin's defense
requires two responses from English observers outside the mission
field if his argument is to stand. They must first admit the possibility
of difference between converts and other Indians, then concede that
they are not able to recognize this difference for themselves (no matter how extensive their personal experiences of Indians). Second, these
observers must agree to rely exclusively on Gookin, Eliot, or other advocates of Praying Indians—the Englishmen with the proper, sustained contact with Praying Indians that, Gookin asserts, is necessary
to distinguish friend from foe.

Thus Gookin continues Eliot's strategy of positioning missionaries
(especially himself) as the only reliable witnesses of events, even to
the point of challenging the reports of captives, whose accounts themselves turn on the power of the eyewitness. Consider Mary Rowlandson's evocative distinction between hearing about and witnessing
horror:

> Now is that dreadfull hour come, that I have often heard of (in time of
> War, as it was the case of others), but now mine eyes see it. Some in our
> house were fighting for their lives, others wallowing in their blood, the
> House on fire over our heads, and the bloody Heathen ready to knock us
> on the head, if we stirred out. Now might we hear Mothers and Chil-
> dren crying out for themselves, and one another, *Lord, What shall we
> do?*[49]

Much less rhetorically effective is Gookin's witness to the loyalty
rather than cruelty of the Praying Indians, spoken to a people either
enduring loss and grief or voyeuristically eager for sensational stories.
What is more, the argument for faithfulness comes from a writer who
had recently reported that Philip, leader of the enemy forces, was near-

ing conversion and was "inclined" toward the English and their way of life. After the war's depredations, few colonists would have agreed with Gookin's conclusions, even if they had read his unpublished account.

"Preying" Indians

That Gookin's account went unpublished signals a significant shift in colonial Indian representation. From 1643 to 1674, mission writings had been controlled by John Eliot, the Commissioners for the United Colonies, and Puritan clergymen. During the war, the mission discourse became available to other authors. The changing articulation and reception of the figure of the Praying Indian not only manifests an understandable hostility to the enemy, but it also documents the access to the Indian discourse by previously silent (or silenced) colonists, who may never have been supportive of mission ideals or convinced by mission rhetoric of Indian regeneracy. Suddenly, we find writers other than missionaries reporting on the conduct and motivation of Indians in New England. One such writer was Nathaniel Saltonstall, a "merchant of Boston," whose sensational, anti-Indian accounts of the war were published in London papers.[50] Wartime chronicles written and published both in New England and London demonstrate that in the 1670s, the Praying Indian was a contested figure who permeated the imaginations of the royal observer, the noncombatant, the pragmatic merchant, the colonial soldier, the orthodox Puritan clergyman, and captive woman alike.

Increasingly, outsiders to the orthodox Puritan elite wrote for an English audience decidedly unsympathetic to rigid Puritan doctrine or political rule. Observers hostile to New England noted the presence of Praying Indians among the enemy and imputed the war to vigorous conversion efforts. In a letter dated 1676, the royal commissioner Edward Randolph reports to the Council of Trade in London that some in New England attributed the conflict

> to an imprudent zeal in the Magistrates of Boston to christianise those heathens, before they were civilized, and enjoining them to the strict observation of their laws, which to people rude and licentious, hath proved even intollerable; and that the more, for while the Magistrates for their profit severely putt the laws in execution against the Indians, the peo-

ple on the other side for lucre and gain intice and provoke the Indians to
the breach thereof.[51]

Randolph reported as well that even those Indians thought to be
civilized and Christian joined with those who had overtly resisted
evangelism: "The praying Indians have been the most barbarous enemies."[52] His report on the "imprudent zeal" of Boston magistrates
took hold; many believed that New England's interlocking system of
evangelism and civil control had provoked the Indians to violence.
Some, such as the Quaker writers Edward Wharton and John Easton,
were openly critical of the Puritans' conduct.[53] Other colonial writers
responded to the pressure of royal criticism and English public opinion by praising English soldiers and offering justification for the war.
They saved their condemnation for Indians, including converts, characterizing Eliot's evangelism as misguided and naïve rather than self-
serving and tyrannical. These writers, including Saltonstall, Thomas
Wheeler, a military captain, and Benjamin Tompson, a teacher and
poet, as well as numerous private letter writers, may have always been
suspicious of Indian evangelism.

Mary Pray, a resident of Providence, wrote to Captain James Oliver
in October 1675, asking for the latest news and offering her own report. Her description of the actions of Praying Indians hints at the
information shared among colonists and between America and England—exchanges that helped to vilify Praying Indians. She reports rumors that Praying Indians aided the enemy even when they appeared
to fight for the English:

> The Indians boast and say those Indians that are caled praying Indians
> never shut [sic, "shoot"] at the other Indians, but up into the tops of the
> trees or into the ground; and when they make shew of going first into
> the swamp they comonly give the Indians noatis how to escape the En-
> glish.[54]

Compare Pray's letter to the letter written by the Rhode Island entre-
preneur William Harris to his friends in England. He confirms her information:

> Some of them called christians and pretended devotion Sometimes gott
> powder and gave or solde it to the enemy Indeans and throw it under
> trees for the enemy to take it and when they goe with the English against

other Indeans some of them shoote up into the tope of the trees as other Indeans have discovered. And Sometimes those called Christian Indeans run away to the enemy a company of fifty or threescore together with other notorious tricks.[55]

The similarity of these letters—both report on the Praying Indians shooting into the trees rather than enemy—suggests the way eyewitness testimony and even pure conjecture circulated within the colonies and across the Atlantic.

By the end of 1676, colonial English forces claimed victory in King Philip's War, but their success had cost all participants considerably. In an unspeakable tragedy for Native peoples, Algonquians suffered nearly forty percent casualties. The war was also one of the most devastating colonial conflicts for settlers: the English lost one in every sixteen men of fighting age, and many outlying English towns were burnt and abandoned.[56] As Slotkin and Folsom note, so widespread was the suffering, "virtually every community and every family would partake of the common grief."[57] To most New Englanders, their losses and suffering had a clear cause: the essentially treacherous nature of their Indian adversaries.

It was at the point of months-long grief and suffering that New England divines began to write about the conflict. Increase Mather, minister at North Church in Boston, and William Hubbard, minister at Ipswich, Massachusetts, attempted to make sense of the war in larger histories rather than provide yet another of the hasty eyewitness accounts characteristic of earlier wartime writings. Indeed, Increase Mather tells us that he takes pen in hand to correct other writers' mistakes, and he is zealous in correcting all manner of errors, from periwigs to more serious breaches of the covenant with God. Although Mather is by no stretch of the imagination pro-Indian, he does approve of the missions. He begins his history with a letter to the reader that reaffirms the mission impulse, calling evangelism "a main design of the *Fathers* of this *Colony*."[58] And perhaps the war itself, he conjectures, "may be to punish us for our too great neglect in this matter."[59]

However supportive of previous mission goals he may have been, Mather did not speak for many during the war when he preached doom for the excesses of the colony, in his sermons or in this text, which did not sell well.[60] Rather, the work of his fellow minister and rival William Hubbard reflected popular opinion more closely. Hubbard asserts in his *Narrative of the Troubles* the beliefs shared by most New Englanders. There is, he declares, an absolute difference between colonists and Indians: "Subtilety, Malice, and Revenge, seems to be as inseperable from [the Indians], as if it were Part of their Essence."[61] Given the Indians' natural treachery, it is hopeless to expect or encourage the reformation—civil or spiritual—hitherto promised by missionaries. Observing the regular outbreaks of violence between English settlers and coastal Indians throughout colonial history, he comments:

> It is hoped that we shall after a few more Experiences of this Nature learn to beware of this subtle Brood, and Generation of Vipers. Ever since *Enmity was put between the Seed of the Woman, and the Seed of the Serpent,* it hath been the Portion of her Seed in every Generation, and in every Nation, to meet with the sad effects of that Enmity; nor can they ever expect to find better dealing from any of the other Sort, further than either Fear of their Power, or Hope of Benefit by their Favour, may induce them to another Disposition. (vol. 2, 95–96)

Although in this passage the English may create a more tractable Indian population by overawing Indians merely with the "Fear of [English] Power" or by bribing them, more direct violence lurks below the surface. After all, in Genesis 3, the proper response of humankind is to crush the serpent that bites. Hubbard's vitriol demonstrates how little force mission rhetoric retained at the end of the war, when even clerical writers turned against Christian Indians. The revision of New England's errand around evangelism had come to an end.

Appropriating Mission Representations

As the letters by William Harris and Mary Pray and the seemingly easy acquiescence of William Hubbard to Praying Indians' vilification demonstrate, the apostasy of Praying Indians, whether witnessed or rumored, fed the imaginations of fearful colonists and English observers. Although eventually the captivity narratives of white women would come to characterize the form, during and just after the war Mary Rowlandson and other writers necessarily draw on and respond to the missionaries' literary precedent of Praying Indians as spiritual captives. From roughly 1643 until 1674, successful propagandists touted the English redemption of Indians from Satanic captivity. And for English readers, the most publicized route Indians took to literacy or to religious and technological transculturation was through the institutions of Indian evangelism that made their spiritual redemption possible. Hence, whenever Indians exhibit mixed cultural signs in wartime literature, the most immediate model is the Praying Indian as described in mission tracts; anti-Indian narratives must dismantle those earlier, laudatory descriptions of Christian Indians to gain credibility for their negative representations. In other words, although most wartime authors attempt to debunk missionaries' praise of Christian Indians, they nevertheless draw on the same tropes and the same "cultural logic" that structured earlier evangelical literature.[62]

In 1677, Benjamin Tompson penned dedicatory verses to William Hubbard's history of King Philip's War. In his poem, Tompson recites a catalogue of genres that make up the literature of English-Indian contact, culminating in Hubbard's history. Beginning with exploration and conquest writings, the list moves on, briefly, to evangelical and linguistic treatments before turning to warfare:

> Former Adventurers did at best beguile,
> About these Natives Rise (obscure as *Nile*)
> Their grand Apostle writes of their Return,
> *William's* their Language; *Hubbard* how they burn,
> Rob, Kill and Roast, Lead Captive, Slay, Blaspheme.[63]

Whatever recognition Tompson affords the first categories of encounter, he places the rhetorical weight of his catalogue on the last form. From his perspective, this form provides the most accurate representation of English-Indian relations and perhaps even acts as a corrective to earlier, more naïve writings. War histories seem, in his characterization, quite different from the earlier genres. However, his description of Hubbard's history hints at an important relationship between wartime representations of Indians and previous depictions. Whatever the demonic or barbaric qualities that Puritans believed could enable Indians to burn, rob, kill, and roast English settlements and English bodies, only a mission-inculcated familiarity with the colonists' religious faith enabled Indians to blaspheme the English God.

To be sure, we see in war literature some representations of Indians that make no reference to the mission tradition. Some writers resort to animal analogies in their descriptions of Indians.[64] Others noted the Indians' method of warfare (which the English termed "skulking"), made it impossible for the English to discern their adversaries, who concealed themselves in trees and bushes. Gookin claims this confusion was deliberate: "The enemy also used this stratagem, to apparel themselves from the waist upwards with green boughs, that our Englishmen could not readily discern them from the natural bushes."[65]

Sometimes this strategy led the English to injure one another, which suggests that English forces may themselves have adopted camouflaging tactics. Then again, they may simply have blundered upon one another while seeking shelter during battle. Increase Mather describes the swamp fight of December 19, 1675, in which the English forces "if they did but see a Bush stir would fire presently, whereby 'tis verily feared, that they did sometimes unhappily shoot *English men* instead of *Indians*."[66] Benjamin Tompson's poetic rendering of this confusion takes these tactics to the extreme. In his 1676 poem *New Englands Crisis*, the forest itself attacks English soldiers:

> The trees stood sentinels and bullets flew
> From every bush (a shelter for their crew).
> Hence came our wounds and deaths from every side
> While skulking enemies squat undescried,
> That every stump shot like a musketeer,
> And bows with arrows every tree did bear.[67]

Enemy or shrubbery: the blurring of these boundaries was confusing, but not completely so. After all, Indians could, finally, be distinguished from the landscape. A more menacing confusion involved non-Christian Indians and Praying Indians, because that distinction could not as easily be made; yet, to mistake the enemy for the convert was to invite death.

If until 1675 mission literature was dedicated to identifying the differences between Praying Indians and their unconverted brethren, wartime literature continually asserted the confusion of friend and foe, "praying" and "heathen." That uncertainty was often expressed in terms taken from mission rhetoric. In Saltonstall's *Present State of New-England*, the author describes English fears "because they cannot know a Heathen from a Christian by his Visage, nor Apparel."[68] Especially distressing to these writers and disorienting to English forces is the presence in enemy ranks of mission-educated Indians who could read and write, were familiar with Puritan forms of worship, understood and spoke English, and had other skills that seventeenth-century English commentators recognized as "civilized." Perhaps the most shocking and frightening aspect of the war for its contemporary historians was the adaptation of English technologies and belief systems by Indian foes for their own purposes. In this way, wartime writings have a continuing literary link to earlier missionary representations.

In *Present State of New-England,* Saltonstall describes the role he assigned to converts during the war:

> They that wear the Name of *Praying Indians,* but rather (as Mr. *Hezekiah Ushur* termed *Preying-Indians*) they have made Preys of much *English* Blood, but now they are all reduced to their several Confinements; which is much to a general Satisfaction in that respect.[69]

This play on words is more than an example of linguistic wit. By transforming the "praying Indian" of evangelism literature into an Indian who preyed on English blood, Saltonstall is remaking the mission figure. The traits that had described Christian converts during an age of an imminent millennium were now seen as marking treachery. In much the same way that Puritan anagrammatists probed names to uncover truths about the life and faith of the recently deceased, this punning reversal reveals to the Puritan reader the whole truth of a no-longer viable Indian identity.[70]

War writers turned earlier tracts' representations of Praying Indians against them. Broken English, mixed dress, Indian literacy—these and other signs of transculturation were equated with the camouflaging bushes and trees. In these writers' view, such traits concealed Indians' perfidy and enabled them to attack and outrage the English. The author of *A Farther Brief and True Narration of the Late Wars Risen in New-England* claims that "most of our mischiefs have flowed from pretended Friends; who have Demeaned themselves exceeding fairly with us till they have had the opportunity secretly and suddainly to endamage us; and then they fly to our avowed Adversaries." These pretended friends hide themselves among Praying Indians; and the author worries that English wrath toward these apostate Indians may serve to "Condemn the Innocent with the Guilty" and bring down on the colonists "the guilt of blotting out the Interest of the Gospel amon[g]st the *Indians.*"[71]

Having joined the forces arrayed against the English, the Praying Indians who continue to display a "civilized" appearance inspire the English with a false sense of security. Before the war, missionaries repeatedly pointed to English-style clothing as a sign of Indians' reformation. In war literature, a "civilized" appearance becomes an enemy Indian's disguise rather than an external manifestation of inward grace. Wearing the clothes as well as the names of Christian converts, Indians draw the English in only to attack them. William Hubbard reports that "a Lad keeping Sheep, was shot at by an *Indian* that wore a Sign, as if he had been a Friend: the *Indian* was supposed to belong to the *Hassanemesit Indians*, at that Time confined to *Malberough*, where they had Liberty to dwell in a Kind of Fort."[72]

In *New Englands Crisis*, Benjamin Tompson makes use of many mission-derived traits to caricature Philip and his followers, including their desire for and use of English dress. English clothing becomes the booty for covetous Indian forces rather than the reward for pious Indian converts; the appropriation of English clothing becomes emblematic of Indian warriors as English soldiers chase "straggling bluecoats" into swamps.[73] At this point in the poem, Tompson may intend to imply a reversal of the Indians' successes during the first stage of the war, because in an earlier rallying speech, clothing heads the list of promises Philip makes to induce warriors to join him:

> Now if you'll fight I'll get you English coats,
> And wine to drink out of their captains' throats.
> The richest merchants' houses shall be ours,
> We'll lie no more on mats or dwell in bowers.[74]

Philip's promises not only replace the mission tradition of gifting Indian converts with English goods and clothing, but they also ironically reverse English practices as reported in accounts sent to London. The author of *A Brief and True Narration* notes that Connecticut used clothing as wartime bounty; the colony promised to give allied Indian soldiers "20 Coats for *Philip*, and one a piece for each of his men, that they shall kill"[75]

In terms of linguistic rather than physical representation, we witness in the narratives and poems written during and just after the war a radical shift in Indian speech. Williams, Eliot, and others who used Indian "broken English" in mission writings did so within a context of "broken-heartedness" and "plain speech." In their writings, dialect was meant to connote authentic expression as well as to invoke the reader's sympathy, as when a newly affected Indian convert hung his head in despair, saying "mee little know Jesus Christ."[76] After hostilities began, when others begin to provide the eyewitness, front-line accounts for which Eliot had been so well known, they adapted his representational tactics but not his sympathies or motivations. In war literature, Hubbard, Tompson, and Saltonstall rely on a more stylized and crude language to alienate readers from the Indian characters.

The revaluation of mission tracts' linguistic representation is especially clear in William Hubbard's account of Benjamin Church's battlefield "converts." These Indians had fought for the enemy and, once captured, had been persuaded to join Church's troops. On approaching an Indian village, one such former enemy points to a wigwam and tells Church

> that was *his Fathers Wigwam*, and ask'd if he must now go and *kill his Father?* No saith Captain *Church*, do but shew me where he is and I will deal with him; do you fall upon some others: to which the said Indian only replyed in broken English. That *very good Speak.*[77]

Hubbard here first explicitly identifies the Indian's expression as broken English, then goes on to gloss it with his understanding of the moment's deeper significance:

> whereby their natural Perfidiousness even to their nearest Relations may be observed, which makes their Treachery towards us their Foreign Neighbours, the less to be wondred at. And therefore till they be reduced to more Civility, some wise Men are ready to fear Religion will not take much Place amongst the Body of them. (276)

This comment on the anecdote pointedly rejects decades of evangelical claims. Eliot and others had, from the beginning, made exactly the same assessment about the potential for Indian conversion, linking "civility" to Indian conversion. But of course, missionaries had also been providing specific evidence of Praying Indians' civility, including their use of the English language, "broken" or not. Hubbard, naturally, rejects these claims. Nor does he recognize that this man had very little choice of how and against whom to wage war or that Church demands his assistance in finding and killing the father—or for that matter, that we have only Church's version of the encounter. Taken prisoner on the battlefield, the Indian soldier obviously assumes that the English would demand such an act of filial betrayal by one of their new "allies." The man's speech may simply express his relief on discovering that he will not be asked to kill his father. Regardless, Hubbard makes clear that as a marker of cultural or religious transformation, English-language skills are apparently meaningless. His particular care to note the man's mode of expression associates it with the profound betrayal of his father and of notions of Christian civility.

Salstonstall's *Present State of New–England* presents one of the most extreme examples of broken English recorded in the war literature. The assumption underlying *Present State* is that both friendly and enemy Indians spoke or understood English, a belief that severs the mission movement's connection of English (however imperfectly used) to regeneracy. Saltonstall reports that in the heat of battle, Captain Samuel Moseley took off his wig and then records the Indians' response: "As soon as the *Indians* saw that, they fell a Howling and Yelling most hideously, and said, *Umh, umh me no stawmerre fight Engis mon, Engis mon get two hed Engis mon got two hed; if me cut off un hed, he got noder, a put on beder as dis;* with such like words in broken *English*."[78] Recent scholarly treatment of passages such as this indicates the necessity for a cultural analysis of Indians' speech in mediated sources, such as mission tracts. Linguists, for instance, have used English reports of Indian speech to develop a history of American Indian Pidgin English. Yet Saltonstall's linguistic representation is radically opposed to that of contemporary mission writers, and must be treated differently.[79]

Saltonstall intends more than a faithful transcription of the Indians' actual language. He draws attention to the form of the speech by admitting it is an approximation: the Indians spoke "such like words." What is more important, he conveys a sense of linguistic inadequacy. Broken English is of a piece with "howling" and hideous "yelling." Furthermore, the Indians' astonishment at the sight of such a common English item as Moseley's wig underscores their ignorance of "civilized" norms and contradicts the evangelists' assertions that anglicized Indians were familiar with and valued English apparel.

The strangeness of this incident also reflects the wartime controversy in New England between ministers and magistrates, clergy and merchants over English standards of behavior and dress. In October 1675, just a month before *Present–State* was published, the General Court passed a law to suppress "proud Excesses in Apparel, hair, etc." Increase Mather in particular railed against "monstrous and horrid *Perriwigs*."[80] And Mather laid blame for the war at least partly at the feet of greedy merchants who exploited and debauched the Indians. As a "merchant of Boston," Saltonstall may be using this incident to counter such attacks. Not only does a valiant and successful Indian fighter such as Captain Moseley wear a wig, but the enemy are frightened and dismayed by it. Saltonstall asserts a laughable naïveté on the part of enemy Indians, despite the common understanding that Praying Indians, who were likely to have been used to Englishmen and their wigs, numbered among the enemy.[81]

The English military leader most admired by an author committed to an extreme vilification of Indians is Captain Samuel Moseley, a notorious Indian hater. Moseley acknowledged no difference between loyal and apostate Praying Indians; so, too, Saltonstall lumps together friend and foe.[82] He makes no linguistic distinction between enemies, who can scarcely recognize articles of English clothing from parts of English bodies, and friendly Indians, who mingle among English colonists in their towns or fight with them on the battlefield. In a later passage, Saltonstall links an equally extreme example of Indian dialect to cannibalism. At an Indian's execution, an English-allied Indian observer rushes to suck the blood of the executed man. When asked why, he replies, "*Umh, Umh, nu* Me stronger as I was before, me be so strong as me and he too, he be ver strong Man fore he die."[83] In Saltonstall's account, Indians who speak English betray themselves as uncivilized and alien rather than demonstrating, as missionaries had insisted, the meaningful reformation of belief or behavior.

The passing of dialect representation from narratives and histories into the realm of poetry signals the symbolic importance of broken English to New England's understanding of the war. Benjamin Tompson devotes a section of his *New England's Crisis* to direct "quotation" of Philip. He makes his Philip concerned primarily with drinking, raping, and the English punishment of these sins. Philip, whom Tompson calls a "greasy lout," says:

> This no wunnegin, so big matchit law,
> Which our old fathers' fathers never saw.
> These English make and we must keep them too,
> Which is too hard for them or us to do,
> We drink we so big whipped, but English they
> Go sneep, no more, or else a little pay.
> Me meddle squaw me hanged, our fathers kept
> What squaws they would, whether they waked or slept.[84]

In recent appraisals, critics have generally discussed this speech as an instance of literary verisimilitude shedding little light either on Tompson's attitude toward Native Americans or his aesthetics of representation.[85] Wayne Franklin suggests that "our understanding of Philip's 'harangue' is hindered by the very raciness of speech which makes it seem real and convincing."[86] Franklin attributes the speech's realism to Tompson's familiarity with Roger Williams' *A Key into the Language of America*, in which Williams defines both "wunnegin" and "matchit." But there is more here than a lively realism. Given John Eliot's earlier representation of Philip in *Indian Dialogues*, or even Mary Rowlandson's contemporaneous descriptions, both of which present Philip as a fluent speaker, what constitutes "realism" in wartime literature must be questioned.[87]

Tompson's representation is fully intelligible only with reference to the figure of the Praying Indian. Philip's speech in *New England's Crisis* begins with verses in which he reminds his audience that their fathers foolishly "sell our land to Englishmen who teach / Our nation all so fast to pray and preach." Thus, Tompson's Philip attributes the war to colonial or imperial expansion masked by Christian evangelism. Tompson may have heard the reports, addressed primarily to an English audience, that Massachusetts authorities had abused the Indians and thereby provoked them. By putting such sentiments into Philip's mouth, he discredits them.

New Englands Tears, a poem printed in London along with prose accounts of war news, shows that Tompson was well aware of the transatlantic interest in Indians and conversion. He assumes that he speaks to an audience familiar with (and hitherto supportive of) New England evangelism, and he does not wish to discourage continued economic support:

> Least such *Moecaenas's* beyond Sea should,
> Restrain their yearly showrs of Goods and Gold,
> Be pleas'd to know there is an hopeful race,
> Who as you oft have been inform'd have grace.
> These are confin'd under Christian Wings,
> And hopes we have never to feel their stings.
> A natural Prison wall'd with Sea and Isles,
> From our Metropolis not many miles,
> Contains their swarms. . . .[88]

Tompson undercuts his affirmation of Christian Indians here. Although English readers may have been "inform'd" of converts' faith, Praying Indians must be confined by Christianity and by Deer Island— the "natural prison." Puritan grace sits uneasily on them, and Puritan colonists uneasily await the day when they may break out of Christian bonds and sting the settlers. Captivity—confinement "under Christian wings"—is here considered natural and necessary.

Tompson's treatment of Philip's speech in *New Englands Crisis* responds to the assumption of some English observers that the Indians' exposure to English missionaries and Puritan doctrine had not prompted regeneracy but instead had provoked a hatred of the English and their ways that was expressed violently. Writers from across the political landscape noted incidents in which Indians' violence was directed in particular toward Christian symbols or representatives. Even writers who favored Indian evangelism, such as Increase Mather and Daniel Gookin, believed that some Indians' anti-Christian sentiments contributed to the conflict. They pointed out that pious Praying Indians were primary objects of the heathens' rage and, as I discuss in chapter 7, attributed John Sassamon's death, which for the English marked the opening of hostilities, to Indians' hatred of Christianity. Gookin called Sassamon the "first Christian martyr of the Indians."[89]

Writers more indifferent to missions slight Sassamon's death, but symbols of Christianity receive similarly violent treatment from Indians in nearly every account. Hubbard reports that Bibles are torn and scattered "in Hatred of our Religion therein revealed."[90] The author of *News from New England* reports that "these devillish Enemies of Religion seeing a man, woman, and their Children, going but towards a meeting-house, Slew them (as they said) because they thought they Intended to go thither." These writers also read Mary Rowlandson's abduction as a specific attack on her husband, the Reverend Joseph Rowlandson, minister at Lancaster. *News from New England* reports Rowlandson's abduction chiefly so that the readers "shall understand the Damnable antipathy [Indians] have to Religion and Piety."[91] This charge is repeated by Saltonstall in *A New and Further Narrative*. He reports on Rowlandson so that his readers "may perceive the malicious hatred these Infidels have to Religion and Piety."[92] These interpretations of the captivity, however, presuppose the Indians' knowledge of Mary Rowlandson's importance (or that of her husband) in terms of religious authority or New England's social hierarchy. Indians with this understanding must have had an intimate knowledge of English customs and religion, a familiarity heretofore ascribed to Praying Indians.

Tellingly, Indians in war literature are knowledgeable enough about English prayers and piety to outrage English sensibilities, not just by their capture of Rowlandson but also by the manner in which they repeatedly undermine English morale. Mather reports that after burning the house of worship in Groton, which they single out for destruction, Indians taunted the Reverend Willard, pastor of the congregation there: *"What will you do for a house to pray in now we have burnt your Meeting-house?"*[93] In battle, Indians hear and understand the English commanders' shouts of encouragement to their own men, yelling back that "God is against them, and for the *Indians."*[94] Thomas Wheeler reports that when Captain Simon Davis encouraged his men with the assurance "that *God is with us, and fights for us, and will deliver us,"* the Indians *"shouted and scoffed* saying: now see how *your God delivers you."*[95] *A Farther Brief and True Narration* reports that "our Enemies proudly exult over us and Blaspheme the name of our Blessed God; Saying, *Where is your O God?* taunting at the Poor Wretches, which . . . they cruelly Torture to Death."[96] The syntax here indicates an imperfect command of the language but suggests that the Indians are calling out a familiar English phrase; the tract's author is not silently substituting a translation.

Simple mimicry could account for the taunts that mirror the English soldiers' own words. But such representations suggest the authors' belief that Praying Indians—bilingual and knowledgeable about Christian practices and beliefs—were among enemy troops and so were responsible for blasphemies and religious outrages.

More revealing than the battlefield cries that echo the English or that make a general reference to God are those moments when enemy Indians specifically parody Christian prayer. The author of *A True Account* notes that on capturing an "elderly *English* man," an Indian offered up an "insulting" prayer: *"Come Lord Jesus, save this poor English man if thou canst, whom I am now about to Kill."*[97] Hubbard alludes to such insults when he hopes that near the end of the war, when the Indians must have been aware of impending defeat, they may themselves have understood their fate as divine punishment:

> Whether it were by any Dread that the Almighty sent upon their execrable Blasphemies, which 'tis said they used in the torturing of some of their poor Captives (bidding *Jesus* come and deliver them out of their Hands from Death if he could) we leave as uncertain, though some have so reported.[98]

The Indians' understanding of English religious expression and practices extends to public forms of Christian worship. Wheeler notes a moment in the siege of Brookfield when the attacking Indians, in perfect parody of approved Praying Indian behavior, act out a Christian worship service:

> The next day being *August 3d*, they continued *shooting & shouting, &* proceeded in their *former wickedness blaspheming the Name of the Lord*, and *reproaching* us *his Afflicted Servants*, scoffing at our *prayers* as they were sending in their shot upon all quarters of the house And many of them went to the Towns *meeting house* (which was within *twenty Rods* of the house in which we were) who mocked saying, *Come and pray, & sing Psalms, &* in Contempt made an hideous noise *somewhat resembling singing.*[99]

Here, Indian speech is represented as degenerating into nonsense. The account is especially vicious as a particular revision of earlier mission representations, in which descriptions of Indian worship, with psalms in an Indian language, were matched to English meter. Here such transculturation is seen as hideous and empty noise "somewhat resembling" human expression.

Of course, given the Indians' intent to shock and humiliate the English, this "psalm" may very well have been "hideous noise." The Indians seem knowingly to have occupied the role of devilish tempters, as in this moment of parody or as in *True Account*, when they challenge their captives and Jesus to prove the power of the Christian God in words that may consciously echo gospel accounts of the crucifixion. Or the English authors may themselves have cast Indian utterances into such a blasphemous register. However Indians put their gospel knowledge to use, whatever the veracity of these reports, wartime literature turns white captives into martyrs and their Praying Indian enemies into tormentors who put their mission-inculcated knowledge of Christianity to evil purposes.

Rowlandson's Praying Indians

The best-known narrative of the war is Mary Rowlandson's account of her captivity, *The Sovereignty and Goodness of God*. Although it was published in 1682, she probably wrote it sometime soon after her return to Boston in 1676. A best-seller in its day, her narrative went through many editions that were published in both Boston and London, and it has become the most studied literary production of the war.[100]

Rowlandson's narrative synthesizes the accounts of divines, soldiers, and observers. She is both a participant in the war, like Thomas Wheeler, and an observer or interpreter of that experience, like Nathaniel Saltonstall or William Hubbard. She is a laywoman but also a minister's wife. The preface to her narrative was probably written by a clergyman, and her husband's last sermon was appended to the first edition. Conversant with the theological mythmaking that shaped full-scale histories of the conflict, she reports her experience as a participant in the war, focusing on her physical and spiritual captivity and her redemption through God's grace.

Unlike any other war publication, Rowlandson's treatment of Praying Indians was doubly legitimated by her status as a captive eyewitness and by the authorization of her clerical husband and prefacer. Her understanding and representation, therefore, of Indians' conversions and perfidy had further-reaching effects than any other wartime production. Her narrative registers both the permanent impression of mission representations on the colonial Indian discourse and the reevaluation of the missionaries' normative Indian figure, a reversal that profoundly influenced her narrative's generic and thematic successors.

Some literary historians consider her account to be the primogenitor of the American captivity narrative, going so far as to call her text "the starting point of a cultural myth affecting America as a whole."[101] Whatever the narrative's status as an archetype, readers have found it to be "homespun and homely," "unembellished," and a transparent account of her contact with Indians rather than a product of conscious artistry. Unlike later participants in the captivity genre, Rowlandson has been assumed by many critics to have held herself apart from Indian culture and resisted assimilation, affirming Puritan gender and racial hierarchies.[102]

Literary historians have more recently asserted the extent and power of her cultural transformation and its challenge to "the rigid hierarchies of Puritan orthodoxy."[103] In readings that call attention to her disruption of Puritan gender norms, critics cite Rowlandson's entry into the Indian economy—she trades her skill as a seamstress for goods and food—and they talk about her increasing understanding of her captives as humans and individuals.[104] These readers cite her "imperfect" restoration to Puritan society in Boston as evidence of the lasting effects of her wilderness experience. She is, they argue, indelibly marked by her time among Indian captors. This cultural conversion, more than her spiritual one, drives continuing critical interest.

My view is closer to the latter set of readings than the former, but both approaches ignore her text's relationship to works that preceded it. Previous readings have failed to note that Rowlandson's captivity narrative owes its content and contemporary prominence in some measure to the rhetoric of Indian conversion published before the war. The physical and material transformation that Rowlandson underwent and describes had been articulated and valued by mission writers as the experiences of Indian converts who were redeemed from spiritual captivity into Puritan civility. Rowlandson's importance to the later American Indian discourse depends less on her ability to see her captors as individuals than on her translation of missionary representations, which overwrites them and erases Indians from positive colonial significance. Most important, Rowlandson's narrative illustrates how completely the period from the Restoration through King Philip's War closed down the possibilities of a viable Praying Indian identity at the center of New England culture.

The gothic landscape described by the mission writers in which Indians were chained by Satan is Rowlandson's New England landscape as well. (At one point, she describes the swamp where her party stayed the night as "a deep Dungeon.")[105] But her account suggests that the earlier writers who had sketched that landscape for their English readers had been misled as to its inhabitants. From the perspective of a captive, Rowlandson understands and represents Indian transculturation as hypocrisy, turning the external signs of Indian regeneracy into mere sophistry and illusion. As a story of "Christian affliction," the narrative centers on a white woman rather than on Indian converts. Thus Rowlandson reinscribes the markers of English-Indian transculturation into the rhetoric of Indian-hating. Whether consciously or not, she is engaged in the same representational battle that Eliot, Gookin, Mather, Hubbard, Saltonstall, and Tompson waged.

Rowlandson's narrative is structured by "removes"—successive geographic and temporal displacements that lead her away from and then back toward her home. Early on, during the first remove, she introduces the topic that troubled other wartime chroniclers—the presence of converted Indians in the ranks of the heathen enemy: "Little do many think what is the savageness and brutishness of this barbarous Enemy, aye even those that seem to profess more than others among them, when the *English* have fallen into their hands."[106] Rowlandson singles out Praying Indians—those who "profess"—for particular description and largely negative judgment, and her representations reflect the dissemination of earlier missionary imagery.

At several moments in her narrative, Rowlandson is careful to note Praying Indians' participation in campaigns against the English.[107] She remarks on an earlier attack on her town of Lancaster: "Those seven that were killed at *Lancaster* the summer before upon a Sabbath day, and the one that was afterward killed upon a week day, were slain and mangled in a barbarous manner, by One-ey'd *John*, and *Marlborough's* Praying *Indians*" (71). Rowlandson's careful distinction between Sabbath and weekday killings is significant, pointing as it does to the special nature of the crimes. Not only did "professing" Indians kill, but they also intensify the horror of the crime by killing on the day they are commanded to keep holy.[108]

Her description of Praying Indians implies that attacks by those Indians who profess Christianity are more vicious than the depredations of the "heathen" because they are so unexpected. In her account, converts continue to occupy the borderlands between heathens and Christians, but their ability to assume the external appearance of Christian makes them even more objectionable than non-Christian Indians. Like military writers who rail against the "skulking" tactics of Indian forces, Rowlandson describes civility and prayer as the camouflage for native dishonor and treachery. During her captivity, she is always in danger of misreading appearances. One Indian offers her the comfort of a good meal, and that gesture temporarily distracts her gaze from an important sign of his "true" barbaric nature:

> As I was eating, another *Indian* said to me, he seems to be your good Friend, but he killed two *Englishmen* at *Sudbury*, and there lie their Cloaths behind you: I looked behind me, and there I saw bloody Cloaths, with Bullet holes in them; yet the Lord suffered not this wretch to do me any hurt. (101)

The juxtaposition of that mangled clothing with the Indian's material generosity to her (as well as his violent appropriation of English clothing) functions not only as a reminder of God's watchfulness but also as a warning not to accept outer manifestations of civility as indicative of an inward state.[109]

Earlier in her narrative, she generalizes such captivity experiences to the wider English society. From a postwar perspective, she warns against a too-sanguine acceptance of such seemingly harmless Indian figures. In her twelfth remove, she describes how she is evicted from home at sword point by a "rude fellow," then she goes on to report, *"Mine eyes have seen that fellow afterwards walking up and down* Boston, *under the appearance of a* Friend-Indian, *and severall others of the like Cut."*[110]

Her use of the words "appearance" and "cut" resonate with earlier missionaries' reliance on cross-cultural dress as a sign of spiritual conversion.[111] During her eleven-week captivity, Rowlandson earned money, food, or goods by making or trading English clothing. Recent critical treatments of her narrative have cited this participation in the Indian economy as a primary measure of her assimilation and transculturation, but few mention the significance of her Indian captors desiring and valuing such clothing. During her captivity, she is asked to make or trade stockings, aprons, shirts, and shifts, and she carefully describes the mixed dress that her master and mistress wear at a dance, which includes ornaments made from both wampum and shillings. Her attention to these details has been deemed proto-ethnographic, as if she were simply recording incidents without ideological inflection.

And perhaps these moments do reflect a desire for verisimilitude or a Puritan aesthetic of providential design, in which she records as many details as possible without interpreting them because she does not know which details have special significance within God's plan. As this minister's wife must have been aware, however, similar descriptions in mission discourse would have elicited commentary and praise. Missionaries had repeatedly assured white New Englanders that Praying Indians loved them, that their adoption of English customs and dress reflected their desire to anglicize and Christianize not only their external appearances but their hearts as well. She departs markedly from this tradition when she records Indian clothing styles and then declines to explain it. Here, hybridity of appearance has no Christian signification.

On occasion, mixed sartorial signs do come under her scrutiny and suspicion, eliciting comment. Other wartime writers found the ease of transformation through attire and the subsequent unreadability of appearance threatening, and Rowlandson is likewise greatly affected by the Indians' English dress:

In that time came a company of *Indians* to us, near thirty, all on horse-
back. My heart skipt within me, thinking they had been *English men* at
the first sight of them, for they were dressed in *English* Apparel, with
Hats, white Neckcloths, and Sashes about their waists, and Ribbonds
upon their shoulders: but when they came near, there was a vast difference between the lovely faces of Christians, and the foul looks of those
Heathens. (94)

Michelle Burnham proposes that the possibility the English clothing
came from stripped English casualties upsets Rowlandson. But these
men are not bedecked haphazardly with trophies; they are carefully
and completely dressed.[112] Immediately preceding this description of
the Indian company, Rowlandson discusses the first letters that Massachusetts authorities and her captors exchanged to negotiate her release. The conjunction of those negotiations and the appearance of
this company suggests that she thought these men were her English
rescuers. It is the newly dislocating experience of Indian bodies inhabiting English clothing (however the clothes were acquired) that
makes the moment notable.

Rowlandson distinguishes between the categories of heathen and
Christian, but contrary to missionary claims, she links the term
"Christian" to a particular racial and national identity: only English
are Christian. Even the two converts, Peter Conway and Tom Dublett,
who successfully negotiate her release, are identified as Indians with
whom she has some fellow-feeling rather than Praying Indians.[113]
Rowlandson instead refines the mission binary of heathen or Christian not only by asserting that Praying Indians are not Christians but
also by citing incidents demonstrating that they are worse than the
heathen enemy.

The above examples of Rowlandson's Indian representations all
seem to come from her direct experience in captivity. However, lest
we consider her narrative an unembellished description of her life in
an Indian community, she includes in the nineteenth remove an extended list of Praying Indians that includes information she could not
have known at the time of her captivity. This seemingly random list
of Praying Indians is actually carefully ordered, making the argument
that these converts are as heathen as their nonpraying brethren, enabled by their mission education to perform unusual acts of treachery.

When she details the steps that the General Court of Massachusetts and her Indian captors took to negotiate her release, she is careful to note that a Praying Indian, whom Salisbury identifies as James Printer, wrote the letter of negotiation for the Indians.[114] The scribe owed his trade to the introduction of reading and writing by missionaries who were concerned about converts' access to scripture. Immediately following this reference to the scribe, Rowlandson describes her encounter with a mission-educated, scripturally literate Praying Indian in terms that argue that putative converts pervert their education for their own ends:

> There was another Praying-*Indian*, who told me, that he had a brother, that would not eat Horse; his conscience was so tender and scrupulous, (though as large as hell, for the destruction of poor *Christians*). Then he said, he read that Scripture to him, 2 Kings, 6. 25. *There was a famine in* Samaria, *and behold they besieged it, until an Asses head was sold for fourscore pieces of silver, and the fourth part of a Kab of Doves dung, for five pieces of silver.* He expounded this place to his brother, and shewed him that it was lawfull to eat that in a Famine which is not at another time. And now, says he, he will eat horse with any *Indian* of them all. (98)

This passage describes a Christian dialogue with exactly the form encouraged and exemplified by John Eliot's missionary "handbook," *Indian Dialogues.* One Indian raises an objection to a desired belief or behavior, and another convinces him of the "right" path by citing and expounding scripture.

Such an appropriation of Christian conventions overturns missionaries' characterizations of Indian piety. What could be more blasphemous than an enemy Indian quoting and expounding a scriptural text for his own evil purpose? And what could be more misleading than missionaries' claims that such exchanges led to Indian regeneracy? Rather than leading one Indian on the path to "civil," English transformation, this dialogue makes the tender-hearted brother *more* Indian as he accedes to his community's dietary necessities. The "preacher" here uses his scriptural knowledge to aid and comfort the enemy. Tellingly, although Rowlandson goes through a similar process of repulsion and acceptance in learning to eat what she calls Indian "trash," she does not connect her hearing of this Praying Indian's exposition of scripture to her ability to eat horsemeat (or even a horse hoof), citing entirely different scripture to explain and justify her actions. Both the scribe in the previous anecdote and the "preacher" here use their mission-inculcated knowledge to aid and comfort the enemy: one makes ransom demands possible because he can compose letters of negotiation; the other, by citing chapter and verse, saves his brother from starvation, possibly to fight another day.

The Praying Indian's application of scripture to his brother's condition is at least as apt as the scripture she takes for her own instruction: *"To the hungry Soul every bitter thing is sweet."*[115] The scripture she uses emphasizes God's role in transforming adverse circumstances for the good of the sufferer. The Praying Indian's selection justifies extreme human responses to those same circumstances. The presence of this Indian "dialogue" in her account also problematizes the role of food in Rowlandson's narrative, for what has been taken as evidence of her transculturation (her consumption of "Indian" food) is shown to have a potentially Christian valence. Moreover, horsemeat seems not to have an essentially Indian connection. For the enemy, too, the meat is unusual and perhaps disgusting food, to be consumed only in moments of great need. Indeed, English accounts of their own warfare diets include horsemeat as an alternative to starvation.[116]

Following Rowlandson's description of the uses to which Indians put their missionary education are several increasingly graphic descriptions of Indian treachery:

> There was another Praying-*Indian*, who, when he had done all the mischief that he could, betrayed his own Father into the *English* hands, thereby to purchase his own life. Another Praying-*Indian* was at *Sudbury*-fight, though, as he deserved, he was afterward hanged for it. There was another Praying *Indian*, so wicked and cruel, as to wear a string about his neck, strung with *Christians* Fingers. (98)

Each example concerns people and events most likely outside of Rowlandson's immediate experience of captivity. Although she may have had some direct encounters with these people or heard rumors about them while travelling with the Indians, these incidents are treated at greater length in other accounts of the war. Hubbard, as I noted above, had learned from Benjamin Church about one familial betrayal. Mary Pray and William Harris were hearing the same rumor of Praying Indian attacks, and Rowlandson's more generalized accounts give the impression of similarly second-hand knowledge. It seems reasonable to assume that she learned about them from other English sources and

includes them here to discredit Praying Indians and to protest their
ready acceptance back into New England society. Because she speaks
as a captive, she gives the weight of eyewitness testimony to what
might otherwise be dismissed (in London, if not in the colonies) as rumor or exaggeration.

Like Rowlandson, Saltonstall also mentions Indians who wear
"mens fingers as bracelets about their Necks."[117] Interestingly, he
does not identify the wearers as Praying Indians. This story in particular bears the marks of a sensational tale told and retold throughout
the colonies as evidence that the Indians were inhuman, deserving of
extermination. By placing the bloody ornament around the neck of a
Praying Indian, Rowlandson signals her perspective on conversion and
on the possibility of Indian spiritual or cultural transformation: it can
never be certain and is most likely a façade for cruelty camouflaged by
the trappings of conversion.[118]

Some Indians who had previously identified themselves (or who were
identified by others) as Praying Indians clearly joined the allied Indian
forces of King Philip's War. Therefore, from the perspective of many
English observers, the Praying identity could not signify a heartfelt
profession of Christian faith. Converts who joined the ranks of the enemy had at best learned the external trappings of Indian Christianity
in order to gain materially or to hide their evil intentions.[119] The positive assessment of Indians who displayed a measure of anglicization
had been violently discredited.

For their part, Indians who fought against the English or with
them—"praying" or not—found in Christian traits the means both to
harass Englishmen and engage them. Shoshanim, known to the English as Sam Sachem of Naswhaway, wrote several letters of negotiation, which reflect his increasingly precarious position as the war
drew to a close. He took part in the negotiations dealing with Mary
Rowlandson's release and was obviously a man of standing in his community.[120] While his early letters were written when the English
looked weak and vulnerable, later letters reflect a change in for-
tune.[121] In a letter addressed to John Leverett, governor of Massachusetts, "Mr. Waban," and "all the chief men our Brethren, Praying to
God," Sam Sachem asks for the good treatment of his wife and other
Indian captives among the English and for further peace negotiations.
He concludes, "We do earnestly entreat you, that it may be so, by Jesus Christ. O! let it be so: Amen. Amen."[122] Not a Christian himself,

Shoshanim evidently had learned the lesson that evangelists had been teaching to any Indians who would listen—call upon Christ, pray to God, and you will successfully negotiate your relationships with English authorities.[123]

How well his tactic worked can be judged by the sachem's ultimate fate and by his discursive treatment. Although the author of *A True Account*, in which this letter of negotiation was published, gives qualified praise to the efforts of Praying Indians in the war effort and describes Waban as "faithfull," other Indians are "bloody wretches" who "plead for themselves by that Sacred name, which they had Blasphem'd." He responds to Shoshanim's prayer for peace in particular with vindictive glee: "Thus doth the Lord Jesus make them to bow before him, and to lick the Dust."[124] Henceforth, an Indian who prayed to God would not be identified as a Praying Indian but rather as a conquered enemy. Shoshanim was hanged in Boston on September 6, 1676.[125]

7 Dying Saints, Vanishing Savages

Dying Indian Speeches in Colonial New England Literature

However much Praying Indians were vilified in wartime literature, special notice was reserved for the most prominent Indian of the war, Metacom, known to the English as "King Philip." In the several contemporary histories of King Philip's War, Metacom's death signals the providential end of the conflict. Although skirmishes continued, the war itself was perceived to be concluded. As much as forty years later, descriptions of Metacom's death and dismemberment continued to assert a providential purpose:

> And in that very place where he first contrived and began his mischief, was he taken and destroyed, and there was he (Like as Agag was hewed in pieces before the Lord) cut into four quarters, and is now hanged up as a monument of revenging Justice.[1]

To wartime chroniclers, King Philip's demise was a sign of God's blessings. Like so many colonial writers before them, they found in the death of an Indian reason to rejoice. As I discuss in chapter 2, the first settlers noted the epidemics that had devastated the inhabitants of coastal communities before their arrival, giving thanks to God for the newly vacant lands. John Winthrop claimed in 1629 that "God hath consumed the natives with a great plague in those parts," and thus Puritan settlers had a "warrant" to settle in New England.[2] In Pequot War descriptions, Puritan victors exulted in the terrible deaths of their foes: "But God was above them, who laughed his Enemies and the Enemies of his People to Scorn, making them as a fiery Oven. . . . Thus did the Lord judge among the Heathen, filling the Place with dead Bodies."[3]

These writers depend on prior vilification as they celebrate such violence. The many who died from disease, they believed, had been willing occupants of the devil's territories and therefore merited death. Philip and his men were viciously stigmatized as brutes whose desire was to spill the blood of English men and to rape English women.[4] From such a viewpoint, the conclusion was obvious: New England needed to be rid of this menace, and in these accounts, the only good Indian is a dead Indian. These authors are uninterested in registering any trace of Indian subjectivity. It doesn't matter *how* the instruments of Satan understand their demise; only white Puritan observers are meant to cash in on the symbolic value of their deaths. By interpreting Indian deaths as providential, Puritan observers assert God's blessing on their invasion, and the colonists construct themselves as the rightful (and righteous) possessors of "New England."[5]

The representation of Indian deaths has, of course, been a prominent a part of later American literature as well. Even those nineteenth-century writers who rejected the virulent Indian-hating rhetoric of early English colonists nevertheless accepted the "fact" of Indian destruction. The trope of the "vanishing Indian" was central to Romantic constructions of national identity, as in this stanza from William Cullen Bryant's "The Disinterred Warrior":

> A noble race! but they are gone,
> With their old forests wide and deep,
> And we have built our homes upon
> Fields where their generations sleep.
> Their fountains slake our thirst at noon,
> Upon their fields our harvest waves,
> Our lovers woo beneath their moon—
> Then let us spare, at least, their graves.[6]

In *The Vanishing American*, Brian Dippie argues that in such poems and in novels by James Fenimore Cooper and others, "Indian remnants *were* the American past," even as the literature registered "sympathy, regret, sadness, despair" at the Indians' tragic fate.[7] However much nineteenth-century authors may have lamented the disappearance of Indians, they agreed with seventeenth-century writers that Indian deaths were necessary and inevitable—whether because of divine will, "natural" inferiority to whites, or manifest destiny.

The sense of the inevitability of Indian disappearance that is shared by seventeenth- and nineteenth-century writers invites the assumption of discursive stasis. Despite some differences, Anglo-American representations of Indians seem always to presume displacement and extinction. But the trope of the vanishing Indian is neither "natural" to colonial literature nor inevitable. Mission writings produced between the Pequot War and King Philip's War disrupt even as they mediate the representational norms that came before and that followed. The mid-century evangelical accounts participated in contemporaneous forms of colonial rhetoric and are forerunners to later Romantic constructions, yet they do not describe all Indians as simply dead, dying, or deserving death. The tenor of the missionaries' descriptions of new Christian believers differs from the glee or thanksgiving with which the news of Indians' violent deaths was reported or the melancholy with which the noble savage was elegized. The death of a savage or the passing of a noble Indian in the nineteenth century served to reassure white readers that Indians could be no real threat, because such descriptions insisted that Indians had no real presence in colonial New England or the early nation. In the mid-seventeenth century, the dying Indian convert's deathbed scene asserted presence: an individual Christian Indian died, but his dying speech addressed a continuing community of believers, and his regenerate state promised a resurrected return.[8]

Let me be clear; no less than descriptions of King Philip's death, the reports of dying Christian Indians are written and read by the English as proof of God's blessings. Moreover, insofar as these descriptions of "Praying Indians" make the continued occupation of native lands palatable to English invaders and their supporters in Europe, the dying speeches are implicated in the more physically violent aspects of colonization. To the extent that evangelistic rhetoric participated in a larger colonial discourse, enabling and justifying physical conquest, the "dying Indian" figure that missionaries produced must be understood not in contrast to the dying Pequots and the Wampanoags or Narragansetts of King Philip's War but as a complementary construction: the "dying Indian savage" makes possible the "dying Indian saint," and vice versa. Nevertheless, by focusing on the spiritual value of individual converts and the survival of their faith community, the mission accounts form something of a counternarrative to the discourse of bloody conquest and the tragic narrative of vanishing Indians—if not in the sense of "opposition," perhaps in the sense of a "counterweight" that balances other aspects of this discourse. This difference allows for some purchase on the questions of representation and Indian agency in these mediated accounts.

Mary Louise Pratt's notion of "anti-conquest" rhetoric in eighteenth-century traveler's narratives helps clarify the discursive distinctions among various dying Indian representations. She uses the term to explain colonial writers' paradoxical assertion of innocence "in the same moment as they assert European hegemony."[9] Whereas both the earlier descriptions of violent deaths and the romantic elegies of later literature are inscribed within the rhetoric of conquest, Puritan missionary articulations are more likely to involve, in Pratt's terms, "strategies of innocence" (7). The missionaries eschew violence, contrasting themselves on the one hand with the New Model Army in England and, on the other, with Spanish conquistadors in America, as I discuss in chapter 1.[10]

What made the figure of the "dying Indian saint" viable was the assertion, counter to wartime beliefs, that not all Indians were instruments of Satan. In the missionaries' terms, if Indians had souls to save, then it behooved the good Christian to spare their lives and work toward their redemption.[11] Further, because Puritan church membership required tangible proof of that redemption, uttered by the redeemed sinner, missionary narratives were interested in representing Christian agency, which meant representing Indian agency as well.

Throughout this book, my analysis of the literature of New England missions has concentrated primarily on the English construction and manipulation of the image. Although recent studies assert that the early seventeenth-century epidemics and the massacre at Mystic Fort in 1637 created a sense of loss among native peoples that made the tenets of Puritan Christianity attractive to some,[12] the texts at the heart of this book are so heavily mediated that it is nearly impossible to uncover the experiences of Indians as Christians. Indeed, the difficulty is so great that most studies of Praying Indians concentrate on reading against the grain for resistance to evangelism. Nevertheless, as historians and ethnographers remind, it is limiting to ignore the desire for and decision to convert and to assume Indians did not participate actively in the formation of new identities. Any discursive figure, once constructed, becomes available for new purposes and new meanings.

In this chapter I examine the figure of the dying Indian saint constructed by English mission writers between 1643 and 1676, and the Praying Indians' own use of the figure. In the deathbed speeches of Praying Indians, though transmitted by white writers, we glimpse a dynamic clergy-laity, English-Indian dialogue. As converts became adept in the conventions of Puritan religious speech, they used their dying speeches to assert the symbolic and lived value of their faith community. Even after the Praying Indian ceased to serve as a norm for Puritans on both sides of the Atlantic, Christian Indians continued to use the identity as an expression of their community's continued viability and presence.

Sixteen forty-three was a significant year for the elaboration of the dying Indian saint. Less than a decade after colonial English writers celebrated the death of their Pequot enemies, two documents, *New Englands First Fruits* and *A Key into the Language of America*, presented competing descriptions of the death of a military ally. In the preface to *A Key*, Roger Williams recounts his encounter with Wequash, a Pequot captain who crossed lines to fight with the English during the Pequot War and participated in the Mystic Fort massacre. Just "two dayes before his Death," Williams makes him a visit. They talk about "his *sicknesse* and *Death*," and Wequash entrusts his son to George Fenwick. Then Williams turns to more important matters: the state of Wequash's soul. Wequash recalls that Williams had taught him about God and assures him that his *"words were never out of my heart to this present."* The minister and convert go on to explore grounds for Wequash's hope of salvation. Wequash notes that he prayed "much" to Christ. Williams responds that "so did many *English, French,* and *Dutch,* who had never turned to *God,* nor loved Him." These words seem to have inspired penitence, for Wequash responds with a confession of sin and faith.[13]

It is easy to see why Williams, a dissident among Puritans, would want to detail this scene. The manner of Wequash's dying suggests a lost soul saved and asserts the importance of Williams's sojourn among the Pequot, Narragansett, and other peoples.[14] Moreover, the account is of a piece with his explicitly polemical writings; the manner of Wequash's passing lends support for Williams's chastisement of "civilized" Christians, which I have described as his book's "prime thesis." Wequash, though Pequot, understands what it means to be a true Christian, even though many "English, French, and Dutch" are hypocritical professors. Though apt as an illustration of Williams's dissident beliefs, this particular anecdote appears in *A Key* not simply because it confirms Williams's views of evangelism but also because he is competing with Bay Colony authorities for discursive control of Wequash's deathbed scene. He includes the story, Williams explains, "since it hath pleased some of my Worthy *Country-men* to mention (of late in print) *Wequash,* the *Pequt Captaine*."[15]

He refers here to *New Englands First Fruits,* also published in 1643. This tract was published in London to describe "the progresse of *Learning*" at Harvard, the newly instituted college, and to reassure English observers that Puritan colonists were indeed spreading the word of God among the heathen, answering charges that they had been ignoring this important duty.[16] With this tract, the Bay Colony laid symbolic claim to Wequash's Christian death. Significantly, when *New Englands First Fruits* reports Wequash's last words, it emphasizes his connections to and gratitude for the English but does not mention Roger Williams, the colony's rival.

Moreover, *First Fruits* constructs Wequash's death as a martyrdom—the result of poisoning by enemy Indians—rather than a natural death, a claim that accentuates the Bay Colony's willingness to exploit the differences among native peoples in contrast to Williams's desire to negotiate these differences. The tract's authors are keenly aware of Wequash's prominence; he is "that famous Indian *Wequash* who was a Captaine, a proper man of person, and of a very grave and sober spirit" (425). Unlike Williams's account, however, the tract does not describe a personal connection between colonial authorities and Wequash. Although *First Fruits* asserts that the example of Wequash "was indeed the occasion of writing all the rest" of the tract, the writers admit that his story had come "to [their] hands very lately" (425). There is no sense of continuing contact or of an unfolding dialogue between minister and convert, as we see in Williams's work. And indeed, such distance may be the point. The impersonal tone reinforces the tract's claims that the good example of the English colonists rather than direct evangelism had been enough to effect conversion. Thus Wequash is offered as anecdotal proof of the Bay Colony's influence on Indians, recounted from a distance by disinterested observers.

Unlike Williams's account, the deathbed scene as recorded by *First Fruits* includes no English clerical intervention. Instead, Indians counsel Wequash, "according to the Indian manner," to send for their own healers, the powwows. Wequash, of course, rejects that advice, giving himself over to the will of Jesus Christ (427). There is no mention of Williams visiting him, although the impression of the whole account suggests some kind of English presence.[17] First, Wequash "did bequeath his Child to the godly care of the English for education and instruction" (although the mechanism of this bequest, i.e. the naming of an English executor or guardian, is not described, perhaps because

Fenwick was Williams's ally). Second, at the moment in the text when Wequash dies, when he "yielded up his soul," clerical sanction is given through the "testimony of Mr. *Sh[epard]* a godly Minister in the *Bay*," who describes Wequash as *"the famous Indian at the Rivers mouth,"* and details his death in terms of third-person ministerial approval.[18]

The Bay Colony's (not to mention Williams's) appropriation of Wequash's deathbed scene exemplifies the genre's significance to subsequent colonial writings. *First Fruits* records the deaths of several other converts, marking a rhetorical shift in emphasis from previous descriptions of military victories. Both the Bay Colony writers and Williams intended their accounts to circulate transatlantically, to win metropolitan support for their efforts. The genre's significance to a New England audience, however, is more difficult to assess. While *A Key* and *First Fruits* certainly demonstrate a general appreciation for the Christian Indian deathbed scene, the documents also reflect the complexities of the New England contact zone: Wequash, a Pequot ally of the English during the war with his people, is visited by Roger Williams, outspoken English separatist, and also receives the endorsement of Bay Colony orthodoxy. At his death, which may have been caused by Indians who resisted the physical and spiritual invasions of the English, he is subject to the advice of non-Christian Indians, who urge him to seek traditional native medical treatment. Such complexities shape the representation of the dying Indian saint throughout the century.

If the 1643 publications initiate this genre in New England, in subsequent writings Puritan missionaries make the descriptions of the dying Indian saint a well-wrought figure. In Eliot's writings, the dying speech is described as one more means of distinguishing Indian Christians from their unconverted brethren. As I discuss in chapter 4, finding the means to make such distinctions in the early days of his mission work was especially important. In Puritan New England churches of the period, believers made public confessions of faith and so identified themselves as "visible saints." Before Indian churches were created, other forms of religious expression were needed to indicate the hopeful signs of regeneration to skeptical English observers. The dying speech, although it was always received with caution among Puritans, was one potent way to assert a Christian identity for the individual and the community.[19]

Although I am tracing the dying speech as it was adapted for missionary representations, as Erik Seeman notes, the genre of deathbed confessions was popular in the seventeenth and eighteenth centuries among the English as well, and its use in mission literature is one more indication of the intersection of metropolitan and colonial writings The "ideal deathbed scene" contains several elements: when death was clearly imminent, friends and family gathered around the afflicted, a minister prayed with and questioned the sufferer about his or her conviction, and finally the dying Christian expressed tentative hope and addressed listeners.[20] This scene became a "powerful cultural norm" (xi). Given its significance, it is not surprising to find English authors extending the genre to Indian converts. New Englanders recorded the last words of Christian Indians for a variety of reasons: out of piety, to defend against charges of cruelty or rapaciousness in their dealings with Indians, or (as in *First Fruits*) to prove that they were fulfilling the terms of their charter.

The deathbed scene of the dying Indian saint closely follows the model Seeman describes. To the elements he identifies, the written accounts add the repudiation of "powwowing" and (often) the entrusting of children to the English. When the first Praying Indian of "ripe years" died, Eliot seized on the opportunity to detail her passing to his English audience. The tract in which Eliot's letter appears glosses the account as "a precious testimony of an Indian woman conceived to dye a Christian."[21] The dying woman is the unnamed wife of Totherswamp—one of the first women to ask a "spiritual question" at a Praying Indian meeting with Eliot. In keeping with her adherence to safe gender norms at that time, her death conforms to all the conventions. She promises to "refuse powwowing," expresses herself "willing to die, and believed [*sic*] to goe to Heaven," and exhorts her children (in a "precious dying speech") to avoid their nonpraying grandparents and uncles and remain in the praying community.

In such accounts of Christian Indian deaths, Eliot is careful to include testimony that supports his particular missionary vision—the founding of Praying Indian towns, for example. He also has an eye for details likely to appeal to a distant audience both intrigued by and skeptical of Christian Indians. For example, in 1651, Eliot described the death of Wamporas, whom he calls "one of our first and principall men."[22] Eliot notes the gathering of friends and family, and records a last conversation in which Eliot, as clerical adviser, questions Wamporas about his conviction and assurance. Happily, Wamporas exhorts his family to continue to participate in Eliot's fledgling mission, urging them to move to the new Praying Indian town of Natick: *"I now shall dye, but Jesus Christ calleth you that live to goe to* Naticke, *that there the Lord might rule over you, that you might make a Church"* (167).

Although here and in most of the account Eliot translates his conversation with Wamporas without comment, at one point he draws attention to language. Eliot reports that "his last words which he spake in this world were these; *Jehova Aninnumah Jesus Christ,* (that is) Oh, Lord, give mee Jesus Christ" (166). Whatever the relation of this transcription to Wamporas's words or feelings, the use of a "native" expression of faith sets this account apart from the myriad other English dying speeches. It creates an effect of authenticity that relies on an English sense of strangeness at seeing the words "Jehova" and "Jesus Christ" set within a Wôpanâak sentence. With this reported speech, Eliot reminds his English audience of this man's redeemed place within a "heathen" community, going so far as to express his belief that "I shall see him againe with Christ in Glory." Finally, Eliot reports, when speech failed Wamporas, "He continued to lift up his hands to Heaven . . . so that they say of him he dyed praying" (167, 166).

The word "they" in this last passage reflects Eliot's awareness of the Praying Indians as an interpretive community and his desire to represent that larger community to the English reader. As he lay dying, Wamporas articulated his understanding of the role affliction played in the Christian's life and expressed his willingness to accept sickness as part of God's plan. According to Eliot, these words "so tooke with them [Indian witnesses], that I observe it in their prayers, that they so reckon up Gods dispensations to them" (166). By recording this reverence for Wamporas's faith, Eliot "authorizes" the community's sentiments literally and figuratively; after all, he records their reaction and translates most of the deathbed scene into English.

One way, therefore, to understand Eliot's writing here is to see his acknowledgment of Wamporas's spiritual leadership as a means of containing and appropriating it. In the 1650s, when Eliot writes down this version of Wamporas's death, he is eager to assert the support of native religious and political leaders for the mission movement. Wamporas's endorsement of the Praying Indian town of Natick "proves" that Christian Indians are willingly deciding that "the Lord," not to mention the Massachusetts Bay Colony, "might rule over them." The death becomes a sign of Eliot's efficacy and touches his own melancholic faith: "Nor am I able to write his Storie without weeping" (167).

Although the anecdote points to successful evangelical-colonial tactics, we may gain some insight into the dynamics of the Praying Indian religious community from this description of Wamporas's death,
which suggests at least local control by the converts themselves over
the life of their religious community. They have selected an element
of his dying speech to remember, and they "flocked together" (167) to
hear Wamporas's final admonitions. However, if his final words were
the only example of the genre, we would have little additional understanding of the role of the dying Indian saint or of the missionary
encounter. The story survives in mission literature because it contributed positively to Eliot's confident assessment of his work, which,
by 1651, had achieved some success. Wamporas's words are almost
seamlessly woven into Eliot's propaganda, obviously congruent with
the missionary's own belief system and with the colonial mission effort as a whole.

To gain a fuller sense of the genre's possibilities, we must adduce additional examples. Eliot's *Dying Speeches & Counsels of such Indians
as dyed in the Lord* seems a natural place to look. Since Eliot published this tract around 1685, some forty years after he began his mission work, we might expect to see in it the apotheosis of the dying
Christian Indian genre, the triumphant celebration of a decades-long
effort and a straightforward elaboration on earlier examples of the
form. Instead, Eliot expresses his sadness and disappointment with
the imminent failure of his work. He mourns the loss of the Praying
Indian community, which he believes will not continue after his
death.

A profound change had occurred between the mid-century celebra-
tions of converted Indians and Eliot's last mission publication. As I
discuss in chapter 6, the outbreak of King Philip's War in 1675 disrupted evangelistic activity and threw Puritan evangelism and the
Praying Indian community into confusion. The war ultimately shifted
colonial Indian policy from assimilation to extermination, and the
rhetorical patterns constructed and made valuable within the mission
discourse became unmoored from their political and theological an-
chors. Wartime narratives clearly staked out the differences between
friend and foe, but the acculturation of Praying Indians to English
ways blurred these certainties. The clash between older missionary
representations and the renewed emphasis on dying savages made
"Praying Indian" a difficult if not untenable identity. In this atmo-
sphere of distrust, the pious deathbed scene of the dying Indian saint,

once circulated to win support for Puritan missions, became a contested genre.

In chapter 6, I discuss wartime accounts of captivity and narratives of King Philip's war, which detail the bloody deaths of the Indian enemy and lament the tragic deaths of the English. Strikingly, however, contemporary accounts of the war begin with the rhetoric of the dying Indian saint rather than the dying savage, as they describe the death of John Sassamon, a Christian Indian. Most observers wrote that the war began after Sassamon was murdered, and his killers, who were Philip's men, were brought to trial, then executed by Plymouth Colony.[23]

Like the competing accounts of Wequash's death, the various descriptions of Sassamon position each writer with respect to his beliefs about English-Indian coexistence. The political position of the three lengthy histories of the war written in the 1670s can be identified simply by reading their varying descriptions of Sassamon. William Hubbard, author of *A Narrative of the Troubles with the Indians in New-England,* notes that Sassamon was killed after his "serious Profession of the Christian Religion."[24] But he does not speculate further on Sassamon's religious convictions, instead connecting his death to his discovery of an Indian plot against the English. Increase Mather's *Brief History of the Warr* clearly links Sassamon's conversion to his murder: "No doubt but one reason why the Indians murthered *John Sausaman,* was out of hatred against him for his Religion, for he was Christianized and baptiz'd, and was a Preacher amongst the Indians."[25] And finally, Daniel Gookin, superintendent of the praying towns, writes of Sassamon's death in his *Historical Account of the Doings and Sufferings of the Christian Indians in New England,* describing it as much more than simple murder: "John Sasamand was the first Christian martyr of the Indians; for it is evident he suffered death upon the account of his Christian profession and fidelity to the English."[26]

Gookin's wholehearted belief in Sassamon's Christian martyrdom reflects missionary efforts to protect Praying Indians from English suspicion and reprisals. Even as Eliot and Gookin tried to assist them materially, they continued to employ the figure of the dying Indian saint. The problem was that while a wide variety of political positions could be satisfied by terming Sassamon a martyr—after all, he was presumably killed by the enemy—the English themselves persecuted Praying Indians within the colonies. Those colonists who continued to support the Praying Indians—Eliot and Gookin were the most prominent—were also suspected of disloyalty. The representation of the dying Indian saint, seemingly so uncontroversial in the prewar years, became an expression of dissent from some colonial wartime policies.

The treatment of Wattasacompanum, known to the English as Captain Tom, illustrates the fault lines of the wartime colony clearly. Wattasacompanum was a Praying Indian and likely the Wutásakómpauin whose conversion narratives were published in *A Further account of the Gospel* in 1660. He was captured while traveling with a group of Indians hostile to the English. But as Jill Lepore explains, along with other Christian Indians, Wattasacompanum had been "compelled to go with the Nipmucks when they came to Hassanemesit in 1675." Wattasacompanum maintained that he was a captive, not a combatant.[27]

Nevertheless, few colonists doubted the justice of his death sentence. To a people frightened for their lives yet convinced of their own godliness, Christian enemies were the worst kind, and an enemy who prayed to God was guilty of blasphemy as well as treachery. Even Daniel Gookin, though professing his belief in "Captain Tom's" innocence, stops short of a vindication, calling him "a prudent, and I believe, a pious man, and had given good demonstration of it many years. I had particular acquaintance with him, and cannot in charity think otherwise concerning him in his life, or at his death, though possibly in this action he was tempted beyond his strength."[28] Gookin's "possibly" is not matched by any uncertainty in Eliot's descriptions. Eliot believed in his innocence and appealed to the governor for a stay of execution, joined by Praying Indians who petitioned the courts for commutation of sentence.[29] Despite these efforts, Captain Tom was executed in 1676.

Eliot's description of the execution is remarkable both for what Jill Lepore calls the "unusual rage"[30] to which he gives vent and also for the rhetorical trope of the dying saint upon which he insists. In the face of general anti-Indian sentiments, when so many English fought and prayed for the destruction of the Indians, Eliot persists in using the narrative of a dying—even persecuted or martyred—saint to describe Captain Tom's death. When he pleaded with the governor for Tom's release, he was told "how bad a man Tom was." Eliot's response makes clear his belief in Tom's state of salvation: "I told him that at the great day he should find that christ was of another mind."[31] His subsequent description of Tom's death echoes his earlier descriptions of Wamporas who "died praying":

On the Ladder he lifted up his hands and said, I did never lift up hand
against the English, nor was I at sudbury, only I was willing to goe away
with the enemise [*sic*] that surprized us. When the ladder was turned he
lifted up his hands to heaven prayer wise, and so held them till strength
failed, and then by degres thei sunk downe. (413)

This description of the execution emphasizes Tom's prayerful attitude
not once, but twice as he "lifted up his hands." The poignant physical
gesture gives eloquent emphasis to his insistence that he "did never
lift up hand against the English."

In the late eighteenth and early nineteenth centuries, such scenes
were described and contained within a vanishing Indian discourse, articulated by writers who turned the "noble savage" image into fiction.
An Indian's death was described with what Roy Harvey Pearce calls
"pity and censure."[32] The attributes Eliot sees as Tom's humility and
piety are understood by later writers as his nobility—savage though it
must be to the Romantic writer.[33] At the moment of Tom's execution,
however, descriptions of the dying saint and of the Praying Indian
more generally are much more challenging, even subversive to Bay
colonists engaged in a devastating war. Apparently, only Eliot's age
protected him from the verbal attacks directed at Gookin for his support of the Praying Indian cause. As Nathaniel Saltonstall reports in
The Present State of New England, when Gookin and Eliot appeared
before the General Court to plead the case of Praying Indians taken by
Captain Samuel Moseley at Marlborough, the court listened to Eliot
on account of his "Gravity, Age and Wisdom." Gookin, however, was
told that "he ought rather to be confined among his Indians, then to
sit on the Bench; his taking the Indian Part so much hath made him a
Byword both among Men and Boys."[34]

Captain Tom's death marks a turning point in the construction of
the Indian saint. One way of characterizing this shift, as I have suggested, is to point to the differences between mid-seventeenth and
mid-nineteenth-century representations of dying Indians. Another
way is to examine changes in Eliot's use of the image before and after
the war. In October 1675, amid general colonial dismay and the chaos
of the first months of the war, Eliot wrote to Robert Boyle, president
of the Society for the Propagation of the Gospel. In his letter, the figure of the dying Indian saint is detached from individual stories and
becomes pure trope. Using the same terms employed to describe the
deaths of Sassamon and, later, Captain Tom, Eliot imagines the end of

his Indian mission. The rhetoric of the dying Indian saint gives shape to his personal and professional grief at the death and discouragement of so many Praying Indians:

> *I must change my ditty now.* I have much to write of lamentation over the work of Christ among our praying Indians, of which God hath called you to be nursing fathers. *The work (in our patent) is under great sufferings. It is killed* in words, wishes, and expression, but not in deeds.[35]

Eliot's words wryly reflect on the success of his earlier work. His promotion of self and converts in letters printed and circulated transatlantically had created the idea of Christian Indians held by many English readers. The limits of his construction were reached during the war, when the Praying Indians' suffering and deaths failed to find a sympathetic local audience.[36] Eliot's opening sentence, "I must change my ditty now," is a strange introduction for the sad news he has to relate. The literal meaning is clear; his letters of praise have turned to letters of sorrow. But the odd tone of this sentence may have to do with Eliot's realization that metropolitan readers had considered his words merely entertainment or that New England observers had disregarded his writings altogether. His "ditty" celebrating the life of his mission turned to dirge. The mission enterprise itself had been murdered.

The "dying saint" here represents the mission as a whole, but because the death is metaphorical, Eliot allows himself a small measure of hope that the trials undergone by converts could serve as spiritual chastisement leading to renewed vigor: "As yet it is (as it were) dead but not buried; nor (I believe) shall be. It is made comformable to Christ (in some poor measure) in dying, but I believe it shall rise again."[37] These words are reminiscent of the optimistic millennialism that surrounded Eliot's reports of the Indians' spiritual resurrection in the 1640s and 1650s, but it is clear from this letter that the power of those early formulations has evaporated. Despite the passage's hopefulness, Eliot here is extraordinarily tentative. His faith in the mission's resurrection reflects the conventional humility of deathbed descriptions in which the Christian's status is "hopeful" but not certain. The heavy use of parentheses and the doubled "I believe" come closer, however, to Gookin's treatment of Captain Tom's death. Eliot knew he was among only a few English colonists who had kept faith with the mission and knew he was nearly alone in his prayers for

its resurrection. This careful letter reflects the singularity of his beliefs but perhaps also admits the possibility that he is wrong, that he
has misjudged the faith of the converts and there will be no resurrection for this Praying Indian community.

After the war, the once vocal and active missionary expresses consistent interest in only one cause: reprinting the Indian Bible. Even in
this area, his requests for funding are tinged with the conviction that
his work would not survive him. In his letters, he acknowledges that
after his death few would remain to carry on the work as he defined
it. His petitions to the New England Company, the organization that
controlled mission funding, are pointed reminders of his unique qualifications and interest in seeing the work completed. But his pleas also
poignantly reflect his failure to educate and inspire a new generation
of New England colonists to shoulder the burden: "I am deep in years,
and sundry say, if I do not procure it [the Indian Bible] printed while I
live, it is not within the prospect of human reason, whether ever, or
when, or how, it may be accomplished."[38]

Eliot's loss of spirit after the war is especially clear in his final publication, *Dying Speeches* This short tract records the deathbed speeches
of eight Praying Indians. The tract is organized by individual testimony, with brief descriptions of the speakers written by Eliot as a
preface to each. As we have seen, at another point in his career, Eliot
would have eagerly recorded evidence of Indians "dying in Christ."
These speeches, however, are perhaps only too final, a reminder that
few new converts were ready to take the place of these Indians as they
passed away. Many of the younger generation of converts had left the
movement since the war, when, as Eliot reported to Boyle, "their souls
received a wound.[39] In Eliot's preface and in his presentation of the
speeches, we can discern the effects of English suspicion, cynicism,
and violence on the missionary and on even the most famous converts.

Eliot's final work indicates his loss of heart immediately. Unlike his
earlier tracts, he explains in the preface, this one is not written out of
his own experiences. Eliot, formerly an expert and eager publicist, has
grown old and does not have the energy to collect firsthand these in-
teresting and revealing testimonies:

> It is an humbling to me that there be no more, it was not in my heart to
> gather them, but Major *Gookins* hearing some of them rehearsed, He
> first moved that *Daniel* should gather them, in the Language as they

were spoken, and that I should translate them into English; And here is presented what was done that way.[40]

Saddest of all is his apology for printing the speeches: "These things are Prin[t]ed, not so much for Publishment, as to save the charge of writeing out of Copyes for those that did desiere them."[41]

The recorded words of one of Eliot's first converts, Antony, at first seems to support Eliot's reading of the mission movement as embattled, embittered, and dying. A sense of loss is nowhere more plain than in these final words of one of Eliot's most faithful and long-lived converts. A preacher and teacher at Natick beginning in 1659, "he was among the first that Prayed to God." Eliot even transformed him into the "Anthony" of the *Indian Dialogues*, who is sent with "William Abahton" to preach to Philip. But Eliot goes on to note Antony's difficulties in later life: "*After the* warrs, *he became a lover of strong drink, was often admonished, and finally cast out from being a Teacher*" (7).

In his speech, Antony is distinguished in his self-understanding and self-representation as a religious leader, albeit a fallen one. Compare the beginnings of other speeches to Antony's. Waban proclaims, "I now rejoyce though I be now a dying" (2). Piambohou says, "I rejoyce and am content and willing to take up my sorrows and sicknesse" (4). And "Old Jacob" exhorts his listeners, "My Brethren: now hear me a few words, stand fast all you people in your praying to God" (6). Antony, by contrast, opens with no such rejoicing or pronouncements. Instead, he immediately indicts himself: "I am a sinner. I doe now confess it, I have long prayed to God, but it hath been like an *Hipocrite*" (7).

Antony's inability to control his drinking to the church's satisfaction is matched by the inability of the Indian church, led by Eliot and Gookin, to "save him": "Love of strong drink is a lust I could not over come . . . though *Major Gookins* and Mr. *Eliot* often admonished me: I confessed, they were willing to forgive me, yet I fell againe" (7). The continual personal failure underscores Eliot's professional one. The elements of Antony's last speech seem to support a sense of the mission's demise. As Eliot fears, these seem to be the last words of a dying community of faith.

And yet, at this moment of despair, we see Antony fully reoccupy his teaching role. Despite having fallen away from righteous leadership, Antony in his dying moments offers advice to the community's first Indian minister: "I say to you *Daniel*, beware that you, love not strong drink as I did, and was thereby undone." He goes on to address the wider community: "Againe I say to you my Children, forsake not praying to God, goe not to strange places, where they pray not to God, but strongly pray to God as long as you live: both you and your Children." In this last speech Antony represents Eliot's vision of the Indian mission, but an earlier one, a vision Eliot has to some extent abandoned. Antony looks forward to the continuation of the Praying Indian community, not its demise.

Another look at Eliot's preface reveals more about the speech represented here. Daniel Takawampbait, Natick's first Indian minister, ordained in 1683,[42] is the clerical attendant to these dying men. Evidently, white missionaries are not ministering at the bedsides, as Eliot hears of these speeches from Daniel Gookin, and Gookin merely heard these speeches "rehearsed," or read to him by Takawampbait. Thus, although these last words come to us embedded in several layers of translation and publication, we are reading a representation of an Indian-only rite within the Praying Indian community. The converts' words clearly stake out a nontragic view of their individual faith and their assumption that the Praying Indian community will persevere. Even as Eliot introduces his transcriptions as a record of a dying community, its members mortally wounded by King Philip's War, the dying men construe themselves as passing their wisdom to a new generation who will continue as they have begun.

In *Pious Persuasions*, Erik Seeman discusses the deathbed confession in New England as a place or space for subversive lay control over the final religious encounter with clergy.[43] In *Dying Speeches*, we see glimpses of that dynamic operating on several fronts. The dying men reverse the cleric-laity relationship when they exhort their new preacher, as in Antony's exhortation of Daniel to "love not drink" or in that of Old Jacob: "Lastly I say to you *Daniel* our Minister be strong in your work." Jacob even goes on to quote the pertinent scriptural text to his minister: "As *Matt.* 5.14.16. *You must bring Light into the world, and make it to shine, that all may see your good work, and glorify your heavenly Father.*"[44]

To be sure, the men's final exhortations serve to support conservative notions of church hierarchy. Ironically, their sentiments ought to have encouraged Eliot. Here, however, although he welcomes evidence of regeneration, the converts' last speeches contrast with his construction of the mission as dying. Within the context of the 1680s Indian church and within this particular tract, the men's final words, seemingly complicit with colonial efforts to circumscribe their lives to praying townships and "safe" ecclesiastical control, can be read as assertions of local elders' power to lead and advise the community.[45] Several of the men seek to mediate the relation of the community to the new minister. Piambohou says, "I hear and rejoyce that God hath confirmed for us a minister in this Church of *Natek*, he is our watchman. And all you people deal well with him, both *men, women* and *children*, hear him every *Sabbath* day, and make strong your praying to God."[46] John Owussumugsen, echoing Wamporas some thirty years earlier, exhorts his brethren:

> Do not go into the woods among non praying people, abide constantly at *Natik*. You my children, and all my kindred, strongly pray to God: Love and Obey the Rulers, and submit unto their judgment, hear diligently your menisters [*sic*]: be obedient to *Major Gookins* and to *Mr. Eliot.* and *Daniel.*[47]

All the dying men challenge Eliot's dismissal of his own work; they clearly see their community as continuing. They seem to take comfort in the perseverance of their children in the Praying Indian church, and they see Daniel Takawampbait as a strong spiritual leader. Like English Puritans considering the significance of individual Christian deaths, the Praying Indians see the loss of only a small part of the whole faith community and in the dying statements, they become exemplars of Christian piety. They assume that Natick will flourish, their children will enter into church fellowship, and the new way of life will survive them. They register the devastation of the war but, unlike Eliot, speak as if restoration is not only possible but probable.

In 1688, two years before his death, John Eliot wrote to Robert Boyle for the last time. Knowing that he was approaching the end of his life, Eliot took his leave of Boyle with thanks for his support and set his mission accounts in order. Here he seems relatively sanguine concerning the continuation of the mission: "The work in general seemeth to my soul to be in and well toward reviving." In closing, Eliot cites Isaiah 1:25–26 as his final prayer to God concerning the New England colonies, but his melancholy over the loss of the Bay Colony's charter, revoked in 1684, pervades the rest of his concerns, and his mournful tone can be seen as applicable to the Indian mission as well: "I will turn my hand upon thee, and purely purge away thy dross and take away all thy tin, and I will restore thy judges as at the first and thy counsellors as at the beginning."[48] In this last letter to Boyle, Eliot finds some comfort in a prophecy that could apply to the final years of his evangelism. Praying Indians had survived the war, but as Eliot indicates, their civil and ecclesiastical institutions had not yet been "revived" more than ten years afterward. Other writers had celebrated the war's "purging" of Indians from New England. But whereas they were willing to consign all Indians to the flames, Eliot here assumes that in the alloy that is the Praying Indian, there is precious metal to be reclaimed.

The prophecy of restoration remained only a promise until Eliot's death and went unfulfilled afterward. Eliot's vision, the praying towns, and the Praying Indians did not regain their prewar status. And although his hopes for the mission in this 1688 letter are more optimistic, *Dying Speeches* was his last published account of Christian Indians. As we have seen, it is a far from reassuring account of anticipated resurrections. Rather, it describes those converts who had survived the fires of war as melting away. In this, Eliot was wrong. The Praying Indian community did not completely unravel, and its members did not immediately live out a postwar "vanishing Indian" narrative. As Jean O'Brien argues in her discussion of the persistence of the first praying town, "Once it had come together, Natick did not easily come apart."[49] Eliot's understanding of his mission does not register this strength, however. Like James Fenimore Cooper more than a century later, Eliot sees Indians as vanishing; his last literary construct is not the dying Indian saint but the trope of the vanishing Indian.

The Praying Indians' use of the genre of the dying speech demonstrates their very different sense of Natick's persistence. The challenge converts posed to Eliot's representation may be illustrated by the ringing self-assertion in Waban's last recorded words. Waban was the first convert to respond to Eliot's missionary efforts, and his words were recorded at every stage of Eliot's work. Here he begins with the hope that his bodily affliction is God's means of calling him to repentance, seizing on Job's suffering as a type for his own experience. Waban's reading of scripture is an ironic counterpoint to Eliot's disinclination to gather and publish these dying speeches:

> Though my body be almost broken by sickness, yet I desire to remember thy name Oh my God, untill I dy I remember those words Job 19.23,

to 28. Oh that my words were now written, oh that they were printed in a book, that they were graven with an iron pen and lead in a rock for ever.[50]

The "dying speeches" thus construct the Praying Indians' vision of their community's present as worth remembering and its future as worth inhabiting. And so, Eliot's bleak vision was met by the Praying Indians' vigorous assertion of their community's present health and future existence. If in his last works Eliot presages Bryant and Cooper, these "dying Indians" may serve as a bridge to later orators and writers—Joseph Johnson, Samson Occom, and William Apess, among others—who challenged white writers' claims of Indian extinction. After living through forty years of English colonial appropriation of their beliefs and identities, Antony and Waban, the "wife of Totherswamp," James Printer, Sam Sachem, Captain Tom, and Ponampam reclaimed, revisioned, and reoccupied the figure of the Christian Indian.

Notes

Chapter 1. Praying Indians and the Mission upon the Hill

1. William London, *A Catalogue of the most vendible Books in* England, *Orderly and Alphabetically Digested* (1658; rpt. London: Gregg-Archive, 1965). In all quotations of primary texts, I have retained orthography and punctuation but silently expanded abbreviations and exchanged i for j, u for v, and vice versa where appropriate. Unless otherwise noted, when quoting biblical passages I use the Authorized (King James) Version, the translation most popular among Puritans.

2. W[illiam] C[astell], *A petition of W. C. exhibited to the high court of Parliament now assembled, for the propagating of the Gospel in America, and the West Indies, and for the settling of our plantations there* (London, 1641), A5v, 10.

3. John Winthrop, *Reasons to Be Considered for . . . the Intended Plantation in New England,* in *The Puritans in America: A Narrative Anthology,* ed. Alan Heimert and Andrew Delbanco (Cambridge: Harvard University Press, 1985), 73.

4. John Cotton, *God's Promise to His Plantations,* in *The Puritans in America: A Narrative Anthology,* ed. Alan Heimert and Andrew Delbanco (Cambridge: Harvard University Press, 1985), 77, 80.

5. Thomas Hooker, "The Danger of Desertion," in *The Puritans in America: A Narrative Anthology,* ed. Alan Heimert and Andrew Delbanco (Cambridge: Harvard University Press, 1985), 68, 69.

6. Edmund S. Morgan, *The Puritan Dilemma: The Story of John Winthrop* (Boston: Little, Brown and Company, 1958), 178. Morgan offers a succinct discussion of this period, its momentous events, and New Englanders' concomitant anxiety. See esp. chapter 12, "New England or Old."

7. Andrew Delbanco, *The Puritan Ordeal* (Cambridge: Harvard University Press, 1989), 188–89.

8. Roger Williams, *A Key into the Language of America,* ed. John J. Teunissen and Evelyn J. Hinz (Detroit: Wayne State University Press, 1973), 90.

9. Most studies of Praying Indians have situated them almost entirely within

American contexts. See Elise Brenner, "To Pray or to Be Prey: That Is the Question: Strategies for Cultural Autonomy of Massachusetts Praying Town Indians," *Ethnohistory* 27, no. 2 (1980): 135–52; Dane Morrison, *A Praying People: Massachusett Acculturation and the Failure of the Puritan Mission, 1600–1690* (New York: Peter Lang Publishing, 1995); Kenneth M. Morrison, "'That Art of Coyning Christians': John Eliot and the Praying Indians of Massachusetts," *Ethnohistory* 21, no. 1 (1974): 77–92; Robert James Naeher, "Dialogue in the Wilderness: John Eliot and the Indian Exploration of Puritanism as a Source of Meaning, Comfort, and Ethnic Survival," *New England Quarterly* 62, no. 3(1989): 346–68. By contrast, Thomas Scanlan notes that this connection between colonial experiences and European identities has been neglected by the "surprising insular" fields of American and English renaissance studies. *Colonial Writing and the New World, 1583–1671* (Cambridge, Cambridge University Press, 1999), 1–2.

10. Delbanco, *Puritan Ordeal,* 189.

11. See Samuel Eliot Morison, *Founding of Harvard College,* 2nd ed. (Cambridge: Harvard University Press, 1968), 304–5, for a discussion of this tract and its publishing history.

12. *New Englands First Fruits,* in Samuel Eliot Morison, *Founding of Harvard College,* appendix D, 2nd ed. (Cambridge: Harvard University Press, 1968), 428.

13. For a discussion of William Castell's 1641 petition protesting the lack of evangelism and its influence on the New England mission, see William Kellaway, *The New England Company, 1649–1776: Missionary Society to the American Indians* (New York: Barnes and Noble, 1961), 4. Francis Jennings suspects that missionary efforts (or the lack of them) depended on economic considerations. Jennings argues that the colony used mission rhetoric to mask its pragmatic political maneuvering as "an altruistic outpouring of religious benevolence." He also charges that the beginnings of Eliot's missionizing may have been spurred by financial needs and were most certainly motivated by political fears that parliament would credit the attacks made against Massachusetts by repatriated New Englanders such as Thomas Lechford (*The Invasion of America: Indians, Colonialism and the Cant of Conquest* [Chapel Hill: University of North Carolina Press,1975], 238).

14. *New Englands First Fruits,* 421. As I discuss above, John Cotton's 1630 sermon, *God's Promise to His Plantations,* may serve as a counterpoint. Of the six actions that young plantations were to take, only the last injunction makes mention of native inhabitants: "Offend Not the poor natives . . . make them partakers of your precious Faith" (19).

15. *New Englands First Fruits,* 431.

16. *The Day-Breaking, if not the Sun-Rising of the Gospell with the* Indians in New-England, 1647, rpt. in *Tracts Relating to the Attempts to Convert to Christianity the Indians of New England,* Massachusetts Historical Society Collections, 3rd ser., 4 (1834), 1–23. The sources most important to the construction of the figure of the Praying Indian are mission tracts, which were published regularly beginning in 1643 with *New Englands First Fruits* and ending in 1671 with *Brief Narrative.* These are often referred to as the "Eliot tracts," but the term is a misnomer. They are in fact compilations of texts: prefaces, letters, lists, reports, narratives. They were written and edited by many men; indeed, *Day-Breaking* was published anonymously and has been attributed to several authors. Throughout the book, I will make citations to the main title of individual tracts, but my

discussions will often pertain to a specific contributor rather than to the accepted "author" of the tract. See my discussion above, pp. 10–11 and n. 18 below.

17. Ralph Bauer argues that "the constructions and reconstructions of New England's colonial Selfs and Others must be read in the context of the changing relationship between the imperial metropolis and the colonial elites as well in the colony's changing Indian relations" ("The 'Principal End of the Plantation': The Praying Indian and the Politics of a New England Colonial Identity, 1630–1700," in *The American Nation, National Identity, Nationalism*, ed. Knud Krakau [Munich: Lit Verlag, 1997], 57). Specifically, the representation of Christian Indians, Bauer argues, helped in "transculturating an English providentialist sense of mission into an American context" ("John Eliot, The Praying Indian, and the Rhetoric of a New England Errand," *Zeitschrift für Anglistik und Amerikanistik* 44, no. 4 [1996]: 332). James Holstun has suggested that colonial exchanges occurred in both directions. He sees Eliot's work as "a translation of Old World writings into a new geographical setting, but like most translations it criticizes and transforms its original" (*A Rational Millennium* [New York: Oxford University Press, 1987], 104).

18. Hilary Wyss defines the mission tract similarly: It "is a form that encompasses a range of stylistic features and performs multiple rhetorical tasks. Though some are single-author documents with a carefully controlled narrative, often they are collections of seemingly random information in the form of letters, contracts, citations, and anecdotes that all point to the efficacy of a certain missionary or missionary group" (*Writing Indians: Literacy, Christianity, and Native Community in Early America* [Amherst: University of Massachusetts Press, 2000], 11). Philip Round makes the point that the meaning of a seventeenth-century text (and, indeed, any text) is "deeply involved in the formal properties of its medium. . . . Printed texts signified not only in the semantic array of their narratives or verses but also in their overall arrangement—in their prefaces, dedicatory epistles, and poems, their engraved frontispieces and author's portraits" (*By Nature and by Custom Cursed: Transatlantic Civil Discourse and New England Cultural Production, 1620–1660* [Hanover: University Press of New England, 1999], 7).

19. Thomas Shepard, *The Clear Sun-shine of the Gospel Breaking Forth upon the Indians in New-England*, 1648, rpt. in *Tracts Relating to the Attempts to Convert to Christianity the Indians of New England*, Massachusetts Historical Society Collections, 3rd ser. 4 (1834), 28.

20. John Dury's remarks both preface and conclude Edward Winslow's tract *The Glorious Progress of the Gospel, amongst the Indians in New England*, 1649, rpt. in *Tracts Relating to the Attempts to Convert to Christianity the Indians of New England*, Massachusetts Historical Society Collections, 3rd ser. 4 (1834), 95.

21. Henry Whitfield, *The Light appearing more and more towards the perfect Day*, 1651, rpt. in *Tracts Relating to the Attempts to Convert to Christianity the Indians of New England*, Massachusetts Historical Society Collections, 3rd ser. 4 (1834), 145.

22. Shepard, *Clear Sun-shine*, 29.

23. As Reiner Smolinski rightly notes, the understanding of a foundational errand for New England depends on a retrospective reading of a few key texts of New England's first generation: "[u]nquestionably, Puritan typology, with its fig-

ural use of language, played a central role in nurturing a uniquely American identity that came to full flower in the nineteenth century." Critics, "divorcing language from doctrine," have misread that identity backward, into Puritan New England writings. What later scholars took to be extravagant claims for New England were instances of figural language—typology—used to counter the dismissal by some of America as the devil's dominion and to claim that Christ's rule did indeed extend into America (Reiner Smolinski, ed., *Threefold Paradise of Cotton Mather: An Edition of "Triparadisus"* [Athens: University of Georgia Press, 1995], 59).

24. "Embarrassed contradiction" is Delbanco's phrase (*Puritan Ordeal,* 96). In his book, a study of the "affective life" of New England immigrants, he argues that predominant feelings were confusion and uneasiness. He describes the migration "not as a confident journey toward the millennium but as a flight from chaos," and he argues that the heroic identity was born later, out of continuing debate over the flight from England (80). Theodore Dwight Bozeman argues that any notion of New England as a pattern for the nations, such as in Edward Johnson's *Wonder-Working Providence,* arises only after the "English Revolution and under the influence of the copious millennial speculation which that event had evoked" (*To Live Ancient Lives: The Primitivist Dimension in Puritanism* [Chapel Hill: University of North Carolina Press, 1988], 116). However critics and historians read the very early years of plantation, most recognize a rhetorical shift in New England literature that accompanied the upheavals in Old England, whether the civil wars, Interregnum, or Restoration.

25. Sacvan Bercovitch, *The American Jeremiad* (Madison: University of Wisconsin Press, 1978), 7.

26. Bozeman, *To Live Ancient Lives,* 274.

27. Richard W. Cogley, *John Eliot's Mission to the Indians before King Philip's War* (Cambridge: Harvard University Press, 1999), 83, 78.

28. See David Katz, *Philo-Semitism and the Readmission of the Jews to England, 1603–1655* (Oxford: Clarendon Press, 1982), 92. Other influential millennialists include Joseph Mede and Johann Heinrich Alsted. Brightman died in 1607, and so wrote well before the period under consideration here, but as Katz explains, "Brightman's works were among the most respected and influential of millenarian writings, and were reissued in England after the onset of the Civil War" (92). For a brief history of millennial thought and theology, see "Transformations of Millennial Thought in America," the introduction to *Millennial Thought in America: Historical and Intellectual Contexts, 1630–1860,* ed. Bernd Engler, Joerg O. Fichte, and Oliver Scheiding (Trier: Wissenschaftlicher Verlag Trier [WVT], 2002), 9–37.

29. Katz, *Philo-Semitism,* 92, 93.

30. Action-based millennialist beliefs took many forms. The Fifth Monarchists, for example, advocated extreme action. In 1661, Thomas Venner led a violent uprising under the slogan, "Live King Jesus," in which they killed their opponents. See Philip F. Gura, *A Glimpse of Sion's Glory: Puritan Radicalism in New England, 1620–1660* (Middletown, Conn.: Wesleyan University Press, 1984), 142.

31. J. F. Maclear argues that "Puritans differed from many English and Continental Protestants in their tendency to view eschatology not primarily as a formal theological scheme . . . but as a description of the cosmic environment in which the regenerate soldier of Christ was now to do battle against the power of

sin" ("New England and the Fifth Monarchy: The Quest for the Millennium in Early American Puritanism," *William and Mary Quarterly*, 3rd ser., 32, no. 2 [April 1975]: 226).

32. The anti-Puritan writer Thomas Lechford reflected these views in his charge that New Englanders were neglecting their duty. He wrote that New Englanders refused to proselytize out of neglect and millenarian complacency: "There hath not been any sent forth by any Church to learne the Natives language, or to instruct them in the Religion; First, because they say they have not to do with them being without, unlesse they come to heare and learn English. Secondly, some say out of Rev. 15. last, it is not probable that any nation more can be converted til the calling of the Jews" (*Plaine Dealing, or News from New England*, ed. J. Hammond Trumbull [Boston: J. K. Wiggin and Wm Parsons Lunt, 1867], 54). Cogley argues that the orthodox New England view traced Indian origins to the Tartars, *John Eliot's Mission*, 97.

33. For additional discussions of Puritan millennialist beliefs in this period, see Bozeman, *To Live Ancient Lives*; Timothy J. Sehr, "John Eliot, Millennialist and Missionary," *Historian* 46 (February 1984): 187–203; Reiner Smolinski, "*Israel Redivivus*: The Eschatological Limits of Puritan Typology in New England," *New England Quarterly* 63, no. 3 (1990): 357–95, and *Threefold Paradise*; and Cogley, *John Eliot's Mission*, 83–90. Although millennialists were interested in Thorowgood's publications, he himself did not articulate a millennial interpretation. See Cogley, *John Eliot's Mission*, 85.

34. Eliot speculated on such a genealogy in *Light Appearing* and contributed directly to the second edition of Thomas Thorowgood's influential treatise *Jews in America*. He also made the most significant colonial contribution to the millennial debate with his *Christian Commonwealth*, published in 1659. For a discussion of Eliot's changing millennial beliefs and shifting speculations on Indian origins, see Cogley, *John Eliot's Mission*, 76–104.

35. Thorowgood, *Jews in America*, 23.

36. *New Englands First Fruits*, 441.

37. Whitfield, *Light appearing*, 145.

38. Shepard, *Clear Sun-shine*, 34.

39. See chapter 4.

40. Eliot's letter appears in Whitfield, *Strength out of Weaknesse; or a Glorious Manifestation of the further Progresse of the Gospel among the Indians in New-England*, rpt. in *Tracts Relating to the Attempts to Convert to Christianity the Indians of New England* Massachusetts Historical Society Collections, 3rd ser., vol. 4 (1834), 158.

41. See Winslow, *Glorious Progress*, 83.

42. See E. Shaskan Bumas, "The Cannibal Butcher Shop: Protestant Uses of Las Casas's *Brevissima relación* in Europe and the American Colonies," *Early American Literature* 35, no. 3 (2000): 108.

43. See Frank Strong, "The Causes of Cromwell's West Indian Expedition," *American Historical Review* 4, no. 2 (January 1899): 233–36.

44. Karen Kupperman, "Errand to the Indies: Puritan Colonization from Providence Island through the Western Design," *William and Mary Quarterly* 3rd ser., 45, no. 1 (1988): 72.

45. For primary sources for the "Black Legend," see Charles Gibson, ed., *The Black Legend: Anti-Spanish Attitudes in the Old World and the New* (New York: Alfred A. Knopf, 1971). See also William S. Maltby's full-length study, *The Black*

Legend in England: The Development of Anti-Spanish Sentiment, 1558–1660 (Durham, N.C.: Duke University Press, 1971).

46. Winslow, *Glorious Progress,* 95.

47. *Day-breaking,* 18.

48. Shepard, *Clear Sun-shine,* 66.

49. Bumas argues that the 1656 English-authored preface to Las Casas's *Brevísima relación* presents Oliver Cromwell as "merely soothing *The Tears of the Indians* (as that translation is called) by attacking Catholics in Ireland and Scotland" ("Cannibal Butcher Shop," 108).

50. Cromwell to Cotton, qtd. in Kupperman, "Errand to the Indies," 91. Kupperman calls Cotton "one of the foremost interpreters of the Bible's prophetic passages" ("Errand to the Indies," 91).

51. Samuel Sewall, *The Diary of Samuel Sewall,* ed. M. Halsey Thomas (New York: Farrar, Straus and Giroux, 1973), vol. 1, 359.

52. Sewall, *Diary,* 359. Kupperman explains: "Cotton argued that the attack on episcopacy in England was the pouring of the fifth vial and that the entire process, the culmination of history, was speeding up" ("Errand to the Indies," 91).

53. David Armitage, "The Cromwellian Protectorate and the Languages of Empire," *Historical Journal* 35, no. 3 (September 1992): 536.

54. See Kupperman, "Errand to the Indies," 95.

55. Sewall, *Diary,* 359.

56. Kupperman, "Errand to the Indies," 94, 97.

57. Armitage, "Cromwellian Protectorate," 540.

58. See Kupperman, "Errand to the Indies," 96. Cromwell's charge to Gookin is reprinted as "Instructions given unto Mr. Daniel Gookin," appendix H of *Memorials of the Professional Life and Times of Sir William Penn,* vol. 2, ed. Branville Penn (London: 1833).

59. For the details of Gookin's life and career, see Richard Cogley, "Daniel Gookin," in *Dictionary of Literary Biography,* vol. 24: *American Colonial Writers, 1606–1734,* ed. Emory Elliott (Detroit: Gale Group, 1984), 150.

60. John Eliot, *A Late and Further Manifestation of the Progress of the Gospel amongst the Indians in New-England,* 1655, rpt. in *Tracts Relating to the Attempts to Convert to Christianity the Indians of New England,* Massachusetts Historical Society Collections, 3rd ser., vol. 4 (1834), 267.

61. Whitfield, *Light Appearing,* 127.

62. Ibid., 137.

63. Bumas, "Cannibal Butcher Shop," 125; Kupperman, "Errand to the Indies," 93.

64. Bumas argues that "tears became something of a liquid trope" ("Cannibal Butcher Shop," 125).

65. John Eliot and Thomas Mayhew, Jr., *Tears of Repentance; or, A further Narrative of the Progress of the* Gospel, 1653, rpt. in *Tracts Relating to the Attempts to Convert to Christianity the Indians of New England,* Massachusetts Historical Society Collections, 3rd ser., vol. 4 (1834), 212.

66. Cogley, *John Eliot's Mission,* 94. Cogley goes on to argue that a few months later, Eliot had determined that New England was a second inaugural point and the millennium's eastern start did not depend on England.

67. Eliot and Mayhew, *Tears of Repentance,* 212.

68. Cogley provides the most recent biography of Eliot in *John Eliot's Mission.*

69. Eliot and Mayhew, *Tears of Repentance*, 212. As Timothy J. Sehr points out, the colonies may have opposed King Charles, but "Bay leaders had argued that submission to authority was essential to the ordered society they desired" (*Colony and Commonwealth: Massachusetts Bay, 1649–1660* [New York: Garland Publishing, 1989], 34).

70. Eliot, *Late and Further Manifestation*, 271.

71. Evangelism in particular seems to have had a significant transatlantic component throughout the colonial period. Frank Lambert argues that the "Great Awakening" of the 1640s was "invented" by "revivalists [who] saw unity in awakenings occurring in diverse communities separated from each other by great distances" (*Inventing the "Great Awakening"* [Princeton: Princeton University Press, 1999], 4).

72. In 1674, Daniel Gookin claimed the number of Praying Indians to be about 1,100. See his *Historical Collections of the Indians in New England*, in Massachusetts Historical Society Collections, vol. 1 (1806), 141–246. Jennings argues, however, that the real number was much lower, that Gookin and missionary John Eliot blurred the distinction between Indians who merely observed the Sabbath or submitted to the praying towns' civil order and those in "full communion" (*The Invasion of America*, 250–51). He places the number of Indians in communion in 1674 at 64–74. I follow the more optimistic count of Praying Indians here: my emphasis is on those people who were culturally as well as (or even instead of) spiritually identifying themselves with the praying community.

73. Jean M. O'Brien, *Dispossession by Degrees: Indian Land and Identity in Natick, Massachusetts, 1650–1790* (Cambridge, UK: Cambridge University Press, 1997), 16.

74. Shepard, *Clear Sun-shine*, 30.

75. *Day-breaking*, 15.

76. James Axtell uses the phrase to describe the spiritual, emotional, and cultural control that accompanied physical coercion (*The Invasion Within* [New York: Oxford University Press, 1985]).

77. Eliot and Mayhew, *Tears of Repentance*, 223.

78. Ibid., 234. On Edmund Browne's role in Puritan evangelism and his antipathy to Praying Indians during and after King Philip's War, which is entirely in keeping with his cynical tone here, see Jenny Hale Pulsipher, " 'Our Sages are Sageles': A Letter on Massachusetts Indian Policy after King Philip's War," *William and Mary Quarterly* 58, no. 2(2001): 431–48.

79. Eliot and Mayhew, *Tears of Repentance*, 239.

80. Shepard, *Clear Sun-shine*, 57. For a discussion of clothing and identity during this period, see Ann M. Little, " 'Shoot that Rogue, for He Hath an Englishman's Coat on!': Cultural Cross-Dressing, on the New-England Frontier, 1620–1760," *New England Quarterly* 74, no. 2 (2001): 238–74.

81. *Day-breaking*, 3.

82. Shepard, *Clear Sun-shine*, 45.

83. Henry Whitfield, *Strength out of Weaknesse*, 178.

84. Eliot and Mayhew, *Tears of Repentance*, 227.

85. Shepard, *Clear Sun-shine*, 62.

86. Holstun interprets this organization as the imposition of "the spatial ideal ruling utopia's distribution of bodies" on the Indians' traditional use of space. See *A Rational Millennium*, 124.

87. Karen Kupperman discusses such exchanges at length in her *Indians & English: Facing Off in Early America* (Ithaca: Cornell University Press, 2000).

88. Consider, as an example, Thomas Morton's trade in guns with Indians, which compounded his sins in the eyes of Pilgrim authorities, who arrested and charged him with unlawful trade in arms. See William Bradford, *Of Plymouth Plantation, 1620–1647* (New York: Modern Library, 1981), 228–32.

89. "Contact zone" is Mary Louise Pratt's term, meant "to invoke the spatial and temporal copresence of subjects previously separated by geographic and historical disjuncures, and whose trajectories now intersect" (*Imperial Eyes: Travel Writing and Transculturation* [London: Routledge, 1992], 7).

90. Scanlan, *Colonial Writing*, 3. Scanlan argues against "assuming that the exploitation and destruction of native populations and their cultures could only signify something to a subsequent, more enlightened, generation." Rather, he suggests, "the native populations figured in complicated and not necessarily predictable ways in the writings of those who were doing the colonizing" (2–3).

91. I rely here on Joshua Bellin's approach to American writing, which he terms "intercultural literary criticism"; i.e., he "views texts as taking shape through, and shaping in turn . . . cultural interrelationships." Bellin insists that American literature—and here, I would interpose, New England mission literature in particular—"emerges from contexts of encounter, from the interaction and intersection of peoples" (*The Demon of the Continent: Indians and the Shaping of American Literature* [Philadelphia: University of Pennsylvania Press, 2001], 5, 2). Bellin eschews an "images approach" to American literature in which Indians are "silent, ineffectual, and . . . unnecessary to (white) history, (white) ideology, (white) literature" (3). He suggests that mission literature is especially responsive to his critical methodology. See his overview of Indian conversions from the seventeenth to the mid-nineteenth century (14–38).

92. In chap. 2, I discuss these land claims and the courts.

93. Wyss, *Writing Indians*, 3.

Chapter 2. Seeing with Ezekiel's Eyes

1. Samuel Morison, *Founding of Harvard College*, 2nd ed. (Cambridge: Harvard University Press, 1968), 319.

2. I allude, of course, to John Winthrop's sermon, "A Modell of Christian Charity," in which he famously warns: "Wee must Consider that wee shall be as a Citty upon a Hill, the eyes of all people are upon us; soe that if wee shall deale falsely with our god in this worke wee have undertaken and soe cause him to withdrawe his present help from us, wee shall be made a story and a by-word through the world" (*The Heath Anthology of American Literature*, 3rd ed., vol. 1, ed. Paul Lauter et al. [Lexington, Mass.: D. C. Heath and Company, 1994], 233).

3. Thomas Thorowgood, *Jewes in America; or, Probabilities that the Americans are of that race* (London, 1650). Among many other works, Dury authored "An Epistolicall Discourse," included in Thorowgood's work; the discourse outlined his hope that "Americans" would be identified as the lost tribes of Israel. William Greenhill, who signed several prefaces and dedications to mission tracts, also published commentaries on the Book of Ezekiel. In *An exposition continued upon the XX, XXI, XXII, XXIII, XXIV, XXV, XXVI, XXVII, XXVIII, and XXIX, chapters of the prophet Ezekiel, with many useful observations thereupon* (Lon-

don, 1658), Greenhill links the prophet's vision of Judah and Israel's union to Menasseh ben Israel's assertion that American Indians were Israelites (460).

4. Michael Warner, "What's Colonial about Colonial America?" in *Possible Pasts: Becoming Colonial in Early America*, ed. Robert Blair St. George (Ithaca: Cornell University Press, 2000), 56.

5. Benedict Anderson makes this argument about Mary Rowlandson and her insistence on seeing an "English landscape" in Massachusetts ("Exodus," *Critical Inquiry* 20, no. 2 [1994]: 314–27).

6. As Zubeda Jalalzai explains, "Though early America fits diversely within concepts of contemporary postcolonial theory, the theories can apply to both the borders between the settlers and the home country and between the settlers and the wilderness" ("Puritan Imperialisms," *Connecticut Review* 23 [Fall 2001]: 72).

7. Theodore Dwight Bozeman, *To Live Ancient Lives: The Primitivist Dimension in Puritanism* (Chapel Hill: University of North Carolina Press, 1988), 194.

8. Thomas Shepard, *The Clear Sun-shine of the Gospel Breaking Forth upon the Indians in New-England*, 1648, rpt. in *Tracts Relating to the Attempt to Convert to Christianity the Indians of New England*, Massachusetts Historical Society Collections, 3rd. ser., vol. 4 (1834), 61, 60.

9. Janice Knight, *Orthodoxies in Massachusetts: Rereading American Puritanism* (Cambridge: Harvard University Press, 1994), 183. Knight calls Shepard "a more complicated and self-divided version of the preparationist line" (180). And her view is borne out by his continued interest in missions despite his reservations about the radical reading given them by John Eliot, John Dury, Thomas Goodwin, John Owen, and other mission writers. Indeed, these latter figures are associated with John Cotton in her study of Puritan "orthodoxies" rather than with Shepard.

10. Shepard, *Clear Sun-shine*, 29. The latter part of the passage is a combination of several biblical phrases of millennial import: "when the whole earth shall be full of the knowledge of the Lord, as the waters cover the Sea" is from Isaiah 11.9, a verse following the end-time vision of lion and lamb lying together; "East and West" may be from Matthew 8.11: "That many shall come from the east and west, and shall sit down with Abraham, and Isaac, and Jacob, in the kingdom of heaven"; and finally, "the song of the lamb" comes from Revelation 15.

11. The distinction between colonists with access to print and those who did not have such access in this period is significant to any discussion of the Praying Indian figure. That there were critics of the mission endeavor is evident even from the tracts, which periodically address charges of mismanagement or defend converts from disparagement. Throughout this period, however, the United Colonies and the General Court in Massachusetts supported Eliot and the Praying Indians. Colonial opposition, even antipathy toward Christian Indians was held in check until King Philip's War, when long-festering suspicions of Indian apostasy came to the fore. See chapter 6 for my discussion of that violence, which was preceded by a shift in the mission's publishing practices.

12. Shepard, *Clear Sun-shine*, 30.

13. Edward Winslow, *The Glorious Progress of the Gospel, amongst the Indians in New England*, 1649, rpt. in *Tracts Relating to the Attempts to Convert to Christianity the Indians of New England*, Massachusetts Historical Society Collections, 3rd ser., vol. 4 (1834), 97.

14. John Eliot, *A Late and Further Manifestation of the Progress of the Gospel amongst the Indians in New-England*, 1655, rpt. in *Tracts Relating to the At-*

tempts to Convert to Christianity the Indians of New England, Massachusetts Historical Society Collections, 3rd ser., vol. 4 (1834), 267.

15. For details about the Act and the appeal from the pulpit, see William Kellaway, *The New England Company, 1649–1776: Missionary Society to the American Indians* (New York: Barnes and Noble, 1961).

16. Philip Round, *By Nature and by Custom Cursed: Transatlantic Civil Discourse and New England Cultural Production, 1620–1660* (Hanover: University Press of New England, 1999), 261.

17. There were, of course, other—and more successful—English missionaries, even within the Bay Colony. Thomas Mayhew preceded Eliot into the mission fields, and his converts survived King Philip's War and persisted even to the present day. Despite Mayhew's real achievements, however, Eliot was the more successful publicist. In mission tracts he represents Mayhew as a latecomer to the work, young and inexperienced.

18. *The Day-Breaking, if not the Sun-Rising of the Gospell with the* Indians in New-England, 1647, rpt. in *Tracts Relating to the Attempts to Convert to Christianity the Indians of New England,* Massachusetts Historical Society Collections, 3rd ser., vol. 4 (1834), 22.

19. Ezekiel 37:7–10.

20. Shepard, *Clear Sun-shine,* 27.

21. As Richard Cogley shows in his discussion of Eliot's millennialist beliefs, when Eliot first began as an evangelist, his ideas about Christian converts and their millennial identity were conservative. See "The Mission and the Millennium," in *John Eliot's Mission to the Indians before King Philip's War* (Cambridge: Harvard University Press, 1999), 76–104. Eliot's caution may explain why at first the application of Ezekiel to converting Indians was hedged by so many exegetical qualifications. In addition, Reiner Smolinski notes that at this time the Puritans read biblical prophecies relating to Israel's return from Babylonian captivity, such as Ezekiel's vision of the dry bones, through millennial typology: the resurrected bones are a type of Jewish conversion to Christianity in the last days, not a metaphoric type of Puritan New England ("*Israel Redivivus*," 368–69). Given this millennialist reading of Ezekiel, the attempt to identify Praying Indians as the prophet's dry bones is extraordinarily significant, because such an identity would conclusively prove that the end times were upon God's people.

22. Shepard, *Clear Sun-shine,* 62.

23. Ibid., 63.

24. Winslow, *Glorious Progress,* 93.

25. John Winthrop, *Reasons to Be Considered for . . . the Intended Plantation in New England,* in *The Puritans in America: A Narrative Anthology,* ed. Alan Heimert and Andrew Delbanco (Cambridge: Harvard University Press, 1985), 73.

26. William Bradford, *Of Plymouth Plantation, 1620–1647* (New York: Modern Library, 1981), 97.

27. Thomas Morton, *New English Canaan,* in *Tracts and Other Papers Relating Principally to the Origin, Settlement, and Progress of the Colonies in North America, from the Discovery of the Country to the Year 1776,* ed. Peter Force, vol. 2, no. 5 (Washington, D.C., printed by P. Force, 1836–46), 19.

28. John Mason, "Brief History of the Pequot War," in *History of the Pequot War,* ed. Charles Orr (1897; rpt. New York: AMS Press, 1980), 30.

29. Winthrop, "Modell of Christian Charity," 228.

30. *Day-breaking,* 16.

31. Henry Whitfield, *The Light appearing more and more towards the perfect Day*, 1651, rpt. in *Tracts Relating to the Attempts to Convert to Christianity the Indians of New England*, Massachusetts Historical Society Collections, 3rd ser., vol. 4 (1834), 126.

32. Ibid., 122.

33. Michael Warner, "New English Sodom," *American Literature* 64, no. 1 (March 1992): 26; Winthrop, "Modell of Christian Charity," 233.

34. John Eliot, *Christian Commonwealth* (1659; rpt. New York: Arno Press, 1972).

35. See James Holstun for a discussion of Eliot's *Christian Commonwealth* and its connection to praying town rule (*A Rational Millennium* [New York: Oxford University Press, 1987], 145–58).

36. Henry Whitfield, *Strength out of Weaknesse; or a Glorious Manifestation of the further Progresse of the Gospel among the* Indians *in New–England*, 1652, rpt. in *Tracts Relating to the Attempts to Convert to Christianity the Indians of New England*, Massachusetts Historical Society Collections, 3rd ser., vol. 4 (1834), 171.

37. Praying Indian conversion narratives were transcribed and printed in two tracts: John Eliot and Thomas Mayhew, Jr., *Tears of Repentance; or, A further Narrative of the Progress of the* Gospel *amongst the Indians in New-England*, 1653, rpt. in *Tracts Relating to the Attempts to Convert to Christianity the Indians of New England*, Massachusetts Historical Society Collections, 3rd ser., vol. 4 (1834), 197–260; and John Eliot, *A further Account of the progress of the* Gospel *amongst the* Indians *in New England* (London, 1660).

38. Jeffrey Richards, *Theater Enough: American Culture and the Metaphor of the World Stage, 1607–1789* (Durham, N.C.: Duke University Press, 1991), 103.

39. Jean O'Brien, *Dispossession by Degrees: Indian Land and Identity in Natick, Massachusetts, 1650–1790* (Cambridge, UK: Cambridge University Press, 1997), 31.

40. Whitfield, *Strength out of Weaknesse*, 171.

41. Most of the documents pertaining to this land dispute are rpt. in the appendix to *The Early Records of the Town of Dedham*, vol. 4, ed. Don Gleason Hill (Dedham, Mass., 1894).

42. *Early Records*, 242.

43. Ibid., 250, 251, 260.

44. Neal Salisbury, "Red Puritans," *William and Mary Quarterly*, 3rd ser., 31, no. 1 (January 1974): 41.

45. *Early Records*, 259.

46. In a January 1662 petition, Eliot detailed the Indians' right to the land by virtue of their association with "Josias, alias Wompituk," whom Eliot claimed had retained a sachem's right to the land until "he did solemnly in Gods presenc, give up his right in these lands, unto God, to make a towne, gather a church, & live in civile order in this place" (*Early Records of the Town*, 259).

47. Shepard, *Clear Sun-shine*, 34

48. The reversal of this lamentation especially echoes earlier works. Compare it to this passage from Thomas Hooker's sermon, *The Danger of Desertion*: "England hath been a mirror of mercies. Yet now God may leave it and make it the mirror of his justice" (*The Puritans in America, a Narrative Anthology*, ed. Alan Heimert and Andrew Delbanco [Cambridge: Harvard University Press, 1985], 66).

49. Shepard, *Clear Sun-shine*, 34.

50. Whitfield, *Light Appearing*, 146.

51. Richard Slotkin makes this point as well: "In the captivity narrative, the Indians become the instruments of God for the chastisement of his guilty people—a reversal of the missionary and war narratives' insistence that the whites are God's means for the salvation or destruction of the Indians" (*Regeneration through Violence: The Mythology of the American Frontier, 1600–1860* [Hanover, N.H.: Wesleyan University Press, 1973], 99).

52. Shepard, *Clear Sun-shine*, 37. Round reads this same moment as evidence of the "ethic of imprecision that signaled civil conversation" in transatlantic exchanges. He contrasts that ethic with that of "Protestant precision and certitude for [Puritan colonists'] immediate circle" (*By Nature and Custom Cursed*, 24). However, the metropolitan response to Shepard's "imprecision" here is certainty and enthusiasm.

53. Samuel Sewall, *The Diary of Samuel Sewall*, ed. M. Halsey Thomas, vol. 1 (New York: Farrar, Straus and Giroux: 1973), 279; also qtd. in Cogley, *John Eliot's Mission*, 103.

54. Cotton Mather, *The Life and Death of the Reverend Mr. John Eliot* (London, 1694), 89.

55. Mather is actually comparing the linguistic capabilities of beavers and Native Americans, but from Mather's Puritan perspective, the capacity for speech and the "Arts" is inextricably connected to the capacity for salvation (*Life and Death*, 86).

56. Mather was interested in evangelism, of course, but his imagery and descriptions of Praying Indians suggest a considerable difference between his perspective and that of Eliot.

57. Renato Rosaldo, *Culture and Truth: The Remaking of Social Analysis* (New York: Beacon, 1989), 70.

58. The prevalence of the "ghostly" Indian in later works is explored by Renee L. Bergland in her recent book, *The National Uncanny: Indian Ghosts and American Subjects* (Hanover, N.H.: Dartmouth College, 2000).

59. William Cullen Bryant, "The Prairies," in *The Heath Anthology of American Literature*, ed. Paul Lauter et al., 3rd ed., vol. 1 (Lexington, Mass.: D. C. Heath and Company, 1994), ll. 65–66.

60. Philip Freneau, "The Indian Burial Ground," in *The Heath Anthology of American Literature*, ed. Paul Lauter et al., 3rd ed., vol. 1 (Lexington, Mass.: D. C. Heath and Company, 1994).

61. William Apess, "Eulogy on King Philip," in *On Our Own Ground: The Complete Writings of William Apess, a Pequot*, ed. Barry O'Connell (Amherst: University of Massachusetts Press, 1992), 284.

Chapter 3. Wielding the Sword of God's Word

1. James Axtell, *The Invasion Within* (New York: Oxford University Press, 1985).

2. John Eliot and Thomas Mayhew, Jr., *Tears of Repentance; or, A further Narrative of the Progress of the Gospel amongst the Indians in New-England*, 1653, rpt. in *Tracts Relating to the Attempts to Convert to Christianity the Indians of New England*, Massachusetts Historical Society Collections, 3rd ser., vol. 4 (1834), 238, emphasis added.

3. Kathleen Bragdon, "Native Languages as Spoken and Written," in *The Language Encounter in the Americas, 1492–1800,* ed. Edward G. Gray and Norman Fiering (New York: Berghahn Books, 2000), 183. Bragdon reviews the scholarship documenting the destructive impact of literacy on colonized people but also argues that "literacy was often a manifestation of group encounters."

4. Many of the Bibles printed in 1663 were lost or destroyed during the war of 1675–76, and so this number includes replacement copies. The print history of the Bible can be found in the entry on John Eliot in James Constantine Pilling, *Bibliography of the Algonquian Languages* (1891; rpt. New York: AMS Press, 1973).

5. For the percentage of literate Native peoples in the region, see Bragdon, "Native Languages as Spoken and Written," 181. Jill Lepore notes that this literacy rate is "decidedly lower" than that for colonists (*The Name of War: King Philip's War and the Origins of American Identity* [New York: Alfred A. Knopf, 1998], 36–37).

6. I follow jessie little doe fermino's direction for the name and spelling of this language ("Recovering Spoken Wampanoag Language," unpublished paper delivered at "Reinterpreting New England Indians and the Colonial Experience," conference sponsored by the Colonial Society of Massachusetts and Old Sturbridge Village [Sturbridge, April 21–22, 2001]). The language is at present better known as "Massachusett," especially in linguistic accounts such as Ives Goddard and Kathleen Bragdon, *Native Writings in Massachusett* (Philadelphia: American Philosophical Society, 1988).

7. Qtd. in Pilling, *Bibliography of the Algonquian Languages,* 157.

8. S. H. Brown, "Eliot's Indian Bible," in *Putnam's Monthly Magazine of American Literature, Science, and Art* 12, no. 9 (September 1868), 359. In Cornell University Library, *Making of America* (1999), cited May 24, 2002, ⟨http://cdl.library.cornell.edu./cgi-bin/moa/moa-cgi?notisid=ABK9283-0012-77⟩.

9. Ironically, the seemingly fixed texts of seventeenth-century scriptural translations are serving as viable resources for this new work. For a description of the work of the Wampanoag Language Reclamation Committee, see Leanne Hinton and Ken Hale, eds., *The Green Book of Language Revitalization in Practice* (San Diego: Academic Press, 2001), 28–32.

10. Leanne Hinton notes that "the loss of language is part of the oppression and disenfranchisement of indigenous peoples. . . . Indigenous efforts toward language maintenance or revitalization are generally part of a larger effort to retain or regain their political autonomy, their land base, or at least their own sense of identity" ("Language Revitalization: An Overview," in *Green Book of Language Revitalization,* 5). Likewise, the repeated insistence that a language is dead, gone, "evermore unspoken" has political effects and perhaps even hastens the language's "demise."

11. Joshua Bellin, *The Demon of the Continent: Indians and the Shaping of American Literature* (Philadelphia: University of Pennsylvania Press, 2001), 73.

12. William Wallace Tooker identifies the captive translator as "Cockenoe-de-Long Island" (*John Eliot's First Indian Teacher and Interpreter, Cockenoe-de-Long Island, and the Story of his Career from the Early Records* [New York: F. P. Harper, 1896]). For Sassamon's biography, see Lepore, *Name of War,* and Yasuhide Kawashima, *Igniting King Philip's War: The John Sassamon Murder Trial* (Lawrence: University of Kansas Press, 2001).

13. Hilary Wyss, *Writing Indians: Literacy, Christianity and Native Community in Early America* (Amherst: University of Massachusetts Press, 2000), 3, 6.

14. Thomas Shepard, *The Clear Sun-shine of the Gospel Breaking Forth upon the Indians in New-England,* 1648, rpt. in *Tracts Relating to the Attempts to Convert to Christianity the Indians of New England,* Massachusetts Historical Society Collections, 3rd ser., 4 (1834), 64.

15. Henry Whitfield, *Strength out of Weaknesse; or, A Glorious Manifestation of the further Progresse of the Gospel among the* Indians *in New-England,* 1652, rpt. in *Tracts Relating to the Attempts to Convert to Christianity the Indians of New England,* Massachusetts Historical Society Collections, 3rd ser., vol. 4 (1834), 167, 155.

16. Francis Bremer, *Congregational Communion: Clerical Friendship in the Anglo-American Puritan Community, 1610–1692* (Boston: Northeastern University Press, 1994), 189. In *By Nature and by Custom Cursed: Transatlantic Civil Discourse and New England Cultural Production, 1620–1660* (Hanover, N.H.: Tufts University Press, 1999), Philip Round discusses the metropolitan-colonial connections created by mission publications, especially in chapter 5, "Come Over and Help Us."

17. The phrase "Eliot tracts" subordinates individual voices to the whole missionary enterprise, a move that can lead to confusion. The anthology *The English Literatures of America,* ed. Myra Jehlen and Michael Warner (New York: Routledge, 1997), for instance, ascribes to John Eliot a letter written by Thomas Mayhew, Jr., and Round attributes a passage from the tracts at one point to Shepard and at another to Eliot (*By Nature and by Custom Cursed,* 24, 262). These are easy mistakes; the tracts jump from author to author, and they present themselves as the coherent product of a unified mind.

18. I have in mind here an analysis similar to the argument Teresa Toulouse makes in "The Sovereignty and Goodness of God in 1682: Royal Authority, Female Captivity, and 'Creole Male Identity,' " *ELH: A Journal of English Literary History* (2000): 925–49. She examines the American versus the English title of Mary Rowlandson's captivity narrative, arguing that the metropolitan erasure of the American main title, *The Sovereignty and Goodness of God,* avoided drawing attention to the problematic—in 1682—issues of colonial sovereignty and royal prerogative. Similarly, I am interested in the varying cultural work each half of the mission tract's title performs.

19. William Spengemann, *A New World of Words: Redefining Early American Literature* (New Haven: Yale University Press, 1994), 73.

20. Round, *By Nature and by Custom Cursed,* 20.

21. See Spengemann, *A New World of Words;* Jim Egan, *Authorizing Experience: Refigurations of the Body Politic in Seventeenth-Century New England Writing* (Princeton, N.J.: Princeton University Press, 1999).

22. Beginning with Columbus's reports, any number of texts describe religious dialogue: Thomas Harriot, *A Report of the New Found Land of Virginia* (1595); John Smith, *A Generall History of Virginia* (1624); William Wood, *New England's Prospect* (1634); Roger Williams, *Key into the Language of America* (1643); and *New Englands First Fruits* (1643) are but a few examples. Of course, Puritan evangelism itself predates this meeting; Thomas Mayhew, Jr. began preaching on Martha's Vineyard in 1643.

23. *The Day-Breaking if, not the Sun-Rising of the Gospell with the* Indians *in New-England,* 1647, rpt. in *Tracts Relating to the Attempts to Convert to Christianity the Indians of New England,* Massachusetts Historical Society Collections, 3rd ser., 4 (1834), 1.

24. William Bradford, *Of Plymouth Plantation, 1620–1647* (New York: Modern Library, 1981), 87.

25. This point begs the question of the Puritans' awareness and understanding of their listeners' beliefs. As I discuss in chapter 4, the tract itself indicates that Puritans had been taught in earlier encounters just what Christian notions Indians might ridicule.

26. *Day-Breaking*, 3.

27. Laura Murray links this prayer to an evolving metaphoric language that characterized early English-Indian mission communication. Of the 1646 prayer in English she notes, "[Eliot's] awareness that strange language carries mystical power places him (although he would never have admitted it, of course) in the company of priests offering prayers in Latin or sachems drawing authority from archaisms" ("Joining Signs with Words: Missionaries, Metaphors, and the Massachusett Language," *New England Quarterly* 74, no. 1 [March 2001], 74).

28. Tzvetan Todorov, *The Conquest of America*, trans. Richard Howard (New York: Harper Perennial, 1984), 39, 42.

29. Eric Cheyfitz, *The Poetics of Imperialism: Translation and Colonization from* The Tempest *to* Tarzan, exp. ed. (Philadelphia: University of Pennsylvania Press, 1997), 115, 114.

30. Thomas Scanlan might see in the homologies between European and American religious encounters the "allegorical structure of colonial desire" (*Colonial Writing and the New World, 1583–1671: Allegories of Desire* [Cambridge, U.K.: Cambridge University Press: 1999], 8). Round also talks about this connection between colonial discourse and "domestic" identity: "First-generation New Englanders . . . were still very much part of an expanding cultural field whose center was London" (*By Nature and by Custom Cursed*, 6).

31. Shepard, *Clear Sun-shine*, 43.

32. Ibid., 43.

33. See *Day-Breaking*: "Nor were wee willing to tell them the story of the calling of *Noahs* children since the flood . . . because it was too difficult" (11).

34. Edward Winslow, *The Glorious Progress of the Gospel amongst the Indians in New England*, 1649, rpt. in *Tracts Relating to the Attempts to Convert to Christianity the Indians of New England*, Massachusetts Historical Society Collections, 3rd ser., vol. 4 (1834), 82.

35. This meeting resonates typologically in many ways. I am stressing the apostolic allusions, but of course Eliot also enacts Christ's calling of the disciples to be fishers of men.

36. Winslow, *Glorious Progress*, 83.

37. Ibid., 82.

38. Moreover, elsewhere in his mission writings Eliot uses the word "render" to draw attention to idiosyncratic translation. In a 1651 tract, he carefully notes that he "rendered the word peculiar treasure" in Exodus 19:5 as "Jewels" (Henry Whitfield, *The Light appearing more and more towards the perfect Day*, 1651, rpt. in *Tracts Relating to the Attempts to Convert to Christianity the Indians of New England*, Massachusetts Historical Society Collections, 3rd ser., vol. 4 (1834), 101–47).

39. *The Geneva Bible: A Facsimile of the 1560 Edition* (Madison: University of Wisconsin Press, 1969), 384, n. *m*. In quotations from the *Geneva Bible*, I have retained original orthography but expanded abbreviations and exchanged i for j, u for v, and vice versa.

40. Shepard, *Clear Sun-shine,* 44, 57.

41. William Wood, *New England's Prospect* (1634; rpt. Boston: Printed for the Prince Society by John Wilson and Sons, 1865), 88.

42. Winslow, *Glorious Progress,* 95.

43. Shepard, *Clear Sun-shine,* 51. The passage goes on to cite other examples of Judeo-Christian words being co-opted as insults: "A sober Indian going up into the countrey with two of his sons, did pray (as his manner was at home) and talked to them of God and Jesus Christ: but they mocked, & called one of his sons Jehovah and the other Jesus Christ: so that they are not without opposition raised by the Powwaws, and other wicked Indians."

44. Whitfield, *Light Appearing,* 139.

45. The word "praying" appears to have been a widespread term used to describe Christian-identified Indians in early America, and the fact that it transcends European colonial usage suggests its indigenous origin. For instance, Illinois Christians, proselytized by the French, were "those who pray." Nevertheless, we must still account for the English preference of the term—particularly if French converts used it as well. See Tracy Leavelle, "Mediation and Meaning on the French-Illinois Religious and Linguistic Frontier," unpublished paper delivered at "New Frontiers in Early American Literature," University of Virginia (August 2002).

46. Robert James Naeher, "Dialogue in the Wilderness: John Eliot and the Indian Exploration of Puritanism as a Source of Meaning, Comfort, and Ethnic Survival," *New England Quarterly* 62, no. 3 (September 1989): 367. Dane Morrison similarly argues that Christianity as constructed in the Praying Indian movement served to address loss, kinship fragmentation, and displacement for some Indians (*A Praying People: Massachusett Acculturation and the Failure of the Puritan Mission, 1600–1690* [New York: Peter Lang, 1995]).

47. The name appears in other colonial discourses as well; it is especially prominent in the record of the Dedham-Natick land disputes, which I discuss in chapter 2.

48. Round sees just this kind of parallel in Eliot's writings, arguing that he described "Algonquian socialization" as "a series of developmental stages that paralleled those the colonists themselves had undergone" (*By Nature and by Custom Cursed,* 260).

49. Eliot and Mayhew, *Tears of Repentance,* 215.

50. Whitfield, *Light Appearing,* 115.

51. Katz, *Philo-Semitism,* 44.

52. *The Whole Booke of Psalmes* Faithfully *Translated into English Metre* (Cambridge, 1640), n.p.

53. Linda Gregerson, "The commonwealth of the word: New England, Old England, and the praying Indians," in *British Identities and English Renaissance Literature,* ed. David J. Baker and Willy Maley (Cambridge, U.K.: Cambridge University Press, 2002), 188; her emphasis.

54. Matthew Brown, "An Epistemology of the Archive: The Eliot Mission and Early American Literary Studies," unpublished paper presented at the *Society of Early Americanists,* 2nd biennial conference (Norfolk, Va., March 2001), 7.

55. Whitfield, *Light Appearing,* 127.

56. *Dedications to the Rev. John Eliot's Indian Version of the Old and New Testament,* Massachusetts Historical Society Collections, 1st ser., vol. 7 (1800), 223. According to Pilling, about forty copies were bound up with a separate En-

glish title page and dedication and sent to England (*Bibliography of the Algonquian Languages*, 136).

57. See Pilling, *Bibliography of the Algonquian Languages*, 128. It is not uncommon for Biblical translations to leave the names of translators off of title pages, but it is telling that Eliot's name *is* attached to the Bible given to Indian converts rather than those given to English collectors.

58. Qtd. in Pilling, *Bibliography of the Algonquian Languages*, 141. Others read this moment quite differently. For instance, Round argues that "Eliot's cultural capital actually rose in the metropolis after the restoration of Charles II" (*By Nature and by Custom Cursed*, 266). Although I agree that the mission continued as an important element of the transatlantic colonial discourse, Eliot's own role was de-emphasized.

59. Pilling, *Bibliography of the Algonquian Languages*, 151.

60. See, for instance, the "Penn Library/exhibition" website, "Cultural Readings: Colonization and Print in the Americas" (January 7, 1998). February 9, 2002 ⟨http://www.library.upenn.edu/special/gallery/kislak/religion/eliotbible⟩.

61. Goddard and Bragdon, *Native Writings in Massachusett*, 225. The editors and translators tried to stay "as close to the Massachusett wording and phrasing as is possible" in their translations. Their English translation "contains a lot of choppy phrasing and resumptive pronouns and would obviously bear editing to improve its style in some places" (xxiii). I have not presumed to edit their translations, and so this discussion of language use is inflected by their translation decisions.

62. The King James Version of Job 34:30 reads, "That the hypocrite reign not, lest the people be ensnared." This verse is glossed by the Geneva Bible, and while the commentary would have been unavailable to petitioners who were not English readers, it nevertheless indicates how this scriptural allusion might have been read by colonial authorities: "When tyrants sit in the throne of justice which under pretence of executing justice are but hypocrites and oppresse the people, it is a signe that God hath drawen back [h]is countenance and favour from that place" (232, n. *y*). While this interpretation could be construed as a divine rebuke to the petitioners themselves, it makes the English colonial government the devil's instrument, for if God withdraws his countenance, the "place" becomes Satan's dominion. Thus the Gayhead petitioners' use of Elihu's words was a Jeremiadical warning to English colonial authorities who claimed Gay Head as under their rule.

63. Goddard and Bragdon, *Native Writings in Massachusetts*, 20.

64. Beverly Olson Flanigan, "American Indian English in History and Literature: The Evolution of a Pidgin from Reality to Stereotype" (Ph.D. diss., Indiana University, 1981), 72.

65. Karen Kupperman, *Indians & English: Facing Off in Early America* (Ithaca: Cornell University Press, 2000), 86.

66. See Beth Craig, "American Indian English," *English World-Wide* 12, no. 1 (1991): 25–61.

67. Eliot and Mayhew, *Tears of Repentance*, 241.

68. John Eliot, *A further Account of the progress of the Gospel amongst the Indians in New England* (London, 1660), 75. I cite subsequent references to the confessions in the text with short titles in order to indicate the dates of delivery. These were recorded in the *Tears of Repentance* (1653) and *Further Account*. In *Tears of Repentance*, Eliot notes that he may have missed elements of Nishoh-

kou's statement, and it is unclear whether the fault lay with Eliot's skill as a translator or Nishohkou's shy manner: "When he had made this Confession, he was much abashed, for he is a bashful man; many things he spoke that I missed, for want of through [*sic*] understanding some words and sentence" (250).

For other discussions of Praying Indian confession narratives, see Richard Cogley, *John Eliot's Mission to the Indians before King Philip's War* (Cambridge: Harvard University Press, 1999); Charles Cohen, "Conversion among Puritans and Amerindians: A Theological and Cultural Perspective," in *Puritanism: Transatlantic Perspectives on a Seventeenth-Century Anglo-American Faith*, ed. Francis Bremer (Boston: Massachusetts Historical Society, 1993); Morrison, *A Praying People*. Morrison especially focuses on those elements in Ponampam's discussion that pertain to early trauma (116–17).

69. See Mayhew and Eliot, *Tears of Repentance: "That all from the rising of the sun to the going down thereof, shall pray unto God"* (240); "But then I heard Gods free mercy in his word, call all to pray, *from the rising of the Sun to the going down thereof*" (241); "That al shal pray from the rising to the sitting Sun" (242).

70. Winslow, *Glorious Progress*, 83.

71. Homi K. Bhabha, *The Location of Culture* (1994; rpt. London: Routledge, 2001), 86; his emphasis.

72. Robert Naeher, quoting James H. Merrell, argues that in the face of European colonial invasion, "native Americans came to view their world as 'every bit as new as that confronting transplanted Africans or Europeans'" ("Dialogue in the Wilderness," 363).

73. Bhabha characterizes such disruptions as undermining what the colonizer has assumed to be immutable. Ponampam's narrative may "so disturb the systematic (and systemic) construction of discriminatory knowledges"—such as the identification of the elect by public confession of faith—"that the cultural, once recognized as the medium of authority, becomes virtually unrecognizable" (*Location of Culture*, 115).

74. In his essay—not an historical study but rather an analysis of contemporary resonances of the Exodus narrative—Warrior discusses the use of the Exodus narrative in liberation theology. He concludes that indigenous peoples throughout the world "will perhaps do better to look elsewhere for our vision of justice, peace, and political sanity" ("A Native American Perspective: Canaanites, Cowboys, and Indians," in *Voices from the Margin: Interpreting the Bible in the Third World*, ed. R. S. Sugirtharajah, 2nd ed. [New York: Orbis Books, 1997], 285).

75. Cheyfitz, *Poetics of Imperialism*, 125; his emphasis.

Chapter 4. Algonquians and Antinomians

1. Roger Williams, *A Key into the Language of America*, ed. John J. Teunissen and Evelyn J. Hintz (Detroit: Wayne State University Press, 1973), 189.

2. See *The Day-Breaking, if not the Sun-Rising of the Gospell with the Indians in New-England*, 1647, rpt. in *Tracts Relating to the Attempts to Convert to Christianity the Indians of New England*, Massachusetts Historical Society Collections, 3rd ser., vol. 4 (1834), 8–9.

3. I exclude *Dying Speeches & Counsels of such Indians as dyed in the Lord* (1685) as a tract comprising a distinct religious genre (see chapter 7).

4. James Ronda, "'We Are Well As We Are': An Indian Critique of Seventeenth Century Christian Missions," *William and Mary Quarterly*, 3rd ser., 24, no. 1 (1977): 66–82; Harold Van Lonkhuyzen, "A Reappraisal of the Praying Indians: Acculturation, Conversion, and Identity at Natick, Massachusetts, 1646–1730," *New England Quarterly* 63 (September 1990), 396–428.

5. *Day-Breaking*, 19.

6. For a succinct account of these religious beliefs and practices, see "Cosmology," in Kathleen J. Bragdon, *Native People of Southern New England, 1500–1650* (Norman: University of Oklahoma Press, 1996). For a broader discussion of English and Algonquian religious beliefs, see Neal Salisbury, *Manitou and Providence: Indians, Europeans, and the Making of New England, 1500–1643* (New York: Oxford University Press, 1982). For the translation of "Manit" as "God," see Kathleen Bragdon, "Native Languages as Spoken and Written," in *The Language Encounter in the Americas, 1492–1800*, ed. Edward G. Gray and Norman Fiering (New York: Berghahn Books, 2000), 179. Karen Kupperman suggests that Native translators were responsible for the choice, which is a likely explanation. But the English nevertheless greatly reduced the significance of the concept when they seized on it as a transparent sign for the Christian God. See *Indians and English: Facing Off in Early America* (Ithaca: Cornell University Press, 2000), 116.

7. *Day-Breaking*, 19.

8. Ibid., 20.

9. Neal Salisbury argues that the colonists' racism made Indian efforts to become communicants much more difficult than those of their white Christian counterparts. See "Red Puritans," *William and Mary Quarterly*, 3rd ser., 31 (January 1974): 27–54.

10. *Acts of the Commissioners of the United Colonies of New England*, vol. 1, ed. David Pulsifer, in *Records of Plymouth Colony*, vols. 9–10, ed. Nathaniel B. Shurtleff (Boston: William White, 1859), 203.

11. There are other ways of reading tears than the interpretation offered by Puritan observers. Dane Morrison argues that "the saints were convinced that remorse was the natural result of the Algonquians' first apprehension of the concept of sin; they could not see that the message of suffering and redemption provided a convincing explanation for the trauma of depopulation and social disintegration" (*A Praying People: Massachusett Acculturation and the Failure of the Puritan Mission, 1600–1690* [New York: Peter Lang, 1995], 44). It is important to recognize the convert's response to the message in terms of his or her situation, but I am interested here in Puritan English readers' understanding of this sign of conversion.

12. For studies of the conversion narrative, see Edmund Morgan, *Visible Saints: The History of a Puritan Idea* (New York: New York University Press, 1963); Patricia Caldwell, *Puritan Conversion Narratives: The Beginnings of American Expression* (Cambridge: Cambridge University Press, 1983); Charles Cohen, "Conversion among Puritans and Amerindians: A Theological and Cultural Perspective," in *Puritanism: Transatlantic Perspectives on a Seventeenth-Century Anglo-American Faith*, ed. Francis Bremer (Boston: Massachusetts Historical Society, 1993), and *God's Caress: The Psychology of Puritan Religious Experience* (New York: Oxford University Press, 1986).

13. James Holstun, *A Rational Millennium* (New York: Oxford University Press, 1987), 130. He goes on to connect discursive and real identities: "But this melancholy acquired a positive function in the formation of new identities. Public confession and weeping become signs of regeneracy and so a way to praying-town status."

14. Of course, by focusing on oral traditions, Eliot may have been accommodating his style to familiar Algonquian modes of community building and worship. While this reciprocity is important, my interest here is in the ways Eliot fit his practice to orthodox English forms of religious expression to win support for his work. Much more work remains to be done on Indian influences on missionary practices. For a discussion of the changes in Eliot's hortatory style, see Morrison, *A Praying People*, 37–74. Laura Arnold suggests the presence of Indian aesthetic responses to contact, as evidenced in Mary Rowlandson's Puritan captivity narrative in "Now . . . Didn't Our People Laugh: Female Misbehavior and Algonquian culture in Mary Rowlandson's *Captivity and Restauration*," *American Indian Culture and Research Journal* 21, no. 4 (1997): 1–28. See also the methods and approaches of Kupperman, *Indians and English*, and Daniel K. Richter, *Facing East from Indian Country: A Native History of Early America* (Cambridge: Harvard University Press, 2001).

15. John Eliot, *A further Accompt of the Progresse of the Gospel amongst the* Indians *in* New England (London, 1659), 20.

16. Eliot describes the Indian meetings and their four "exercises" in a letter included in Thomas Shepard's tract, *The Clear Sun-shine of the Gospel Breaking Forth upon the Indians in New-England*, 1648, rpt. in *Tracts Relating to the Attempts to Convert to Christianity the Indians of New England*, Massachusetts Historical Society Collections, 3rd ser., vol. 4 (1834), 52–55.

17. For an alternate, brief discussion of Praying Indian questions, see David Murray, *Forked Tongues: Speech, Writing & Representation in North American Indian Texts* (Bloomington: Indiana University Press, 1991), 127–31.

18. *Day-Breaking*, 4.

19. Robert Naeher examines spiritual questions for what they can tell us about Indian volition within Christianity. He argues that "by their questions, the Indians directed Eliot to expand on those aspects of his message most important to them and consequently to tailor it to their new needs and traditional sensitivities" ("Dialogue in the Wilderness: John Eliot and the Exploration of Puritanism as a Source of Meaning, Comfort, and Ethnic Survival," 62, no.3 [September 1989], 367).

20. Shepard, *Clear Sun-shine*, 50.

21. *Day-Breaking*, 4.

22. Van Lonkhuyzen discusses the reasons why Cutshamekin, a traditional sachem, would have resisted the mission message as political encroachment, while Waban and others less politically influential may have seen in Christianity a means to power "A Reappraisal," 406–7.

23. In *A Praying People*, Morrison suggests that through their questions, Indians "acted according to the lights of their culture to unlock the mysteries of another people" (50). And that, in exchanges such as these, Praying Indians were teaching Eliot "the language of the remnant," with which he would unwittingly "integrat[e] into a cogent piece the views of the Dissenting Protestant and the remnant Algonkian" (55). For other discussions of Eliot's religious dialogues with

Algonquians, see Naeher, "Dialogue in the Wilderness"; Ronda, " 'We Are Well' "; and Van Lonkhuyzen, "A Reappraisal."

24. Referring to the use of catechism, Holstun argues that "the missionaries encounter some resistance to their attempt to inscribe Christian doctrine in the conscience of the Indians, but they characterize this resistance not as the opposition of an alternative reason but as the recalcitrance of an inanimate raw material that can be overcome by mere repetition" (*A Rational Millennium*, 128).

25. James Constantine Pilling, *Bibliography of the Algonquian Languages* (1891; rpt. New York: AMS Press, 1973), 169.

26. Qtd. in Pilling, *Bibliography*, 130.

27. Richard Baxter, *A Call to the Unconverted to Turn and Live* (London, 1658), 183.

28. Shepard, *Clear Sun-shine*, 57.

29. Neal Salisbury, "Red Puritans," *William and Mary Quarterly*, 3rd ser., 31 (January 1974): 44.

30. Shepard, *Clear Sun-shine*, 47.

31. Edward Winslow, *The Glorious Progress of the Gospel, amongst the Indians in New England*, 1649, rpt. in *Tracts Relating to the Attempts to Convert to Christianity the Indians of New England*, Massachusetts Historical Society Collections, 3rd ser., 4 (1834), 85.

32. Shepard, *Clear Sun-shine*, 45. Morrison discusses several categories of questions proposed by Algonquian converts (*A Praying People*, 50–57). The question of Christ's origins, he suggests, "taught . . . nascent converts that the English held no monopoly on the powerful Jehovah" (53).

33. *Day-Breaking*, 16.

34. Ibid., 11.

35. Henry Whitfield, *The Light appearing more and more towards the perfect Day*, 1651, rpt. in *Tracts Relating to the Attempts to Convert to Christianity the Indians of New England*, Massachusetts Historical Society Collections, 3rd ser., 4 (1834), 133.

36. Winslow, *The Glorious Progress*, 84.

37. Winslow, *Light Appearing*, 122.

38. Shepard, *Clear Sun-shine*, 42.

39. Winslow, *Glorious Progress*, 96.

40. Shepard, *Clear Sun-shine*, 47.

41. John Eliot, *A Late and Further Manifestation of the Progress of the Gospel amongst the Indians in New-England*, 1655, rpt. in *Tracts Relating to the Attempts to Convert to Christianity the Indians of New England*, Massachusetts Historical Society Collections, 3rd ser., 4 (1834), 265.

42. Myra Jehlen, "History before the Fact: Or, Captain John Smith's Unfinished Symphony," *Critical Inquiry* 19 (Summer 1993): 644–92.

43. Holstun, *Rational Millennium*, 135.

44. James Holstun, introduction to *Pamphlet Wars: Prose in the English Revolution* (London: Frank Cass and Co., 1992), 1.

45. See John Winthrop, *A Short Story of the Rise, Reign, and Ruine of the Antinomians, Familists, and Libertines* in *The Antinomian Controversy, 1636–1638*, ed. David Hall (Durham, N.C.: Duke University Press, 1990), 209, 210 n. 7. In his study of seventeenth-century clergy, David Hall notes, "Out of this mood of disenchantment with the laymen came a number of important changes

in administrative procedure. The synod of 1637 sharply condemned the practice of allowing members to ask questions at the end of sermons and public lectures" (*The Faithful Shepherd: A History of the New England Ministry in the Seventeenth Century* [Chapel Hill: University of North Carolina Press, 1972], 111). In discussing the synod of 1637 and "male cultural production," Philip Round argues that the synod squeezed out women's discursive options, "gendering the discourse of the New England Way in such a fashion that henceforth only men could hope to speak it (*By Nature and by Custom Cursed: Transatlantic Civil Discourse and New England Cultural Production, 1620–1660* [Hanover, N.H.: University Press of New England, 1999], 131).

46. Francis Bremer, *Congregational Communion: Clerical Friendship in the Anglo-American Puritan Community, 1610–1692* (Boston: Northeastern University Press, 1994), 189.

47. Richard Cogley specifically suggests a link between Eliot's evangelism and his millennial beliefs: "The most subtle indication of Eliot's attitudes toward the Indians was his argument for an American millennium." Whereas, he notes, other divines only rarely gave American such pride of place, "the Apostle was transformed by his exposure to the natives." See *John Eliot's Mission to the Indians before King Philip's War* (Cambridge: Harvard University Press, 1999), 248–49.

48. Jim Egan, *Authorizing Experience: Refigurations of the Body Politic in Seventeenth-Century New England Writing* (Princeton: Princeton University Press, 1999).

49. Stephen Foster, *The Long Argument: English Puritanism and the Shaping of New England Culture, 1570–1700* (Chapel Hill: University of North Carolina Press, 1991), 168.

50. See Bremer, *Congregational Communion*, 149.

51. Thomas Lechford, *New-Englands advice to Old-England; or, Some observations upon New-Englands government, compared with the ancient government of Old-England* (London, 1644).

52. Bremer, *Congregational Communion*, 156. See also Foster, *Long Argument*, 168.

53. Bremer, *Congregational Communion*, 157.

54. Qtd. in ibid., 139.

55. Twenty-eight leading English divines (some repatriated from New England) signed various mission tracts: John Arthur, Simeon Ashe, Samuel Bolton, William Bridge, Edmund Calamy, William Carter, Joseph Caryl, Thomas Case, John Downam, John Dury, Thomas Goodwin, William Gouge, William Greenhill, George Griffith, Stephen Marshall, Phillip Nye, Edmund Reynolds, Lazarus Seaman, Sidrach Simpson, John Owen, William Spurstow, William Steele, William Strong, Ralph Venning, Nathan Ward, Jeremiah Whitaker, Henry Whitfield, Edward Winslow.

56. Shepard, *Clear Sun-shine*, 32.

57. David Hall, ed., *The Antinomian Controversy, 1636–1638: A Documentary History*, 2nd ed. (Durham, N.C.: Duke University Press, 1990), 200.

58. Bremer, *Congregational Communion*, 157.

59. Bremer cites Thomas Edwards as arguing that the "true story of New England is one of great heresies, etc., caused by Independency" even as he countered the Dissenting Brethren's advocacy of toleration by pointing to "examples of New England intolerance" (ibid., 158).

60. Shepard, *Clear Sun-shine*, 47.
61. S[amuel] R[ichardson], *Fifty Questions Propounded to the Assembly, to answer by the Scriptures: Whether corporall punishments may be inflicted upon such as hold different opinions in Religion* (London, 1647), n.p.
62. Shepard, *Clear Sun-shine*, 55.
63. Mary Beth Norton, *Founding Mothers & Fathers: Gendered Power and the Forming of American Society* (New York: Vintage Books, 1997), 4. Van Lonkhuyzen also suggests that Indian women welcomed this particular mission redefinition of gender roles, as it discouraged abuse: "There is evidence that the praying movement's redefinition of gender roles, though resisted by men, was an important attraction among women especially because it discouraged wife beating and alcohol abuse." The evidence he relies on, however, comes entirely from evangelical reports ("A Reappraisal of the Praying Indians," 413).
64. Indian women rarely appear as individuals in mission narratives. The first female questioner described here appears later in Winslow's *Glorious Progress of the Gospel*, in which her dying moments are described (see my discussion in chapter 7), and an unnamed "kinswoman" is a character in Eliot's *Indian Dialogues* (see chapter 5).
65. Norton, *Founding Mothers & Fathers*, 397.
66. Round, *By Nature and by Custom Cursed*, 144; Round's insertion.
67. As Round explains, "To New Englanders . . . Winthrop's story [of witchcraft, midwifery, and monstrous births] proved that the gendered disorder that had rocked the Bay Colony could be traced directly back to the *metropolis*. . . . As they had in Hutchinson's court trial, where witnesses had tried to trace the source of her errors back to her prophecy at St. Paul's, New England print apologists attempted to make their experience of gender disorder a transatlantic issue" (*By Nature and by Custom Cursed*, 150).
68. *Day-Breaking*, 15.
69. Jean O'Brien discusses Cutshamekin's leadership before and after joining the Natick community in *Dispossession by Degrees: Indian Land and Identity in Natick, Massachusetts, 1650–1790* (Cambridge: Cambridge University Press, 1997).
70. Shepard, *Clear Sun-shine*, 55.

Chapter 5. Kinfolk and Penitents

1. John Eliot, *John Eliot's Indian Dialogues: A Study in Cultural Interaction*, ed. Henry Bowden and James Ronda (Westport, Conn.: Greenwood Press, 1981), 61.
2. See Thomas Scanlan, *Colonial Writing and the New World, 1683–1671* (Cambridge: Cambridge University Press, 1999), 155. Other studies of *Indian Dialogues* include David Murray, *Forked Tongues: Speech, Writing & Representation in North American Indian Texts* (Bloomington: Indiana University Press, 1991), and Frank Kelleter, "Puritan Missionaries and the Colonization of the New World: A Reading of John Eliot's *Indian Dialogues* (1671)," in *Early America Re-explored: New Readings in Colonial, Early National, and Antebellum Culture*, ed. Klaus H. Schmidt and Fritz Fleischmann (New York: Peter Lang, 2000), 71–106.
3. Scanlan's arguments about *Indian Dialogues* are compelling. However, my

attention is not on the ways the Indians in the text can be seen as models for or allegorical types of the English colonists but rather on elements that seem decidedly unallegoric—on the sales job the tract makes of Praying Indians' identity and their purpose in the colony, not as they reflect on the colonists or on the English nation.

4. Scanlan, *Colonial Writing*, 157.

5. Nancy Armstrong and Leonard Tennenhouse, *The Imaginary Puritan: Literature, Intellectual Labor, and the Origins of Personal Life* (Berkeley: University of California Press, 1992), 204.

6. *Records of Plymouth*, vol. 3, ed. Nathaniel B. Shurtleff (Boston: William White, 1859), 192. Since I am following the inscription of Metacom in writings produced by English settlers and focusing on the cultural work of Praying Indian figures in chapters 5 and 6, I refer to Metacom and Wamsutta by their English names.

7. See Francis Jennings's reconstruction of Alexander's death in *The Invasion of America: Indians, Colonialism and the Cant of Conquest* (Chapel Hill: University of North Carolina Press, 1975), 288–90.

8. For accounts of events leading up to open hostilities, including the treaty of Taunton, see Jennings, *Invasion of America*, 293–94. Other accounts of King Philip's War include James D. Drake, *King Philip's War: Civil War in New England, 1675–1676* (Amherst: University of Massachusetts Press, 1999); Jill Lepore, *The Name of War: King Philip's War and the Origins of American Identity* (New York: Alfred A. Knopf, 1998); and Yasuhide Kawashima, *Igniting King Philip's War: The John Sassamon Murder Trial* (Lawrence: University of Kansas Press, 2001).

9. See John Eliot, *A Brief Narrative of the progress of the Gospel amongst the Indians in New England in the Year 1670, 1671*, rpt. as "Eliot's Brief Narrative," in *Old South Leaflets* 1:21 (Boston: Old South Meeting House, n.d.), 7. For descriptions of Praying Indians and praying towns in this period, see J. W. Ford, *Some Correspondence between the Governors and Treasurers of the New England Company in London and the Commissioners of the United Colonies in America* (London: Spottiswoode, 1896), 29; and Daniel Gookin, *Historical Collections of the Indians in New England*, Massachusetts Historical Society Collections, vol. 1 (1806), 141–246.

10. Eliot, *Brief Narrative*, 3.

11. John Eliot, "Letters of John Eliot," Massachusetts Historical Society Proceedings 17 (1879–80): 249.

12. Scanlan employs a different set of references to fix the significance of *Indian Dialogues* to transatlantic colonial English culture: the publication appeared "neatly between Charles's secret Treaty of Dover (1670) and his second *Declaration of Indulgence*" (156). His attention to chronology underscores my contention that tracking the circumstances of publication is especially important

13. Eliot, *Indian Dialogues*, 94.

14. See Waban's confessions in John Eliot and Thomas Mayhew, Jr., *Tears of Repentance; or, A further Narrative of the Progress of the Gospel amongst the* Indians *in New-England*, 1653, rpt. in *Tracts Relating to the Attempts to Convert to Christianity the Indians of New England*, Massachusetts Historical Society Collections, 3rd ser., 4 (1834), 231–32. Eliot explains the disappointed reaction of the listening English elders: "This Confession being not so satisfac-

tory as was desired, Mr. *Wilson* testified, that he spake these latter expressions with tears." Waban's poor performance may have been due to lack of preparation. Unlike most of the other confessors, he appears to have delivered his narrative only once. He may have been uncomfortable with the process in general; when the Praying Indians came together to offer their confessions in 1659, Waban called in sick (Eliot, *Further Account*, 30).

15. Scanlan terms the dialogue "explosive" (*Colonial Writings and the New World*, 156), while Bowden and Ronda are pained by its claims (*Indian Dialogues*, 48).

16. Nevertheless, the text provides corroboration for Bowden and Ronda's conclusion. Philip made his home at Pokenoket, and the dialogue refers to his father Onsamequin, known as Massasoit.

17. One of those dispatched to Philip was the ill-fated John Sassaman, whose death in 1675 sparked the war. This group of Indian missionaries may have hoped to take advantage of the recent change in Wampanoag leadership to influence the new sachem toward Christianity. And after his brother's death, Philip may have realized that he needed as much information as possible about the English if he were to survive as sachem. See Lepore for an excellent discussion of Sassaman's role in the events leading up to the conflict (*Name of War*, 21–47).

18. John R. Swanton identifies Missogkonnog as a Nipmuck town, "location uncertain" (*Indian Tribes of North America*, Bureau of American Ethnology, Bulletin 145 [Washington, D.C.: U.S. Government Printing Office, 1952], 23).

19. James Walker, "James Walker's Letter to Governor Prince," Massachusetts Historical Society Collections, 1st ser., 6 (1799), 198.

20. On June 27, 1671, Eliot writes to Richard Baxter promising to send his friend a copy of "a few instructive dialogs which are also partly historical" (F. J. Powicke, "Some Unpublished Correspondence of the Reverend Richard Baxter and the Reverend John Eliot, 'The Apostle to the American Indians,' 1656–1682," *Bulletin of the John Rylands Library* 15 [July 1931], 462).

21. See chap. 4.

22. Henry Whitfield, *The Light appearing more and more towards the perfect Day*, 1651, rpt. in *Tracts Relating to the Attempts to Convert to Christianity the Indians of New England*, Massachusetts Historical Society Collections, 3rd ser., 4 (1834), 139.

23. Indeed, in 1674, Gookin reports that Eliot and an agent for Uncas, a key Mohegan leader, did have a rather edgy encounter, in which Eliot seems to have agreed to leave secular rule alone and concentrate his energies on religious conversion:

> There was a person among them, who sitting mute a great space, at last spake to this effect: That he was agent for Unkas, sachem of Mohegan, who challenged right to, and dominion over, this people of Wabquissit. And said he, Unkas is not well pleased, that the English should pass over Mohegan river, to call his Indians to pray to God.
>
> Unto which speech Mr. Eliot first answered, that it was his work to call upon all men every where, as he had opportunity, especially the Indians, to repent and embrace the gospel; but he did not meddle with civil right or jurisdiction. (*Historical Collections*, 191)

For Uncas's role in seventeenth-century New England politics, see Drake, *King Philip's War*, 29–31, 106–110.

24. Scanlan, *Colonial Writing and the New World*, 170, 169.

25. Eliot's political tract *A Christian Commonwealth* was burned in 1660, and he was forced to recant his work.

26. Winslow, *Light Appearing*, 141.

27. Eliot, *Indian Dialogues*, 132.

28. Interestingly, Danforth was present at one of the trials of Indian confessors. See John Eliot, *A further Account of the Progresse of the Gospel amongst the* Indians *in New England*, 1659, rpt. in *Tracts Relating to the Attempts to Convert to Christianity the Indians of New England*, Massachusetts Historical Society Collections, 3rd ser., 4 (1834), 75. Could Danforth's sense of New England's declensions have been influenced by his witness of Indian piety?

29. There is a distant echo here of Danforth's phrasing of the colonists' reasons for emigrating: "You have solemnly professed before God, angels, and men that the cause of your leaving your country, kindred, and fathers' houses and transporting yourselves with your wives, little ones, and substance over the vast ocean into this waste and howling wilderness, was your liberty to walk in the faith of the Gospel with all good conscience according to the order of the Gospel and your enjoyment of the pure worship of God according to His institution without human mixtures and impositions" (*Brief Recognition of New England's Errand into the Wilderness*, in *Early American Writing*, ed. Giles Gunn [New York: Penguin Books, 1994], 202).

30. Scanlan, *Colonial Writing and the New World*, 186.

31. Eliot, *Indian Dialogues*, 72.

32. Ibid., 126. Such sentiments appear in other exchanges as well. In a speech that flatters Bay Colony authorities, Praying Indian John Speen tells a character simply identified as "Penitent," "I do not doubt but the Governor and Magistrate of the Massachusetts will be easily entreated to interpose in so good a work, which may tend to the bringing in so many people to the service of Jesus Christ" (162).

33. Ibid., 133. I am indebted to Peter Sattler for bringing this moment to my attention. Sattler makes the case that in this representation of Philip's inner self we can see Eliot's "novelistic" tendencies: "In trying to scrape away the veneer of human custom and native declension (*'abrasa tabula'*), Eliot is searching for what we might now call a Cartesian or proto-Lockean self. He is engaged in some of the thinking that Ian Watt sees eventually giving rise to the novel and its formally situated concerns. He wants to examine people at their most basic and watch the motions of their souls" ("Approaching Dialogue: Eliot, Formalism, and the Novel," unpublished paper delivered at the Society for Early Americanists biannual conference, Norfolk, 2001), 9–10.

34. Editors Bowden and Ronda tentatively identify the character Piumbukhou as Piambow or Piam Boohan (*Indian Dialogues*, 163 n. 3), but it seems more likely that he is meant to represent the Piumbuhhou whose confessions appear in *Further Account*.

35. Roger Williams, *A Key into the Language of America*, ed. John J. Teunissen and Evelyn J. Hinz (Detroit: Wayne State University Press, 1973, 194).

36. Eliot, *Indian Dialogues*, 69.

37. David Murray, *Forked Tongues: Speech, Writing & Representation in North American Indian Texts* (Bloomington: Indiana University Press, 1991), 127.

38. Eliot, *Indian Dialogues*, 67.

39. Bowden and Ronda identify Peneovot as "a character of Eliot's own invention" (*Indian Dialogues*, 165, n. 31).

40. Thomas Shepard, *The Clear Sun-shine of the Gospel Breaking Forth upon the Indians in New-England*, 1648, rpt. in *Tracts Relating to the Attempts to Convert to Christianity the Indians of New England*, Massachusetts Historical Society Collections, 3rd ser., 4 (1834), 57.

41. Other relevant texts include Proverbs 24:13: "My child, eat honey, for it is good, and the drippings of the honeycomb are sweet to your taste. Know that wisdom is such to your soul."

42. See Eliot, *Indian Dialogues*, 70–74, 84, 86.

43. Editors Bowden and Ronda themselves gloss the word with reference to Williams (*Indian Dialogues*, 164, n. 12).

44. See chap. 2 for my discussion of the missionary's linguistic representation of Praying Indians.

45. Richard Baxter, *The Call to the Unconverted to Turn and Live* (London, 1658), 112.

46. Ronda identifies the kinswoman's speech here as an argument common to many Indians who were in contact with European proselytizers, and he deduces that this is a moment of real Indian resistance to the mission message (" 'We Are Well As We Are': An Indian Critique of Seventeenth Century Christian Missions," *William and Mary Quarterly*, 3rd ser., 24, no. 1 [January 1977]: 66–82).

47. Eliot, *Indian Dialogues*, 82; see my discussion of Totherswamp's wife in chap. 4.

48. Sattler suggests that a "formalist" analysis of Eliot's work reveals how closely he is working with tropes and style that approach later American fiction: *Indian Dialogues* "actually achieves (now and then) what so few early American texts even attempt—the representation of convincing, differentiated, individuated native characters" ("Approaching Dialogue," 13).

49. See Nancy Armstrong and Leonard Tennenhouse, *The Imaginary Puritan: Literature, Intellectual Labor and the Origins of Personal Life* (Berkeley: University of California Press, 1992), 196–216.

50. Nancy Armstrong, "Captivity and Cultural Capital in the English Novel," *Novel: A Forum on Fiction* 31, no. 3 (Summer 1998): 373.

51. Armstrong writes, "Our point . . . was . . . to consider that genre [the captivity] as one which simultaneously connected and distinguished two anglophone cultures" ("Captivity and Cultural Capital," 373).

52. Eliot, *Indian Dialogues*, 136.

53. Scanlan, *Colonial Writing and the New World*, 172. Scanlan also links this anti-Catholic moment to desires for a new commonwealth: "Eliot provides his readers with an intermediate goal that is far less dangerous and extreme than trying to overthrow the English throne. In a sense, Eliot says to his readers that the fight against monarchy can begin in their own back yards." I see the antimonarchism of *Indian Dialogues* as much more muted. Indeed, the later years of Eliot's mission were devoted by the commissioners of the United Colonies to the king, as I discuss in chapter 2. Moreover, I see Eliot's presentation of Philip as more respectful and positive than does Scanlan. Nevertheless, Scanlan's argument is a finely nuanced one, and my disagreement is primarily one of emphasis.

54. Eric Hinderaker, "The 'Four Indian Kings' and the Imaginative Construction of the First British Empire," *William and Mary Quarterly*, 3rd ser., 53, no. 3 (1993): 489. In addition to Hinderaker's excellent study, see Richmond P. Bond,

Queen Anne's American Kings (Oxford: Clarendon Press, 1952), and Richard D. Altick, *The Shows of London* (Cambridge: Belknap Press/Harvard University Press, 1978) for accounts of the visit and the events leading up to it.

55. Hinderaker includes copies of engravings from the John Verelest paintings ("The 'Four Indian Kings,' " 510–13).

56. William Smith, *The History of the Province of New-York*, ed. Michael Kammen (Cambridge: Belknap Press/Harvard University Press, 1972), 1:136.

57. Joseph Addison, *Addison and Steele: Selections from* The Tatler *and* The Spectator, ed. Robert J. Allen (New York: Rinehart, 1957), 98.

58. Hinderaker, 488. Hinderaker cites Thomas Harriot, John Smith, and William Wood, all of whom can plausibly be said to articulate a coherent image of the Indian based on exploratory contact rather than the experience of the settler-colonist ("Four Indian Kings," 488, n. 3).

Chapter 6. Satan's Captives, "Preying" Indians, and Mary Rowlandson

1. John Eliot, *John Eliot's Indian Dialogues: A Study in Cultural Interaction*, ed. Henry W. Bowden and James P. Ronda (Westport, Conn.: Greenwood Press, 1980), 63.

2. James Axtell, *The European and the Indian: Essays in the Ethnohistory of Colonial North America* (Oxford: Oxford University Press, 1981), 59.

3. Mary Louise Pratt borrows the term "transculturation" from "ethnographers [who] have used this term to describe how subordinated or marginal groups select and invent from materials transmitted to them by a dominant or metropolitan culture," *Imperial Eyes: Travel Writing and Transculturation* (London: Routledge, 1992), 6.

4. For an account of the English treatment of Praying Indians during the war, see Jenny Hale Pulsipher, "Massacre at Hurtleberry Hill: Christian Indians and English Authority in Metacom's War," *William and Mary Quarterly*, 3rd ser., 53, no. 3 (July 1996): 459–86. Studies that discuss the representation of Native Americans after the war include Louise Barnett, *The Ignoble Savage: American Literary Racism 1790–1890* (Westport, Conn.: Greenwood Press, 1975); Robert F. Berkofer, *The White Man's Indian: Images of the American Indians from Columbus to the Present* (New York: Vintage Books, 1979); Francis Jennings, *Invasion of America: Indians, Colonialism and the Cant of Conquest* (Chapel Hill: University of North Carolina Press, 1975); Roy Harvey Pearce, *Savagism and Civilization: A Study of the Indian and the American Mind*, rev. ed. (Berkeley and Los Angeles: University of California Press, 1988); Raymond William Stedman, *Shadows of the Indian: Stereotypes in American Culture* (Norman: University of Oklahoma Press, 1982).

5. Jill Lepore agrees that the accounts of the war that were printed "transformed New England's natives into irredeemable monsters" (*The Name of War: King Philip's War and the Origins of American Identity* [New York: Alfred A. Knopf, 1998], 45).

6. Henry Whitfield, *The Light appearing more and more towards the perfect Day*, 1651, rpt. in *Tracts Relating to the Attempts to Convert to Christianity the Indians of New England*, Massachusetts Historical Society Collections, 3rd ser., vol. 4 (1834), 142.

7. Henry Whitfield, introduction to *Strength out of Weaknesse*, 1652, rpt. in

Tracts Relating to the Attempts to Convert to Christianity the Indians of New England, Massachusetts Historical Society Collections, 3rd ser., vol. 4 (1834), 161; Whitfield, *Light appearing*, 104.

8. Daniel Gookin, *Historical Collections of the Indians in New England*, in Massachusetts Historical Society Collections, vol. 1 (1792), 200. The phrases "miserable Captives and "slaves to the devil" come from Mayhew's letter in Whitfield, *Strength out of Weaknesse*, 185–86; "poor captivated men" appears in John Eliot and Thomas Mayhew, Jr., *Tears of Repentance*, 1653, rpt. in *Tracts Relating to the Attempts to Convert to Christianity the Indians of New England*, Massachusetts Historical Society Collections, 3rd ser., vol. 4 (1834), 202.

9. Edward Winslow, *The Glorious Progress of the Gospel, amongst the Indians* in New England, 1649, rpt. in *Tracts Relating to the Attempts to Convert to Christianity the Indians of New England*, Massachusetts Historical Society Collections, 3rd ser., vol. 4 (1834), 95; Whitfield, *Strength out of Weaknesse*, 156.

10. John Eliot, *A Late and Further Manifestation of the Progress of the Gospel amongst the Indians in New-England*, 1655, rpt. in *Tracts Relating to the Attempts to Convert to Christianity the Indians of New England*, Massachusetts Historical Society Collections, 3rd ser., 4 (1834), 266; Whitfield, *Strength out of Weaknesse*, 155.

11. I discuss the self-proclaimed parallels between New England missionaries and soldiers in the New Model Army in "The Mission upon the Hill: New England Evangelism, 1643–1653," in *Millennial Thought in Historical Context: From Puritanism to the Civil War*, ed. Bernd Engler, Joerg F. Fichte, and Oliver Scheiding (Trier: Wissenschaftlicher Verlag Trier [WVT], 2002), 133–63.

12. Whitfield, *Light appearing*, 139.

13. Ibid., 113. Henry Van Lonkhuyzen notes that sachems and powwows, "who had the most to lose if the social order were upset, were typically against Christianity" ("A Reappraisal of the Praying Indians: Acculturation, Conversion, and Identity at Natick, Massachusetts, 1646–1730," *New England Quarterly* 63 [September 1990], 405).

14. Whitfield, *Strength out of Weaknesse*, 158.

15. See E. Shaskan Bumas's discussion of the 1656 translation by John Phillips, "The Cannibal Butcher Shop: Protestant Uses of Las Casas's *Brevíssima relación* in Europe and the American Colonies," *Early American Literature* 35, no. 3 (2000): 117–26. Phillips is quoted on p. 125.

16. The trope of captivity—particularly the Hebrew scripture story of slavery in Egypt or of Babylonian captivity—has been central to liberation theologies that speak to the dispossessed worldwide. See James Treat, ed., *Native and Christian: Indigenous Voices on Religious Identity in the United States and Canada* (New York: Routledge, 1996) for essays on liberation theology in contemporary Native Christian communities.

17. There are manifold studies of the captivity narrative in the Anglo-American tradition. Roy Harvey Pearce provided an early survey of the form, which is still influential today ("The Significances of the Captivity Narrative," *American Literature* 19, no. 1 [March 1947]: 1–20). His discussion of the form has been extended, revised, and challenged by generations of critics who followed. See Michelle Burnham, *Captivity and Sentiment: Cultural Exchange in American Literature, 1682–1861* (Hanover, N.H.: University Press of New England, 1997); Christopher Castiglia, *Bound and Determined: Captivity, Culture-crossing, and White Womanhood from Mary Rowlandson to Patty Hearst* (Chicago: Univer-

sity of Chicago Press, 1996); Kathryn Zabelle Derounian, "The Publication, Promotion, and Distribution of Mary Rowlandson's Indian Captivity Narrative in the Seventeenth Century," *Early American Literature* 23, no. 3 (1988): 239–61, and "Puritan Orthodoxy and the 'Survivor Syndrome' in Mary Rowlandson's Indian Captivity Narrative," *Early American Literature* 22, no. 1 (1987): 82–93; Tara Fitzpatrick, "The Figure of Captivity: The Cultural Work of the Puritan Captivity Narrative," *American Literary History* 3, no. 1 (1991): 1–26; Annette Kolodny, *The Land before Her: Fantasy and Experience of the American Frontiers, 1630–1860* (Chapel Hill: University of North Carolina Press, 1984); Pauline Turner Strong, *Captive Selves, Captivating Others: The Politics and Poetics of Colonial American Captivity Narratives* (Boulder, Colo.: Westview Press, 1999); Teresa Toulouse, " 'My Own Credit': Strategies of (E)valuation in Mary Rowlandson's Captivity Narrative," *American Literature* 64, no. 4 (1992): 655–76, and "The Sovereignty and Goodness of God in 1682: Royal Authority, Female Captivity, and 'Creole' Male Identity," *ELH* 67, no. 4 (Winter 2000): 925–49. Hilary Wyss links missionary tracts to captivity narratives, finding parallels between the construction of the evangelical self, surrounded by heathens, and the captive self, surrounded by savages (*Writing Indians: Literacy, Christianity, and Native Community in Early America* [Amherst: University of Massachusetts Press, 2000], 13).

18. Whitfield, *Strength out of Weaknesse*, 182.

19. For an account of Algonquian captivity practices, see Strong, *Captive Selves*.

20. Eliot and Mayhew, *Tears of Repentance*, 214.

21. The best-known example of such a captivity is that of Pocahontas, who converted to English Protestantism and married the Englishman John Rolfe. She learned her doctrine, of course, from those who had tricked and kidnapped her, but this context is often forgotten in the retellings of her legend, which stress instead Pocahontas's role as a pacific and beautiful go-between who legitimizes English colonial settlement. Pauline Turner Strong argues that the full story of Pocahontas's interaction with the English must include her captivity, which (along with the captivities of other Indians) "subverts the dominant opposition in Anglo-American representations of captivity in the New World: the opposition between the Colonial Captive and the Captivating Savage" (*Captive Selves*, 20). But this subversion has been contained, she argues, by the careful neglect of Indian "captivity as a historical practice." Similarly, the story of the spiritual salvation of Praying Indians, described and celebrated by English missionaries, does not recognize the physical captivity or at least constraint that makes it possible. Rather, these accounts of spiritual redemption elide the Indians' captivity by the English completely or otherwise erase any trace of its figurative significance.

22. Eliot and Mayhew, *Tears of Repentance*, 234.

23. John Eliot, *A further Account of the progress of the* Gospel *amongst the* Indians *in New England* (London, 1660), 58.

24. "Dives" is a name associated with the rich man in the parable of Lazarus. See Luke 16: 19–31.

25. For a full-length history of the conflict, see Alfred A. Cave, *The Pequot War* (Amherst: University of Massachusetts Press, 1996). See also Michael Fickes, " 'They Could Not Endure that Yoke': The Captivity of Pequot Women and Children after the War of 1637," *New England Quarterly* 73, no. 1 (2000): 58–81.

26. Most studies of Eliot's mission and translation work rely on William Wal-

lace Tooker's research into the identity and biography of this man, who served as Eliot's primary translator; see *John Eliot's First Indian Teacher and Interpreter Cockenoe-de-Long Island* (New York: Francis P. Harper, 1896). While the historical details Tooker provides are useful, the name "Cockenoe" seems to be a description of his translating services rather than a personal name: "This name . . . no matter how varied in the records of Long Island and elsewhere . . . finds its parallel sounds in the Massachusetts of both Eliot and Cotton, in the verb *kuhkinneau*, or *kehkinnoo* . . . and therefore indicating by a free translation "an interpreter or teacher" (21).

27. Winslow, *Glorious Progress*, 90.

28. John Eliot's *A further Accompt of the Progresse of the Gospel amongst the Indians in New England* (London, 1659) describes one such gathering, a fast day in November 1658, during which several Praying Indians preached sermons on biblical texts.

29. Douglas Edward Leach remarks that in the early part of the war, Philip "remained something of a ghost leader" and argues that once the war spread beyond Plymouth, "Philip lost his control of the situation. . . . There is no evidence that Philip ever exercised supreme command over the various warring tribes" (*Flintlock and Tomahawk: New England in King Philip's War* [New York: W. W. Norton, 1958], 101, 241).

30. Although most seventeenth-century accounts cite this incident as the central cause of the war because an impassioned Philip was angered by the execution or feared that he too would be suspected and treated in like manner, the onset of the war had several causes. For instance, Philip and the Plymouth colony competed for land, not just for English farming and Indian hunting but also for grazing rights for Indian and English herds of swine. Scholarship on King Philip's War is extensive, and the works cited below are merely representative. For causes of the war, see Virginia Anderson, "King Philip's Herds: Indians, Colonists, and the Problem of Livestock in Early New England," *William and Mary Quarterly* 51, no. 4 (1994): 601–24; Philip Ranlet, "Another Look at the Causes of King Philip's War," *New England Quarterly* 6, no. 1 (1988): 79–100; and James P. Ronda and Jeanne Ronda, "The Death of John Sassamon: An Exploration in Writing New England History," *American Indian Quarterly* 1, no. 2 (1974): 91–102. For book-length histories of the war, see Russell Bourne, *Red King's Rebellion: Racial Politics in New England, 1675–1678* (New York: Oxford University Press, 1990); James D. Drake, *King Philip's War: Civil War in New England, 1675–1676* (Amherst: University of Massachusetts Press, 1999); Leach, *Flintlock and Tomahawk*; and esp. Lepore, *Name of War*. The introduction and notes by Richard Slotkin and James K. Folsom, *So Dreadfull a Judgment: Puritan Responses to King Philip's War, 1676–1677* (Middleton, Conn.: Wesleyan University Press, 1978) usefully detail the contexts of several major wartime publications. For colonial contexts of the war, see Francis Jennings, *Invasion of America: Indians Colonialism and the Cant of Conquest* (Chapel Hill: University of North Carolina Press, 1975), which treats the conflict as the second Puritan war of conquest. For transatlantic contexts, see Stephen Saunders Webb, *1676: The End of American Independence* (New York: Knopf, 1984), esp. 221–24.

31. *Calendar of State Papers: Colonial Series—America and West Indies*, ed. Noel Sainsbury, vol. 9 (London: Eyre and Spottiswode, 1893), 351.

32. For a contemporary account of the attack on Brookfield and Praying Indian involvement, see Thomas Wheeler's narrative, "A Thankfull Remembrance of

Gods Mercy to several Persons at Quabaug or Brookfield," in *So Dreadfull a Judgment: Puritan Responses to King Philip's War, 1676–1677*, ed. Richard Slotkin and James K. Folsom (Middleton, Conn.: Wesleyan University Press, 1978), 207–33. James the Printer is the Christian Indian who is perhaps best known as one who fought against the English. He appears in Anon., *A True Account of the Most Considerable Occurrences that have hapned in the Warre between the English and the Indians in New-England* (London, 1676): "A Revolter he was, and a fellow that had done much mischief, and staid out as long as he could, till the last day but one of a Proclamation set forth, to encourage such *Indians* as had a desire to return to the *English*" (5). For other contemporary accounts of the printer's activities during and after the war, see Daniel Gookin, *An Historical Account of the Doings and Sufferings of the Christian Indians in New England in the Years 1675, 1676, 1677*, in *Transactions and Collections of the American Antiquarian Society* 2, no. 6 (1836) (rpt.; New York: Arno Press, 1972), and Mary Rowlandson, *The Sovereignty and Goodness of God*, ed. Neal Salisbury (Boston: Bedford Books, 1997).

33. Gookin, *Historical Account*, 449.

34. Ibid., 497. As Jenny Hale Pulsipher's recent publication of Edmund Browne's letter to the Bay Colony magistrates makes clear, influential colonists, even those who had supported Indian evangelism, turned against Praying Indians after the start of the war. Edmund Browne, minister at Sudbury—a town attacked during the conflict—asked that Indians within the colonies be restricted in their movement and disarmed. See " 'Our Sages are Sageles': A Letter on Massachusetts Indian Policy after King Philip's War," *William and Mary Quarterly* 58, no. 2 (April 2001): 431–48.

35. See Salisbury's description of Indian efforts to negotiate Rowlandson's release in his introduction, "Mary Rowlandson and Her Removes," in *Sovereignty and Goodness* (33).

36. Natick Indians served as soldiers for the English, "thereby they have gained much in the affections of the *English* who have had some Jealousie about them" (*True Account*, 3).

37. See Richard Cogley, "Daniel Gookin," in *Dictionary of Literary Biography*, vol. 24: *American Colonial Writers, 1606–1734*, ed. Emory Elliot (Gale Literary Databases, cited August 24, 2002). For a brief biography of Gookin and his spiritual conversion narrative, see Mary Rhinelander McEarl, "Thomas Shepard's Record of Relations of Religious Experience, 1648–1649," *William and Mary Quarterly* 48, no. 3 (July 1991): 432–66.

38. Gookin, *Historical Collections*, 200.

39. Ibid., 167.

40. Ibid., 168.

41. Of cider, Gookin writes, "Some of the worst of [Indians] are too prone to abuse unto drunkenness: though others of them that are Christians, use it or other strong drink with great sobriety." As for clothing, "The Christian and civilized Indians do endeavour, many of them, to follow the English mode in their habit." Ibid., 151–52. This characteristic of cross-cultural dress is particularly resonant in a discussion of captivity, as it is such an important aspect of white people's captivity experience. Being stripped and re-clothed in Indian dress is described as a kind of baptism into the captors' culture. See Ann Little, " 'Shoot That Rogue, for He Hath an Englishman's Coat On!': Cultural Cross-Dressing on

the New England Frontier, 1620–1760," *New England Quarterly* 74, no. 2 (2001): 228–74.

42. Gookin, *Historical Collections*, 165.

43. The Hassanemesit Praying Indians might be classified as another category of "captive." Lepore points out that when Hassanemesit residents were given the choice to go with the Nipmucks who came to their town or to lose all their provisions and be sent destitute to the English, they were presented with a "false choice" that resulted, essentially, in captivity to either the Nipmucks or to the English (*Name of War*, 136–45).

44. Gookin, *Historical Account*, 433, 443.

45. See chapter 2.

46. Gookin, *Historical Account*, 479.

47. All sides were engaging in strategies of division; Jennings reads the trial of Sassamon's alleged murderers as an attempt by the English to "drive a wedge" between Praying Indians and pagan Indians; see *Invasion of America*, 296.

48. Gookin, *Historical Account*, 454.

49. Rowlandson, *Sovereignty and Goodness*, 69.

50. Saltonstall wrote several tracts: *The Present State of New-England* (London, 1675), *A Continuation of the State of New-England* (London, 1676), and *A New and Further Narrative* (London, 1676). Lepore provides a table of contemporary wartime publications in *Name of War* (50–51).

51. *Documents Relative to the Colonial History of the State of New-York*, vol. 3, ed. John Brodhead (Albany: Weed, Parsons and Company, 1853), 242.

52. *Calendar of State Papers*, 466.

53. E[dward] W[harton], *New-England's Present Sufferings* (London, 1676); John Easton, *Relacion of the Indyan Warre* (London, 1676).

54. Mary Pray to James Oliver, October 20, 1675, Massachusetts Historical Society Collections, 5th ser., vol. 1 (1871),106.

55. William Harris, *A Rhode Islander Reports on King Philip's War: The Second Harris Letter of August, 1676*, ed. Douglas Edward Leach (Providence: Rhode Island Historical Society, 1963), 66. Gookin notes the rumors, but chalks them up to rank prejudice: "I am not ignorant that some officers and soldiers in the army who had conceived much animosity against all Indians, disgusted our Christian Indian soldiers, and reported ultimately concerning them, saying they were cowards and skulked behind trees in fight, and that they shot over the enemies' heads, and such like reproaches; but as the proverb says, Ill will speaks no good" (*Historical Account*, 444).

56. For the extent of the devastation on both sides, see Strong, *Captive Selves*, 85, and Slotkin and Folsom, *So Dreadfull a Judgment*, 3–4.

57. Slotkin and Folsom, *So Dreadfull a Judgment*, 4.

58. Increase Mather, "A Brief History of the Warr with the Indians in New-England," in *So Dreadfull a Judgment: Puritan Responses to King Philip's War, 1676–1677*, ed. Richard Slotkin and James K. Folsom (Middleton, Conn.: Wesleyan University Press, 1978), 82.

59. Mather, *Brief History*, 84. Webb writes that Mather's sentiments would have marked him as "an old-fashioned, isolationist saint" in cosmopolitan coffeehouses (*1676*, 222).

60. See Anne Kusener Nelsen, "King Philip's War and the Hubbard-Mather Rivalry, *William and Mary Quarterly*, 3rd ser., 72, no. 4 (October 1970): 615–29.

61. William Hubbard, *Narrative of the Troubles with the Indians in New-England*, rpt. in *History of the Indian Wars in New England*, ed. Samuel G. Drake (New York: Burt Franklin, 1865), vol. 2, 207.

62. I am drawing here on Nancy Armstrong's notion of the relation between American captivity narratives and the later English novels that followed. In particular, she argues for the dependence of novelists such as Austen on the very figurations she criticized: "When Austen deliberately set about to debunk the same tropes of captivity that Radcliffe exploited, she nevertheless entered into a collaboration with her gothic counterpart that would preserve the cultural logic I am tracking" ("Captivity and Cultural Capital," 381). Similarly, the authors of captivity narratives and war histories "preserve" the cultural logic of earlier mission representations by working within its structures but drawing opposite conclusions.

63. Benjamin Tompson, "Upon the Elaborate Survey of New-Englands Passions from the Natives, By the Impartial Pen of that Worthy Divine Mr. William Hubbard," in Hubbard, *Narrative of the Troubles*, vol. 1, 24.

64. To Hubbard, Indians are "wolves continually yelling and gaping for their Prey." Thomas Wheeler relates that "they did *roar against* us like so many *wild Bulls.*" Hubbard, *Narrative of the Troubles*, vol. 1, 100; Wheeler, "Thankfull Remembrance," 247.

65. Gookin, *Historical Account*, 441.

66. Mather, *Brief History*, 90. Mather also comments on the confusion of Indians and English: "The darkness was such as an English man could not be discerned from an Indian" (114). The confusion of Indian and English soldiers is exceptional in wartime literature and signals Mather's perspective on human ontology. Mather alone among published wartime authors continued to assert the universal nature of the soul, even among Indians and English.

67. Benjamin Tompson, *New Englands Crisis*, in *So Dreadfull a Judgment*, 220.

68. Saltonstall, *Present State of New-England*, 7.

69. Ibid., 19.

70. For a discussion of anagrams, see Jeffrey Walker, "Anagrams and Acrostics: Puritan Poetic Wit," in *Puritan Poets and Poetics: Seventeenth-Century American Poetry in Theory and Practice*, ed. Peter White (University Park: Pennsylvania State University Press), 1985.

71. Anon., *A Farther Brief and True Narration of the Late Wars Risen in New-England* (London: 1676), 4.

72. Hubbard, *Narrative of the Troubles*, 1, 95. Hassanamesit was an established praying town with an especially vexed position during the war; see Lepore, *Name of War*, 136–45.

73. Benjamin Tompson, *New Englands Crisis*, in *So Dreadfull a Judgment: Puritan Responses to King Philip's War, 1676–1677*, ed. Richard Slotkin and James K. Folsom (Middleton, Conn.: Wesleyan University Press, 1978), 220. Slotkin and Folsom identify "blue-coat" as a term of derision referring to the clothing of servants or of the poor (232, n. 22).

74. Ibid., 218.

75. Anon., *A Brief and True Narration of the Late Wars Risen in New-England* (London, 1675), 6.

76. Anon., *The Day-Breaking if not the Sun-Rising of the Gospell with the Indians in New-England*, 1647, rpt. in *Tracts Relating to the Attempts to Convert*

to *Christianity the Indians of New England,* Massachusetts Historical Society Collections, 3rd ser., 4 (1834), 12.

77. Hubbard, *Narrative of the Troubles,* vol. 2, 276.

78. Saltonstall, *Present State of New-England,* 12.

79. See, for instance, Douglas Leechman and Robert Hall, "American Indian Pidgin English: Attestations and Grammatical Peculiarities," *American Speech* 30 (1955): 163–71.

80. Mather, *Brief History,* 105; Increase Mather, "An Earnest Exhortation to the Inhabitants of New-England," in *So Dreadfull a Judgment: Puritan Responses to King Philip's War, 1676–1677,* ed. Richard Slotkin and James K. Folsom (Middletown, Conn.:Wesleyan University Press, 1978), 177.

81. Hubbard even recounts one incident in which an Indian fighting on behalf of the English made good his escape by resorting to a similar, although purposeful subterfuge to get himself out of a tight spot. He held his hat up on a stick, drawing fire, and escaped while the enemy was reloading (*Narrative of the Troubles,* vol. 1, 176).

82. See Lepore for an account of Moseley's subordination of a plan to reunite Praying Indians traveling with Nipmucks with their friends and families who had remained with the English (*Name of War,* 142).

83. Saltonstall, *Present State of New-England,* 13.

84. Tompson, *New Englands Crisis,* 218.

85. There is some confusion about the word "sneep." Peter White argues that it is a dialect form of "sleep" (*Benjamin Tompson: Colonial Bard* [University Park: Pennsylvania State University Press, 1980], 101, n. 8). Wayne Franklin cites the English word "sneep," which he notes is defined in the *Oxford English Dictionary* as "to rebuke," a meaning that gives a sense to the passage I find most plausible ("The Harangue of King Philip in *New Englands Crisis (1676),*" *American Literature* 51, no. 4 [January 1980]: 536–40.

86. Franklin, "Harangue of King Philip," 537.

87. Rowlandson, *Sovereignty and Goodness,* 96, 103–4.

88. Benjamin Tompson, *New Englands Tears,* in White, *Benjamin Tompson,* 114. "Moecaena" was the patron of Virgil and other poets, and the name was synonymous with generous philanthropy. Perhaps Tompson is trying to suggest that like-minded Englishmen might do well to transfer their generosity from Indian missions to the sponsorship of deserving New England poets.

89. Gookin, *Historical Account,* 441.

90. Hubbard, *Narrative of the Troubles,* vol. 1, 71.

91. Anon., *News from New England* (London, 1676), 5, 3.

92. Saltonstall, *New and Further Narrative,* 4.

93. Mather, *Brief History,* 113.

94. Wharton, *New England's Present Sufferings,* 4.

95. Wheeler, *Thankfull Remembrance,* 247.

96. Anon., *Farther Brief and True Narration,* 4.

97. Anon., *True Account,* 2.

98. Hubbard, *Narrative of the Troubles,* vol. 1, 213.

99. Wheeler, *Thankfull Remembrance,* 248–49.

100. For a discussion of Rowlandson's widespread popularity and the narrative's publishing history, see Derounian, "Publication, Promotion, and Distribution."

101. Slotkin and Folsom, *So Dreadfull a Judgment,* 302.

102. For "homespun and homely," see Jason Russell, *Summary of Dissertations on the Indian in American Literature, 1775–1875* (Ithaca: Cornell University Press, 1932); for "unembellished," Louise Barnett, *The Ignoble Savage: American Literary Racism, 1790–1890* (Westport, Conn.: Greenwood Press, 1975), 81. Slotkin contrasts her authorship with the "conscious artistry" of Cotton Mather (*Regeneration through Violence: The Mythology of the American Frontier, 1600–1860* [Hanover, N.H.: Wesleyan University Press, 1973], 102).

103. Castiglia, *Bound and Determined*, 48.

104. See Amy Lang's introduction to Rowlandson in *Journeys in New Worlds: Early American Women's Narratives*, William L. Andrews, ed. (Madison: University of Wisconsin Press, 1990), 24.

105. Rowlandson, *Sovereignty and Goodness*, 80.

106. Ibid., 71.

107. Rowlandson's editor, Neal Salisbury, suggests that she may have been consciously attacking Gookin's benevolent portrayal of Praying Indians; see his introduction, "Mary Rowlandson and Her Removes," in *Sovereignty and Goodness*, 41.

108. Although I do not see a direct connection between this moment in Rowlandson's text and transcribed Indian confessions, Nishohkou's wonder at the English colonists' own Sabbath breaking (quoted above) takes on greater significance when set against Rowlandson's text.

109. Notably, she does not comment on the fact that another of her captors helped her to this clearer understanding of her benefactor.

110. Rowlandson, *Sovereignty and Goodness*, 87. Ironically, one such "Friend Indian" was James the Printer, who scribed for Philip, writing the letters that negotiated her release. Taking advantage of an English amnesty offer, he returned to Boston and probably helped print a postwar edition of Eliot's translation of the Bible and set type for Rowlandson's narrative (see n. 35 above).

111. *Oxford English Dictionary* gives a definition of "cut" that was current in the seventeenth century and referred to fashion: "the shape to which, or style in which a thing is cut; fashion, shape (of clothes, hair, etc.)."

112. Michelle Burnham, "The Journey Between: Liminality and Dialogism in Mary White Rowlandson's Captivity Narrative," *Early American Literature* 28, no. 1 (1993): 69.

113. On first seeing them, Rowlandson says, "Though they were *Indians*, I gat them by the hand, and burst out into tears; my heart was so full that I could not speak to them" (*Sovereignty and Goodness*, 97). Later, she links them to the Englishman negotiating her release, who asks the two men to serve as witnesses to those negotiations: "Then Mr. *Hoar* called *his own Indians*, *Tom* and *Peter*, and bid them go and see whither he [Rowlandson's master] would promise [the terms of ransom] before them three" (103; emphasis added).

114. Rowlandson, *Sovereignty and Goodness*, 98, n. 65.

115. Ibid., 81. The allusion is to Proverbs 27.1.

116. Saltonstall describes English troops killing and consuming their horses. He recounts how an English company pursued the enemy "till our Horses were tired, our men faint, and our victuals spent; Insomuch that several horses were killed and eaten, whereof the General (the worthy *Josiah Winslow* Esquire, Governor of *New-London*), eat his part, and in all, as well hardships as dangers, was not wanting to encourage his men by his own valiant example" (*New and Further Narrative*, 2).

117. Ibid., 14.

118. Rowlandson's possible sources for these stories also indicate that hers is an antimission viewpoint. Even if Hubbard, Saltonstall, and Rowlandson write about these incidents independently, they are obviously drawn to similar evidence of converts' treachery.

119. The author of *A True Account* notes that *"Natick* or *Praying Indians"* first fought alongside English troops quite late in the war. But, he argues, the delay is not "to be wondred at, considering the hurry this War hath put us into; the disappointment we have met with by the Treachery of several of that Nation, on whose Friendship we thought we might have depended, as having deserved other things at their hands: and that some few of the praying *Indians* have been carried away with the present outrage of their Nation" (3).

120. See Salisbury's introduction to *Sovereignty and Goodness*, 33, as well as the letter to John Leverett, April 12, 1676, 133, in the same edition.

121. Hilary Wyss describes Sam Sachem's letters as shifting from Algonquian confidence and rhetorical (not to mention political) control over the terms of negotiation to a painful acquiescence to English conventions (*Writing Indians*, 39–41, 45–47).

122. Mattamuck et al., letter to John Leverett et al., July 6, 1676, in Rowlandson, *Sovereignty and Goodness*, 141.

123. Wyss agrees: "Sam Sachem sees Christianity and Christian Indians as a potential avenue of negotiation" (*Writing Indians*, 45).

124. *True Account*, 7, 6.

125. See Hubbard, *Narrative of the Troubles*, vol. 1, 200, 281. Bourne also describes Shoshanin's role in the war (*Red King's Rebellion*, 167 and passim).

Chapter 7. Dying Saints, Vanishing Savages

1. Increase Mather, *A Brief History of the War with the Indians in New-England*, in *So Dreadfull a Judgment: Puritan Responses to King Philip's War, 1676–1677*, ed. Richard Slotkin and James K. Folsom (Middletown, Conn.: Wesleyan University Press, 1978), 139.

2. John Winthrop, *Reasons to Be Considered for . . . the Intended Plantation in New England*, in *The Puritans in America: A Narrative Anthology*, ed. Alan Heimert and Andrew Delbanco (Cambridge: Harvard University Press, 1985), 73.

3. John Mason, "Brief History of the Pequot War," in *History of the Pequot War*, ed. Charles Orr (1897; rpt. New York: AMS Press, 1980), 30.

4. Benjamin Tompson's poem "New England's Crisis" vividly expresses these fears in a "quoted" speech of Philip to his troops:

> Now if you'll fight I'll get you English coats,
> And wine to drink out of their captains' throats.
> The richest merchants' houses shall be ours,
> We'll lie no more on mats or dwell in bowers.
> We'll have their silken wives take they our squaws,
> They shall be whipped by virtue of our laws.
> (Slotkin and Folsom, *So Dreadfull a Judgment*, 218)

5. For extended discussions of the history, meaning, and representation of cross-cultural violence in colonial New England, see Alfred A. Cave, *The Pequot*

War (Amherst: University of Massachusetts Press, 1996); Francis Jennings, *The Invasion of America: Indians, Colonialism and the Cant of Conquest* (Chapel Hill: University of North Carolina Press, 1975); Jill Lepore, *The Name of War: King Philip's War and the Origins of American Identity* (New York: Alfred A. Knopf, 1998); and Richard Slotkin, *Regeneration through Violence: The Mythology of the American Frontier, 1600–1860* (Hanover, N.H.: Wesleyan University Press, 1973).

6. William Cullen Bryant, "The Disinterred Warrior," in *The Poetical Works of William Cullen Bryant* (1903; rpt. New York: AMS Press, 1969), 107.

7. Brian Dippie, *The Vanishing American: White Attitudes and U.S. Indian Policy* (Middletown, Conn.: Wesleyan University Press, 1982), 24.

8. Although this chapter focuses on the deathbed narratives of Christian Indians produced between 1643 and 1685, the genre continued into the eighteenth and nineteenth centuries, especially in mission accounts written by both Indians and white authors. For instance, William Apess's *The Experiences of Five Christian Indians of the Pequot Tribe,* in *On Our Own Ground: The Complete Writings of William Apess, a Pequot,* ed. Barry O'Connell (Amherst: University of Massachusetts Press, 1992) is a challenging variation on the pattern. And Experience Mayhew's lengthy *Indian Converts; or, Some Account of the Lives and Dying Speeches of a Considerable Number of the Christianized Indians of Martha's Vineyard, in New-England* (London, 1727) provides a wealth of information and poses the same challenges of mediation and cultural exchange as Eliot's work. For a discussion of these works, see Hilary Wyss, *Writing Indians, Literacy, Christianity, and Native Community in Early America* (Amherst: University of Massachusetts Press, 2000), 52–80.

9. Mary Louise Pratt, *Imperial Eyes: Travel Writing and Transculturation* (London: Routledge, 1992), 7.

10. Although Eliot and others in the mission tracts distinguish their efforts from the violence of Spanish conquistadors, the rhetorical rather than historical nature of the disavowals of violence are clear when they are set beside the history of the mission. Puritan missionaries certainly employed violent rhetoric in their descriptions of attempts to "reduce" Indians to civility, and they had no qualms about instituting flogging as a punishment for civil infractions in the praying towns. Moreover, as Neal Salisbury notes, although the "institutional arrangement [of mission administration] reinforced the mission's subordinate position in an Indian policy that was primarily military," Eliot accepted the situation; he "seriously questioned neither the premise nor the implications of the arrangement" ("Red Puritans," *William and Mary Quarterly* 3rd ser., 31, no. 1 (January 1974): 31.

11. This emphasis on the Indian soul is, of course, a long-standing element of missionary colonial discourse. Bartolomé de las Casas provides perhaps the first prominent articulation in his *Brevísima relacíon de la destruccíon de las Indias.*

12. If the tenets were not attractive in and of themselves, the association or alliance with English Christians may have been. The reasons for conversion were varied, ranging from a desire to strengthen kinship and community ties, to a desire to protect lands, to a desire to fulfill spiritual needs. For discussions of the motivation for conversion and the participation of Indian converts in Christian identity formation, see James Axtell, *After Columbus: Essays in the Ethnohistory of Colonial North America* (New York: Oxford University Press, 1988), 100–

121; Dane Morrison, *A Praying People: Massachusett Acculturation and the Failure of the Puritan Mission, 1600–1690* (New York: Peter Lang Publishing, 1995), 1–36; Robert Naeher, "Dialogue in the Wilderness: John Eliot and the Indian Exploration of Puritanism as a Source of Meaning, Comfort, and Ethnic Survival," *New England Quarterly* 62 (September 1989): 346–68; Jean O'Brien, *Dispossession by Degrees: Indian Land and Identity in Natick, Massachusetts, 1650–1790* (Cambridge: Cambridge University Press, 1997), esp. 51–58; and Harold Van Lonkhuyzen, "A Reappraisal of the Praying Indians: Acculturation, Conversion, and Identity at Natick, Massachusetts, 1646–1730," in *New England Quarterly* 63 (September 1990): 396–428.

13. Roger Williams, *A Key into the Language of America*, ed. John J. Teunissen and Evelyn J. Hintz (Detroit: Wayne State University Press, 1973), 88.

14. On Williams's complex and changing views of Indian evangelism, see W. Clark Gilpin, *The Millenarian Piety of Roger Williams* (Chicago: University of Chicago Press, 1979), and Anne Myles, "Dissent and the Frontier of Translation: Roger Williams's *A Key into the Language of America*," in *Possible Pasts: Becoming Colonial in Early America*, ed. Robert Blair St. George (Ithaca: Cornell University Press, 2000).

15. Williams, *A Key*, 87.

16. Anon., *New Englands First Fruits*, in *Founding of Harvard College*, ed. Samuel Eliot Morison, 2nd ed., appendix D (Cambridge: Harvard University Press, 1968), 420.

17. The account implies that that no minister is present at the deathbed, suggesting that only Williams visited him in that capacity.

18. *New Englands First Fruits*, 427.

19. Experience Mayhew discusses the problematic nature of the deathbed confession in his *Indian Converts*. His preface makes clear both the Puritan suspicion of eleventh-hour conversions and indicates the racism that made these confessions doubly suspect to a white audience:

> Tho I could have mentioned many of our *Indians*, who have discovered very probable Signs of true Repentance in the Time of their last and long Sicknesses, many of them dying of Chronical Diseases; yet considering the Doubtfulness of a Death-bed Repentance, I have not put any into my Catalogue of Penitents, in whom a remarkable Change did not appear while they were well and in Health. (x)

He concludes: "Tho I could give several Instances of this kind [i.e., deathbed conversions], that would not be despised, if the Persons instanced in were of our own Nation" (xi).

20. Erik Seeman, *Pious Persuasions: Laity and Clergy in Eighteenth-Century New England* (Baltimore: Johns Hopkins University Press, 1999), 288–89.

21. Edward Winslow, *The Glorious Progress of the Gospell, amongst the Indians in New England*, 1649, rpt. in *Tracts Relating to the Attempts to Convert to Christianity the Indians of New England*, Massachusetts Historical Society Collections, 3rd ser., vol. 4 (1834), 79.

22. Henry Whitfield, *Strength out of Weaknesse*, 1652, rpt. in *Tracts Relating to the Attempts to Convert to Christianity the Indians of New England*, Massachusetts Historical Society Collections, 3rd ser., vol. 4 (1834), 166.

23. Lepore discusses Sassamon's role at length (*Name of War*, 21–47).

24. William Hubbard, *Narrative of the Troubles with the Indians in New-En-*

gland, rpt. in *History of the Indian Wars in New England*, ed. Samuel G. Drake (New York: Burt Franklin, 1865), 15.

25. Mather, *Brief History*, 87.

26. Daniel Gookin, *An Historical Account of the Doings and Sufferings of the Christian Indians in New England in the Years 1675, 1676, 1677*, in *Transactions and Collections of the American Antiquarian Society* 2, no. 6 (1836) (rpt.; New York: Arno Press, 1972), 440.

27. For a description of Wattasacompanum's capture, defense, and execution, including John Eliot's protest on his behalf, see Lepore, *Name of War*, 143–45.

28. Gookin, *An Historical Account*, 476.

29. John Eliot, "Eliot's Records of the Church in Roxbury," *New England Historical and Genealogical Register* 33 (1879): 413, and "Documents Illustrating Gookin's History of the Christian Indians," *Transactions and Collections of the American Antiquarian Society* 2, no. 6 (1836): 527–34 (rpt.; New York: Johnson Reprint Corporation, 1971), 527–28.

30. Lepore, *Name of War*, 145.

31. Eliot, "Eliot's Records," 413.

32. Roy Harvey Pearce, *Savagism and Civilization: A Study of the Indian and the American Mind*, rev. ed. (Berkeley and Los Angeles: University of California Press, 1988), 55.

33. Just how easily the rhetoric of Captain Tom's defense can become assimilated into the romantic discourse of the noble savage is suggested by Samuel G. Drake's biography of "Capt. Tom, alias Wattasacompanum." Drake writes that the captain's treatment by the English provokes "melancholy interest" (*The Aboriginal Races of North America* [New York: Hurst & Company, 1880], 744.

34. Nathaniel Saltonstall, *The Present State of New-England* (London, 1675), 40. For discussions of attacks on Gookin and others, see James D. Drake, *King Philip's War: Civil War in New England, 1675–1676* (Amherst: University of Massachusetts Press, 1999), 144; Douglas Edward Leach, *Flintlock and Tomahawk: New England in King Philip's War* (New York: W. W. Norton, 1958), 147–52; and Lepore, *Name of War*, 140–41.

35. John Eliot, "Letters of John Eliot," *Massachusetts Historical Society Proceedings* 17 (1879): 251.

36. Tellingly, Gookin's war history was not published, and as Lepore suggests, Eliot probably understood the local presses too well to try to publish his own account (Lepore, *Name of War*, 44). One wonders if Eliot expected this letter to Boyle to be printed, as so many of his other letters had been. If so, his construction of the mission as a dying Indian saint may have been written with public circulation in mind.

37. Eliot, "Letters of John Eliot," 251.

38. John Eliot, "Eliot's Letters to Boyle," *Massachusetts Historical Society Collections*, 1st ser., 3 (1794), 182. The note of dejection may also have to do with the tactical necessity for humility; this passage comes from a letter seeking to explain away Eliot's importunity in printing the Old Testament before receiving permission from Boyle to do so.

39. Eliot, "Letters to Boyle," 181.

40. John Eliot, *Dying Speeches & Counsels of such Indians as dyed in the Lord* (Cambridge, Mass., [1685]), 1.

41. Again, as in his apology to Boyle for moving ahead with a second edition of the translated Bible, Eliot here employs conventional expressions of humility.

But in the context of declining numbers of converts and declining support from the English, Eliot's words suggest he no longer expected much of a readership for such mission publications.

42. O'Brien, *Dispossession by Degrees*, 88.

43. Seeman, *Pious Persuasions*, 67–78.

44. Eliot, *Dying Speeches*, 6.

45. This reading of the *Dying Speeches* tract attends to the English context of the relations. The accounts of dying converts also suggest the preservation of traditional practices within the Praying Indian community. As is clear from the number of non-Christian Indians who attended Wequash at his death, the gathering of friends and loved ones is not some sort of English imposition. Indeed, Cogley notes that the archaeological record of praying-town cemeteries shows that converts shaped their funeral practices from a variety of new and traditional practices (*John Eliot's Mission to the Indians*, 244).

46. Eliot, *Dying Speeches*, 5.

47. Ibid., 9. Cogley argues that the dying speeches often emphasize the resurrection of the soul rather than of the body. This dissent from orthodox Puritan belief, he suggests, may mean that converts "accepted only those Christian doctrines that were consonant with traditional Indian beliefs." A more likely interpretation, he argues, is that "the Christian beliefs and practices that were most meaningful to Waban, Piambohou, and other long-term participants in the mission were those that could be interpreted in a traditional manner" (*John Eliot's Mission to the Indians*, 243). Cogley continues: "The credit for perceiving and stressing these theological points of overlap surely belonged to the leading proselytes and not to Eliot" (243). I would also stress the converts' role in this late construction of the "dying Indian saint," an identity on which they insist in their deathbed testimonies.

48. Eliot, "Eliot's Letters to Boyle," 188.

49. In her history of Natick, O'Brien focuses on the "connection between land and identities, and the means by which land served to mark the place of Indian people in New England" (*Dispossession by Degrees*, 10). She examines the construction of "friend Indians" after the war of 1675 and the continuation of the Natick community in the decades that follow. Clearly, however, the mission ideal as Eliot articulated it did not survive the war intact. He mourns this specific "dying Indian" construct, which is not resurrected.

50. Eliot, *Dying Speeches*, 2.

Index